"Anyone interested to know why
and its host Taliban regime from Afghanistan, and five years after the killing of Osama bin Laden, jihadist Islam is still on the march must read this brilliant collection of essays."

—**Professor Efraim Karsh**, King's College London and Bar-Ilan University, author of *Islamic Imperialism: A History*

"I find this collection of essays heartbreakingly rational, masterfully reasoned, entirely clear, prescient—and therefore utterly heartbreaking—because the handwriting was on the very sky, from the moment Khomeini held our diplomats hostage—and by 2001, you and your team at the ARI were on duty speaking out against the willful blindness, cowardice, irrationality, and denial that has characterized the failure of American foreign policy under both Republican and Democratic presidents."

—**Phyllis Chesler, Ph.D.,** author of fifteen books, including *The New Anti-Semitism* and *An American Bride in Kabul,* fellow, the Middle East Forum

"This brilliant collection of editorials and interviews is a moral *tour de force*.... Onkar Ghate and Elan Journo offer a clear and consistent presentation of what a moral and rational American foreign policy ought to look like. The essays also offer original and insightful analyses of the West's suicidal questioning of its own right to exist. The shameful appeasement, the destructive altruism behind our war efforts, and the tragic ways our government has become an agent for the self-defense of the citizens of enemy countries at the expense of its own citizens are all expertly and impressively highlighted. This original and intellectually honest book dares to identify the only antidotes to the current crisis we face in fighting Islamic terrorism: reason, rational self-interest and a merciless strategy designed to vanquish the enemy. This book will inspire and infuriate many in our culture. It provides that rare combination of philosophical principles applied to concrete political problems. The solutions provided here are the only viable ones in our culture today."

—**Jason D. Hill, Ph.D.,** professor of philosophy, DePaul University

"[A] cornucopia of topical essays that relate to the crisis in which we find ourselves as 2016 draws to a close.... Since 9/11 and even before, the West has been loath to comprehend the threat of spreading Islamic extremism, now so correctly called 'totalitarianism.' ... This book should be a primer for leaders around the globe and a text to be read by students hoping to go out into the working world in leadership positions. Highly recommended."

—**Carol Gould,** broadcaster and author of *Don't Tread on Me: Anti-Americanism Abroad* and *Spitfire Girls*

FAILING TO CONFRONT ISLAMIC TOTALITARIANISM

WHAT WENT WRONG AFTER 9/11

SECOND EXPANDED EDITION

To Jacob Dinkel,

Thank you for your dedication to ARI's mission and your ongoing support of our work.

FAILING TO CONFRONT ISLAMIC TOTALITARIANISM
WHAT WENT WRONG AFTER 9/11

SECOND EXPANDED EDITION

With my gratitude and best wishes,

E. Journo

ONKAR GHATE AND ELAN JOURNO

WITH ADDITIONAL CONTRIBUTIONS BY
LEONARD PEIKOFF, YARON BROOK, AND KEITH LOCKITCH

AYN RAND INSTITUTE PRESS

CONTENTS

PREFACE TO THE SECOND EDITION

We published this book in 2016, a collection of essays dating all the way back to 2001, to show how from the very beginning irrational ideas have disastrously undermined America's responses to the September 11 attacks. We're issuing this second edition in 2021 because the failure to confront Islamic totalitarianism has been compounding and wreaking havoc. One major consequence is a climate of fear that must not be accepted as a "new normal."

In 2015, jihadists burst into the offices of *Charlie Hebdo* and shot to death members of the French magazine's staff—for "insulting Islam." Five years later, speaking at the trial of alleged conspirators in the attack, a survivor of the massacre decried the fact that the magazine now operates under heavy security: "We are living under siege, in Paris, in 2020."

Elsewhere in Paris, while that trial was unfolding, a jihadist attacked a middle school teacher, Samuel Paty, and beheaded him. Why? Paty had shown some students a cartoon from *Charlie Hebdo*—"during a moral and civic education class discussion about freedom of speech."

This climate of fear haunted the creation of an illuminating documentary, *Islam and the Future of Tolerance* (2018). It's a frank conversation between Sam Harris and Maajid Nawaz (a former Islamist) about the religion of Islam, the Islamist threat, and attempts to silence discussion on these issues. Its funding came, not from any major TV network or streaming platform, but the crowdfunding site Kickstarter. Numerous backers, fearing for their safety, withheld their names from the film's website and end credits. In a note to supporters, the filmmakers acknowledged, "we may end up being targets. That's a risk we are willing to take."

Shortly after the first edition of this book was published, a squad of student "thought police" at UCLA Law School tried to ban it. Why? Because they felt the title, and by implication the book, was "offensive." In a grim irony, this incident, which prompted comment in the *Washington Post* and elsewhere, happened at a panel discussion on how America's leaders have appeased jihadist attacks on freedom of speech.

The wider cultural phenomenon reflects a growing taboo against honest, rational discussion of the ideas of Islam, a taboo brought on by confusions, willful distortions and the "jihadist's veto"—the very real threat that anyone critically discussing Islam might be deemed a blasphemer and murdered.

This book presents the Ayn Rand Institute's distinctive analysis of what's wrong with America's response to the Islamist threat since 9/11. We argue that the fundamental problem lies in irrational philosophic ideas that permeate—and subvert—American foreign policy. You can see those ideas at work in the failure properly to understand the nature and goals of the Islamists—in the self-effacing policies leading to unwinnable wars in Afghanistan and Iraq—in the self-crippling battlefield rules of engagement that hamstring our military—in our continuing appeasement of the enemy and our evasion of the scale of the problem—and in the failure of Western leaders to uphold the secular principle of freedom of speech.

This book's first edition was subtitled *From George W. Bush to Barack Obama and Beyond.* The expanded edition—newly subtitled *What Went Wrong After 9/11*—spans two more presidential administrations, underscoring the profound impact of philosophic ideas in foreign policy, regardless of who sits in the Oval Office.

The new material, in parts 5 and 6, includes two essays deserving special emphasis, both originally published in *New Ideal,* the journal of the Ayn Rand Institute.

"Jihadists: Understanding the Nature of the Enemy" argues that the enemy is an ideological movement rooted in Islam. Their conflict with us is not about anyone's race, nor is it fundamentally animated by material (political or economic) factors. Theirs is an ideas-driven movement, one with factional infighting and disputes, but with a clear goal that followers *choose* to embrace.

"Trivializing the Islamist Menace" observes that the George W. Bush-era view of the "terrorist threat" exaggerated the problem by portraying it as "existential." But critics of that view ended up trivializing the problem, leaving us ill-equipped to deal with a growing menace. The essay offers a rational perspective on the seriousness of the Islamist threat.

Part 7 now includes the essay "What Should a Distinctively American Foreign Policy Do?," first published in *A New Textbook of Americanism: The Politics of Ayn Rand* (2018). Informed by an Objectivist perspective, it argues for the necessity of defining foreign policy by reference to rational moral principles.

We've also prefaced each of the book's parts with a brief note providing context about events and issues discussed in that part. And we've retained (with slight revisions) the Introduction, which spotlights the distinctiveness of the Institute's approach and why our analysis has been borne out by events. That uniqueness comes from the intellectual framework we embrace: Ayn Rand's philosophy of Objectivism.

Finally, in connection with the second edition of this book, we wish to thank Ben Bayer, Thomas Bowden, Simon Federman, Keith Lockitch, Donna Montrezza, Anu Seppala, Carla Silk, and Agustina Vergara Cid.

INTRODUCTION TO THE FIRST EDITION

The present state of the world is not the proof of philosophy's impotence, but the proof of philosophy's power. It is philosophy that has brought men to this state—it is only philosophy that can lead them out.
— Ayn Rand, 1961

Look around the world, and you will see something that would have shocked anyone living in the aftermath of 9/11. Following the worst attack on American soil since Pearl Harbor, with thousands of our citizens killed, Americans were rightly outraged—and their (healthy) response was to demand retaliation. Our leaders in Washington insisted that the people who attacked us would be made to pay. No longer would anyone dare think of the United States as a "paper tiger." The prevailing mood conveyed a clear message: America was entitled to defend itself. The nation was primed to unleash its full military might to annihilate the threat.

Now consider just *some* of the brazen attacks in the last year and a half: the massacre at the Paris office of the magazine *Charlie Hebdo*; shootings at free-speech events in Copenhagen and in Garland, Texas; the suicide bombings and murder spree across Paris; the mass shooting in San Bernardino, California; the bombing of the Brussels airport and subway; the slaughter at a gay nightclub in Orlando, Florida.

The events of the last year and a half reflect a long-standing trend, one that was supercharged in the last decade and a half: the ascent of the Islamist cause. That movement is strong materially, capable of inflicting harm, controlling territory, subjugating people. And, what's more significant: the movement is strong in its morale, exhibiting an astounding confidence. Iran's state-backing for jihadist groups (according to the U.S. State Department) is "undiminished," and the regime seeks nuclear capability. Five-plus years after bin Laden's death, the al-Qaeda network lives on. The Taliban in Afghanistan has reconquered about as much territory as it held prior to the U.S.-led war. Across the Middle East, the Islamic State rampages. The group has conquered parts of Iraq and Syria, and it has distinguished itself through unspeakable barbarity. You might expect that to put potential recruits off, but in fact Islamic State is a magnet for foreign fighters, including many from Europe and North America.

Let that sink in: *Since 9/11, countless individuals have eagerly enlisted to fight for the cause of Islamic totalitarianism.*

At the same time, many Americans are exhausted, resigned, demoralized. Our military forces—mighty, brave, determined—were sent into Afghanistan and Iraq, two winnable wars that became quagmires. Materially, the Islamists are far weaker than the enemies we faced in World War II. Then, we eliminated the threat to our lives and freedom in less than five years. Since 9/11, however, we've been told that this must be a "long war." George W. Bush viewed Afghanistan and Iraq as unwinnable. Indeed, Afghanistan is the longest war in America's history. Barack Obama further scaled back expectations, pointedly ruling out a World War II-like "victory" (a word he feels uncomfortable using).

We have reached a new normal: Clouding our daily lives is the persistent threat of jihadist attacks. And, for fear of incurring the wrath of Islamists, many newspapers, magazines, and publishing houses (such as Yale University Press and Random House) engage in self-censorship. What we're seeing is the twilight of the freedom of speech.

Suppose that in the wake of 9/11 you told people that this grim reality lay ahead. They would have been astounded. Indignant even. Some might have dismissed it as far-fetched. After all, our military strength is unmatched in all of world history. And yet, far from defeated, Islamic totalitarianism is on the march. No one would have predicted the situation we face today.

We at the Ayn Rand Institute predicted it.

We warned against precisely that kind of disaster. We pinpointed the fundamental problem subverting American foreign policy. We championed an uncompromising solution.

In the aftermath of 9/11, ARI placed full-page ads in the *Washington Post* and the *New York Times* explaining the attack and presenting an incisive warning. The "greatest obstacle to U.S. victory," wrote ARI's founder Leonard Peikoff, is not our enemies, but "our own intellectuals." They advocated the same ideas that had encouraged the enemy. "Fifty years of increasing American appeasement in the Middle East have led to fifty years of increasing contempt in the Muslim world for the U.S.," wrote Peikoff. The irrational ideas shaping American foreign policy had led to 9/11, and every indication pointed to one conclusion: those dominant ideas, unless rejected, would subvert the U.S. military response and our national security. America is a military superpower, but it lacks the self-confidence and moral certainty needed to understand and fight for its own self-defense.

Tragically our analysis—articulated in countless ARI op-eds, essays, media interviews, talks—has proved correct.

We argued that properly conceptualizing the enemy—identifying its character, its goals—is necessary in order to defeat it. Our enemy is defined, not primarily by their use of terrorist means, but by their ideological ends. They fight to create a society dominated by Islamic religious law. We call the movement Islamic totalitarianism—a cause long inspired and funded by patrons such as Saudi Arabia, the Gulf states and, above all, Iran. Yet the last two administrations not only failed to define the enemy, but evaded this responsibility. Witness the destructive consequences all around you. Over time the necessity of understanding the enemy has only grown more urgent.

We argued that a proper war is one fought in self-defense to safeguard the individual rights of Americans. We argued that such a war must seek to eliminate the objective threats to our lives, using all necessary force. Yet Bush's supposedly "muscular" policy was in fact animated by "compassion" and the allegedly moral ideal of selfless service to the needy. That's true of the overarching goal of Bush's crusade for democracy—giving the needy and oppressed of the Middle East the vote—and of its implementation on the ground. Far from unleashing a "shock and awe" campaign, Washington engaged in "nation building" and subjected our soldiers to absurd, self-sacrificial battlefield constraints. Those same constraints on our soldiers—stemming from the doctrines of Just War Theory and embodied in international norms of war—persist under Obama's administration.

We identified the predictable consequences of the ideas shaping America's foreign policy. Our forward-looking assessments were proven correct.

The democracy crusade, we argued, would empower jihadists across the Middle East. It did; see Iraq, Afghanistan, Lebanon, Egypt, the Palestinian territories.

On the battlefield the self-effacing rules of engagement, we argued, would encourage the Iraq insurgency and the remnants of the Taliban. They did.

We argued that the widely celebrated "surge" in Iraq—deploying thousands more U.S. soldiers to quell the insurgency through bribes and appeasing gestures—could only paper over, not end, the fundamental enmities and that more violence would return. It did.

Allowing insurgents to go undefeated, we warned, would enable the most vicious, effective killers to survive and reemerge. They did; one such insurgent group became the core of Islamic State.

The policy of appeasement, we argued, would only empower such enemies as Hamas and Hezbollah. It did; witness the Islamist-Israeli wars in 2006, 2008/9, 2012, 2014.

We argued that the prevailing response to the Danish cartoons crisis was pathetic. The West's inability to uphold so vital a right as the freedom of speech, we warned, would further inspire the jihadists. It did; recall *Charlie Hebdo*.

The diplomatic outreach to Iran, begun under Bush and consummated by Obama's team, would further encourage the standard bearer of the jihad, the Iranian regime; a nuclear deal—we warned a decade before it was signed—would fuel Iran's hostility. It did.

From the outset, we at ARI spelled out what a real war actually looks like; we highlighted the sharp contrast between that and the supposedly "tough" policy of the Bush administration in Iraq and Afghanistan. The wrong lesson, we warned, would be to regard Bush's (policy) failure as discrediting the use of military force in self-defense. That misconception, however, is now pervasive. Many (wrongly) believe that our military—despite being unrivaled—is ineffectual and, if used, counterproductive. We warned that that insidious premise was leading America to disarm itself, even as threats mount. And indeed that premise goes a long way to explaining how Obama's nuclear deal with Iran was seen as even remotely plausible. Obama posed the alternatives as another Middle East war—*another Iraq*—or the Iran deal. If "war" means another quagmire, everyone should reject it.

From the outset, we at ARI exposed the perverse ideas about morality that permeated, and therefore subverted, U.S. foreign policy. We warned that by subordinating military victory to allegedly moral constraints, Washington's policy would undermine our national security. The ruinous consequences of that policy abound.

What makes ARI's approach distinctive—and why our analysis has been borne out—is the intellectual framework that we embrace: Ayn Rand's philosophy of Objectivism. Thus our work fits in none of the conventional categories, such as conservative, libertarian, progressive, "realist," "isolationist," neoconservative. That ARI's perspective on U.S. foreign policy has been borne out is a testament to the real-world value of our philosophic framework. Objectivism begins by embracing a basic orientation to facts; *reality is,* and in the quest to live we must use our reason to discover reality's nature and learn to act successfully in it. The philosophy's moral code teaches us what is in our self-interest, what produces happiness, and what a proper society looks like. Rand once explained: "I am not primarily an advocate of capitalism, but of egoism; and I am not primarily an advocate of egoism, but of reason. If one recognizes the supremacy of reason and applies it consistently, all the rest follows." It is this philosophic outlook that led us to identify and take seriously the threat of Islamic totalitarianism, and then properly conceive what actions our self-defense required.

When looking at the cultural and political events of the day, we at ARI view them in a wider context, we identify issues in fundamental terms, and we recognize the profound role of philosophic ideas in shaping the world. We take our function to be in line with Ayn Rand's conception of the proper role of intellectuals in society: "The intellectual is the eyes, ears and voice of a free society: it is his job to observe the events of the world, to evaluate their meaning and to inform the men in all the other fields." This is the role all of ARI's intellectuals—whether writing on philosophy, foreign policy, law, economic issues—seek to live up to everyday, whereas our culture's leading intellectual voices have long ago abandoned it.

The major presentation of our view of what went wrong after 9/11 is *Winning the Unwinnable War: America's Self-Crippled Response to Islamic Totalitarianism,* edited by Elan Journo. In that book of in-depth essays, we show how conventional, dominant ideas about morality subverted American security.

The present book *echoes* that theme, but it conveys ARI's distinctive philosophic viewpoint in bite-size portions. In the op-eds, essays, blog posts, and interviews that we selected for inclusion here, you will see how irrational philosophic ideas warped foreign-policy thinking and crippled us in action. You will also learn that victory is achievable—if we take certain necessary steps (a detailed account can be found in *Winning the Unwinnable War*). The book's final part sketches out how an Objectivist approach to foreign policy stands apart in today's intellectual landscape.

We at ARI fight for a future of reason, individualism, and freedom. We ask you to join us. How? The book's final section, "What You Can Do," provides concrete suggestions. Read, watch, listen to the recommended ARI content—then distribute it to others and speak up for your ideas and values.

Join us, and your support will multiply ARI's impact and fuel our mission. We make people aware of the philosophy of Objectivism because we believe that Objectivism is indispensable for understanding the world, defining values, and achieving one's own happiness. To convey that, we educate people about Rand's philosophy and we spotlight Objectivism's cash value in an individual's life and in society. From that philosophic perspective, we write and speak about crucial political-cultural issues of the day. What you'll find in the pages that follow is that the arena of U.S. foreign policy offers stark, life-and-death illustrations of the value of Objectivism for understanding the world and guiding our action.

Can we end the Islamist menace and secure our right to life, liberty, and the pursuit of happiness on earth? Yes—easily—if we adopt the right ideas.

ELAN JOURNO   ONKAR GHATE

"END STATES WHO SPONSOR TERRORISM"

Leonard Peikoff October 2, 2001*

The following article appeared as a full-page advertisement in the New York Times.

Fifty years of increasing American appeasement in the Mideast have led to fifty years of increasing contempt in the Muslim world for the U.S. The climax was September 11, 2001.

Fifty years ago, Truman and Eisenhower surrendered the West's property rights in oil, although that oil rightfully belonged to those in the West whose science, technology, and capital made its discovery and use possible. The first country to nationalize Western oil, in 1951, was Iran. The rest, observing our frightened silence, hurried to grab their piece of the newly available loot.

The cause of the U.S. silence was not practical, but philosophical. The Mideast's dictators were denouncing wealthy egotistical capitalism. They were crying that their poor needed our sacrifice; that oil, like all property, is owned collectively, by virtue of birth; and that they knew their viewpoint was true by means of otherworldly emotion. Our Presidents had no answer. Implicitly, they were ashamed of the Declaration of Independence. They did not dare to answer that Americans, properly, were motivated by the selfish desire to achieve personal happiness in a rich, secular, individualist society.

The Muslim countries embodied in an extreme form every idea—selfless duty, anti-materialism, faith or feeling above science, the supremacy of the group—which our universities, our churches, and our own political Establishment had long been upholding as virtue. When two groups, our leadership and theirs, accept the same basic ideas, the most consistent side wins.

After property came liberty. "The Muslim fundamentalist movement," writes Yale historian Lamin Sanneh, "began in 1979 with the Iranian [theocratic] revolution..." (*New York Times,* 9/23/01). During his first year as its leader, Ayatollah Khomeini,

---

* We are honored to reprint this essay with Dr. Peikoff's permission. Note that he has not reviewed or endorsed any of the other content in this book.

urging a Jihad against "the Great Satan," kidnapped fifty-two U.S. diplomatic personnel and held them hostage; Carter's reaction was fumbling paralysis. About a decade later, Iran topped this evil. Khomeini issued his infamous Fatwa aimed at censoring, even outside his borders, any ideas uncongenial to Muslim sensibility. This was the meaning of his threat to kill British author Rushdie and to destroy his American publisher; their crime was the exercise of their right to express an unpopular intellectual viewpoint. The Fatwa was Iran's attempt, reaffirmed after Khomeini's death, to stifle, anywhere in the world, the very process of thought. Bush Sr. looked the other way.

After liberty came American life itself. The first killers were the Palestinian hijackers of the late 1960s. But the killing spree which has now shattered our soaring landmarks, our daily routine, and our souls, began in earnest only after the license granted by Carter and Bush Sr.

Many nations work to fill our body bags. But Iran, according to a State Department report of 1999, is "the most active state sponsor of terrorism," training and arming groups from all over the Mideast, including Islamic Jihad, Hamas, and Hezbollah. Nor is Iran's government now "moderating." Five months ago, the world's leading terrorist groups resolved to unite in a holy war against the U.S., which they called "a second Israel"; their meeting was held in Tehran. (Fox News, 9/16/01)

What has been the U.S. response to the above? In 1996, nineteen U.S. soldiers were killed in their barracks in Saudi Arabia. According to a front-page story in the *New York Times* (6/21/98): "Evidence suggesting that Iran sponsored the attack has further complicated the investigation, because the United States and Saudi Arabia have recently sought to improve relations with a new, relatively moderate Government in Teheran." In other words, Clinton evaded Iran's role because he wanted what he called "a genuine reconciliation." In public, of course, he continued to vow that he would find and punish the guilty. This inaction of Clinton's is comparable to his action after bin Laden's attack on U.S. embassies in East Africa; his action was the gingerly bombing of two meaningless targets.

Conservatives are equally responsible for today's crisis, as Reagan's record attests. Reagan not only failed to retaliate after 241 U.S. marines in Lebanon were slaughtered; he did worse. Holding that Islamic guerrillas were our ideological allies because of their fight against the atheistic Soviets, he methodically poured money and expertise into Afghanistan. This put the U.S. wholesale into the business of creating terrorists. Most of them regarded fighting the Soviets as only the beginning; our turn soon came.

For over a decade, there was another guarantee of American impotence: the notion that a terrorist is alone responsible for his actions, and that each, therefore, must be tried as an individual before a court of law. This viewpoint, thankfully, is fading; most people now understand that terrorists exist only through the sanction and support of a government.

We need not prove the identity of any of these creatures, because terrorism is not an issue of personalities. It cannot be stopped by destroying bin Laden and the al-Qaeda army, or even by destroying the destroyers everywhere. If that is all we do, a new army of militants will soon rise up to replace the old one.

The behavior of such militants is that of the regimes which make them possible. Their atrocities are not crimes, but acts of war. The proper response, as the public now understands, is a war in self-defense. In the excellent words of Paul Wolfowitz, deputy secretary of defense, we must "end states who sponsor terrorism."

A proper war in self-defense is one fought without self-crippling restrictions placed on our commanders in the field. It must be fought with the most effective weapons we possess (a few weeks ago, Rumsfeld refused, correctly, to rule out nuclear weapons). And it must be fought in a manner that secures victory as quickly as possible and with the fewest U.S. casualties, regardless of the countless innocents caught in the line of fire. These innocents suffer and die because of the action of their own government in sponsoring the initiation of force against America. Their fate, therefore, is their government's moral responsibility. There is no way for our bullets to be aimed only at evil men.

The public understandably demands retaliation against Afghanistan. But in the wider context Afghanistan is insignificant. It is too devastated even to breed many fanatics. Since it is no more these days than a place to hide, its elimination would do little to end terrorism.

Terrorism is a specific disease, which can be treated only by a specific antidote. The nature of the disease (though not of its antidote) has been suggested by Serge Schmemann (*New York Times*,

9/16/01). Our struggle now, he writes, is "not a struggle against a conventional guerrilla force, whose yearning for a national homeland or the satisfaction of some grievance could be satisfied or denied. The terrorists [on Tuesday]...issued no demands, no ultimatums. They did it solely out of grievance and hatred—hatred for the values cherished in the West as freedom, tolerance, prosperity, religious pluralism and universal suffrage, but abhorred by religious fundamentalists (and not only Muslim fundamentalists) as licentiousness, corruption, greed and apostasy."

Every word of this is true. The obvious implication is that the struggle against terrorism is not a struggle over Palestine. It is a clash of cultures, and thus a struggle of ideas, which can be dealt with, ultimately, only by intellectual means. But this fact does not depreciate the crucial role of our armed forces. On the contrary, it increases their effectiveness, by pointing them to the right target.

Most of the Mideast is ruled by thugs who would be paralyzed by an American victory over any of their neighbors. Iran, by contrast, is the only major country there ruled by zealots dedicated not to material gain (such as more wealth or territory), but to the triumph by any means, however violent, of the Muslim fundamentalist movement they brought to life. That is why Iran manufactures the most terrorists.

If one were under a Nazi aerial bombardment, it would be senseless to restrict oneself to combatting Nazi satellites while ignoring Germany and the ideological plague it was working to spread. What Germany was to Nazism in the 1940s, Iran is to terrorism today. Whatever else it does, therefore, the U.S. can put an end to the Jihad-mongers only by taking out Iran.

Eliminating Iran's terrorist sanctuaries and military capability is not enough. We must do the equivalent of de-Nazifying the country, by expelling every official and bringing down every branch of its government. This goal cannot be achieved painlessly, by weaponry alone. It requires invasion by ground troops, who will be at serious risk, and perhaps a period of occupation. But nothing less will "end the state" that most cries out to be ended.

The greatest obstacle to U.S. victory is not Iran and its allies, but our own intellectuals. Even now, they are advocating the same ideas that caused our historical paralysis. They are asking a reeling nation to show neighbor-love by shunning "vengeance." The multiculturalists—rejecting the concept of objectivity—are urging us to "understand" the Arabs and avoid "racism" (i.e., any condemnation of any group's culture). The friends of "peace" are reminding us, ever more loudly, to "remember Hiroshima" and beware the sin of pride.

These are the kinds of voices being heard in the universities, the churches, and the media as the country recovers from its first shock, and the professoriate et al. feel emboldened to resume business as usual. These voices are a siren song luring us to untroubled sleep while the fanatics proceed to gut America.

Tragically, Mr. Bush is attempting a compromise between the people's demand for a decisive war and the intellectuals' demand for appeasement.

It is likely that the Bush administration will soon launch an attack on bin Laden's organization in Afghanistan and possibly even attack the Taliban. Despite this, however, every sign indicates that Mr. Bush will repeat the mistakes made by his father in Iraq. As of October 1, the Taliban leadership appears not to be a target. Even worse, the administration refuses to target Iran, or any of the other countries identified by the State Department as terrorist regimes. On the contrary, Powell is seeking to add to the current coalition these very states—which is the equivalent of going into partnership with the Soviet Union in order to fight Communism (under the pretext, say, of proving that we are not anti-Russian). By seeking such a coalition, our President is asserting that he needs the support of terrorist nations in order to fight them. He is stating publicly that the world's only superpower does not have enough self-confidence or moral courage to act unilaterally in its own defense.

For some days now, Mr. Bush has been downplaying the role of our military, while praising the same policies (mainly negotiation and economic pressure) that have failed so spectacularly and for so long. Instead of attacking the roots of global terrorism, he seems to be settling for a "guerrilla war" against al-Qaeda, and a policy of unseating the Taliban passively, by aiding a motley coalition of native tribes. Our battle, he stresses, will be a "lengthy" one.

Mr. Bush's compromise will leave the primary creators of terrorism whole—and unafraid. His approach might satisfy our short-term desire for retribution, but it will guarantee catastrophe in the long term.

As yet, however, no overall policy has been solidified; the administration still seems to be groping. And an angry public still expects our government not merely to hobble terrorism for a while, but to eradicate it. The only hope left is that Mr. Bush will listen to the public, not to the professors and their progeny.

When should we act, if not now? If our appeasement has led to an escalation of disasters in the past, can it do otherwise in the future? Do we wait until our enemies master nuclear, chemical, and biological warfare?

The survival of America is at stake. The risk of a U.S. overreaction, therefore, is negligible. The only risk is underreaction.

Mr. Bush must reverse course. He must send our missiles and troops, in force, where they belong. And he must justify this action by declaring with righteous conviction that we have discarded the clichés of our paper-tiger past and that the U.S. now places America first.

There is still time to demonstrate that we take the war against terrorism seriously—as a sacred obligation to our Founding Fathers, to every victim of the men who hate this country, and to ourselves. There is still time to make the world understand that we will take up arms, anywhere and on principle, to secure an American's right to life, liberty, and the pursuit of happiness on earth.

The choice today is mass death in the United States or mass death in the terrorist nations. Our Commander-In-Chief must decide whether it is his duty to save Americans or the governments who conspire to kill them

PART 1

The Self-Crippled Response

Less than a month after 9/11, U.S. and allied forces began a military operation in Afghanistan half-heartedly targeting the Taliban and al-Qaeda. And ever since the Iranian Revolution and the seizure of the U.S. embassy in Tehran in 1979–80, we have known that Iran is the wellspring of Islamic totalitarianism.

But the Bush administration focused on Iraq. On March 20, 2003, U.S. forces began "Operation Iraqi Freedom" with airstrikes, followed by a massive ground invasion. The Iraq campaign became the centerpiece of the Bush administration's crusade for democracy.

In March 2004, jihadists detonated 10 bombs on commuter trains in Madrid, Spain, killing 193 people and injuring nearly 2000. The following year, jihadist suicide bombers attacked London's transit system during the morning rush hour, killing 56 and injuring 700.

In 2005, to gauge the phenomenon of self-censorship, journalists at the Danish newspaper *Jyllands-Posten* commissioned and published several cartoons about Islam. By early 2006, that decision had led to boycotts, deadly protests and a global crisis over freedom of speech.

Innocents in War?

Onkar Ghate January 18, 2002

If President Bush makes the solemn decision to go to war with Iraq in self-defense, he must not shackle our nation—as he did in Afghanistan—with his own personal religious or altruistic notions. As president, he has no right to worry about civilian causalities in enemy territory. As president, his chosen obligation is to achieve U.S. victory while safeguarding the lives of each and every one of the courageous individuals who have volunteered to defend America.

The government of a free nation is simply the agent of its citizens, charged with one fundamental responsibility: to secure the individual rights—and very lives—of its citizens through the use of retaliatory force. An aspect of this responsibility is to uphold each citizen's right to self-defense, a responsibility our government in part meets by eliminating terrorist states that threaten U.S. citizens.

If, however, in waging war our government considers the deaths of civilians in terrorist states as a cost that must be weighed against the deaths of our own soldiers (or civilians), or as a cost that must be weighed against achieving victory over the enemy, our government thereby violates its most basic function. It becomes not an agent for our self-defense, but theirs.

Morally, the U.S. government must destroy our aggressors by whatever means are necessary and minimize U.S. casualties in the process.

To be victorious in war, a free nation has to destroy enough of the aggressor to break his will to continue attacking (and, then, dismantle his war apparatus and, where necessary, replace his government). In modern warfare, this almost always necessitates "collateral damage," i.e., the killing of civilians.

In fact, victory with a minimum of one's own casualties sometimes requires a free nation to deliberately target the civilians of an aggressor nation in order to cripple its economic production and/or break its will. This is what the U.S. did in WWII when it dropped fire bombs on Dresden and Hamburg and atomic bombs on Hiroshima and Nagasaki. These bombings were moral acts. The destruction of Hiroshima and Nagasaki, for instance, precipitated Japan's surrender and so achieved victory with no further

U.S. casualties. In that context, to sacrifice the lives of hundreds of thousands of U.S. soldiers in a ground attack on Japan would have been morally monstrous.

But, it will be objected, is it not more monstrous to kill all those innocent civilians?

No. The moral principle is: the responsibility for all deaths in war lies with the aggressor who initiates force, not with those who defend themselves. (Similarly, if in self-defense you shoot a hit man about to kill you, and also strike the innocent bystander the hit man was deliberately using as a shield, moral responsibility for the bystander's death lies with the hit man not you.)

Moreover, the objection contains a mistaken assumption: it is false that every civilian in enemy territory—whether we are speaking of Hitler's Germany or Hirohito's Japan or the Taliban's Afghanistan or Hussein's Iraq—is innocent.

Many civilians in the Middle East, for example, hate us and actively support, materially and/or spiritually, those plotting our deaths. Can one seriously maintain, for instance, that the individuals in the Middle East who celebrated by dancing in the streets on September 11 are innocent?

Other civilians in enemy states are passive, unthinking followers. Their work and economic production, however meager, supports their terrorist governments and so they are in part responsible for the continued power of our enemies. They too are not innocent—and their deaths may be unavoidable in order for America to defend itself. (Remember too that today's civilian is tomorrow's soldier.)

But what of those who truly are innocent?

The civilians in enemy territory who actually oppose their dictatorial, terrorist governments are usually their governments' first innocent victims. All such individuals who remain alive and outside of prison camps should try to flee their country or fight with us (as some did in Afghanistan).

And the truly innocent who live in countries that initiate force against other nations will acknowledge the moral right of a free nation to bomb their countries and destroy their governments—even if this jeopardizes their own lives. No truly innocent civilian in Nazi Germany, for example, would have questioned the morality of the Allies razing Germany, even if he knew he may die in the attacks. No truly innocent individual wishes to become a tool of or a shield for his murderous government; he wishes to see his government toppled.

Thus it should be unsurprising that a European think tank reported last year that "a significant number of those Iraqis interviewed, with surprising candor, expressed their view that, if [regime change] required an American-led attack, they would support it."

As a free nation our goal is our own defense, not civilian deaths, but we must not allow human shields, innocent or otherwise, to deter us from defending ourselves.

The U.S. government recognized the truth of this on September 11 when, in order to defend those citizens it could, it ordered the shooting down of any more airplanes-become-missiles, even though this meant killing not only the terrorists but also the innocent American civilians captive onboard.

The government must now recognize that the same principle applies to civilian captives in Iraq and the rest of the Middle East.

War is terrible but sometimes necessary. To win the war on terrorism, we must not let a mistaken concern with "innocents" deter us. As a free nation, we have the moral right to defend ourselves, even if this requires mass civilian casualties in terrorist countries.

America Is Not Winning the War

Onkar Ghate August 29, 2002

As we pause on September 11 to remember the stockbrokers, policemen, firefighters and many other fallen Americans, it is vital also to reflect on the progress of the war. For it was precisely to prevent future September 11ths that America responded with force. How goes the war?

Tragically, not well.

To wage a war in self-defense you must know who your enemy is. But our enemy remains unidentified and, therefore, untargeted. Ours is a war against "terrorism"—a form of violence, not an ideological opponent intent on killing us. Our enemies, however, are dedicated to a fundamentalist interpretation of Islam, which extols faith, mindless obedience, sacrifice to state and God, primitivism, theocracy. This is why they are at war with the "Great Satan," America, the foremost embodiment of the opposite values: reason, individualism, the selfish pursuit of happiness, secularism, capitalism. bin Laden understands this: "Hostility toward America," he declares, "is a religious duty." But our politicians, schooled in pragmatism and range-of-the-moment non-thinking, cannot conceive of an ideologically motivated conflict. An individual terrorist brandishing a bomb, like bin Laden, may still be real to them, but the movement for which he fights, Islamic fundamentalism, is not. Thus, we try to kill a few terrorists—but leave untouched the main militant Islamic states breeding the terrorists. We have no long-term plan to achieve victory in the war because we cannot identify the enemy that must be incapacitated. Ask yourself: Would America have been victorious in WWII if our goal had been to destroy "kamikaze-ism," not Japanese totalitarianism?

Worse, to the extent that our policy makers glimpse the mystical ideology operative in the Middle East, they consider it a positive force. As pragmatists, they are intellectually blind to the historical evidence of centuries of religious wars and are led, instead, by their own religious feelings. They can grasp no connection between faith taken seriously as the ruling principle of every aspect of man's life—and the attempt to physically force such dogma on nonbelievers. The terrorists, on this approach, are inexplicable aberrations, deluded interpreters of true faith, who, mysteriously, try to spread their mystical doctrines by appeal not to a rational argument but to a gun. We therefore treat as allies such enemies of reason as Saudi Arabia, which spawns Islamic fundamentalists and finances their suicide bombers, and Pakistan, which trained the Taliban and punishes blasphemy with death. Our government even courts Iran, the spearhead of militant Islamic fundamentalism, and works with Iranian officials to foster "religious values" at U.N. conferences.

Predictably, the administration's actions, guided as they are not by reason but by emotion (including emotions of outrage), are chaotic and contradictory. No one knows what—if anything—America will do next in the war because we ourselves don't know what we'll do or why. Bush pays lip service to the correct idea that you are either for America's ideals or against them, but undermines our strongest ally in the war, Israel. He even promises the Palestinians a provisional state, thereby teaching every would-be killer that to the terrorist go the spoils. In typically empty rhetoric Bush declares that there is an axis of evil in the world, but allows Syria to head the U.N. Security Council and pursues dialogue with axis-of-evil-members North Korea and Iran—all terrorist states according to his own government.

Without actual principles, where will such a mentality turn for moral guidance? The answer is: to others and their moral views. So Bush—programmed by feelings formed from millennia of assertions that it is evil to uphold one's own interests, that the strong must sacrifice to the weak, that the meek shall inherit the earth—undercuts any genuine action taken in America's self-defense. In Afghanistan, for instance, morally unsure of his right to safeguard American lives, Bush feared world disapproval over civilian casualties. He would neither commit the number of American ground troops required to capture the enemy nor authorize the kind of massive bombing necessary to kill the enemy before it fled. The result: hundreds of Taliban and al-Qaeda escaped to plot further American destruction. In the Middle East, uncertain of America's right unilaterally to defend its interests, the administration obsesses with "coalition-building" (which includes shunning Israel and courting Saudi Arabia) and refuses to proclaim the superiority of America's ideals over those of medieval barbarism.

Lacking the moral conviction to uphold its values abroad, America increasingly and self-destructively turns inward, shifting its focus to such relatively trivial questions as whether airline pilots should be armed or government bureaucracies reshuffled. Because of our inaction on foreign soil, we resign ourselves to more terrorist attacks like that of September 11.

How then goes the war? An objective answer must be: badly. But our cause is not yet lost. We lack not the wealth nor the skilled military necessary to defeat the enemy, only the ideas and the will. If we articulate and practice a rational foreign policy, one actually premised on America's self-interest, we will prevail. Nothing more is needed to achieve victory than to replace the pragmatism and self-sacrifice now dictating America's actions with the principles of reason and rational self-interest; nothing less will do.

* * *

This article originally appeared in the *Greenville News*.

Don't Blame Our Intelligence Agencies—Blame Our Unprincipled Foreign Policy

Onkar Ghate April 2, 2004

The 900-page congressional report criticizing the operations of the FBI and CIA in the months prior to the September 11 attacks misses the fundamental point. Whatever incompetence on the intelligence agencies' part, what made September 11 possible was a failure, not by our intelligence agencies—but by the accommodating, range-of-the-moment, unprincipled foreign policy that has shaped our government's decisions for decades.

September 11 was not the first time America was attacked by Islamic fundamentalists engaged in "holy war" against us. In 1979 theocratic Iran—which has spearheaded the "Islamic Revolution"—stormed the U.S. embassy in Tehran and held fifty-two Americans hostage for over a year. In 1983 the Syrian- and Iranian-backed group Hezbollah bombed a U.S. marine barracks in Lebanon, killing 241 servicemen while they slept; the explosives came from Yasser Arafat's Fatah movement. In 1998 al-Qaeda blew up the U.S. embassies in Kenya and Tanzania, killing 224 individuals. In 2000 al-Qaeda bombed the USS *Cole* in Yemen, killing seventeen sailors.

So we already knew that al-Qaeda was actively engaged in attacking Americans. We even had evidence that agents connected to al-Qaeda had been responsible for the 1993 bombing of the World Trade Center. And we knew in 1996 that bin Laden had made an overt declaration of war against the "Satan" America.

But how did America react? Did our government adopt a principled approach and identify the fact that we were faced with a deadly threat from an ideological foe? Did we launch systematic counterattacks to wipe out such enemy organizations as al-Qaeda, Hezbollah and Fatah? Did we seek to eliminate enemy states like Iran? No—our responses were short-sighted and self-contradictory.

For instance, we initially expelled Iranian diplomats—but later sought an appeasing rapprochement with that ayatollah-led government. We intermittently cut off trade with Iran—but secretly negotiated weapons-for-hostages deals. When Israel had the courage to enter Lebanon in 1982 to destroy the PLO, we refused to uncompromisingly support our ally and instead brokered the killers' release. And with respect to al-Qaeda, we dropped a perfunctory bomb or two on one of its suspected camps, while our compliant diplomats waited for al-Qaeda's terrorist attacks to fade from the headlines.

At home, we treated our attackers as if they were isolated criminals rather than soldiers engaged in battle against us. In 1941 we did not attempt to indict the Japanese pilots who bombed Pearl Harbor—we declared war on the source. Yet we spent millions trying to indict specific terrorists—while we ignored their masters.

Despite emphatic pronouncements from Islamic leaders about a "jihad" against America, our political leaders failed to grasp the ideology that seeks our destruction. This left them unable to target that enemy's armed combatants—in Palestine, Iran, Iraq, Syria, Saudi Arabia—and the governments that assist them. Is it any wonder then that, although our intelligence agencies prevented many planned attacks, they could not prevent them all?

Unfortunately, little has changed since September 11. Our politicians' actions remain hopelessly unprincipled. Despite the Bush administration's rhetoric about ending states that sponsor terrorism, President Bush has left the most dangerous of these—Iran—untouched. The attack on Iraq, though justifiable, was hardly a priority in our war against militant Islam and the countries (principally, Saudi Arabia and Iran) that promote it. Moreover, when Bush does strike at militant Islam, he does so only haltingly. Morally unsure of his right to protect American lives by wiping out the Taliban and al-Qaeda, Bush feared in Afghanistan world disapproval over civilian casualties. Consequently, he reined in the military forces (as he also did in Iraq) and allowed numerous Taliban and al-Qaeda fighters to escape. And Bush continues to allow their comrades in arms in the Middle East to go unharmed. He pretends that the Palestinians and Islamic militants attacking Israel—and who have attacked Americans in the past and will try again in the future—are, somehow, different from the killers in Afghanistan and deserving of a "peace" plan.

Instead of taking consistent, principled action to destroy our terrorist adversaries, politicians from both parties continue to focus on details like reshuffling government bureaucracies and haggling over how much criticism of Saudi Arabia the 900-page congressional report can contain. Thus, too unprincipled to identify the enemy and wage all-out war, but not yet completely blind to their own ineffectualness, our leaders resignedly admit that we're in for a "long war" and that there will be more terrorists attacks on U.S. soil.

There is only one way to prevent a future September 11: by rooting out the amoral, pragmatic expediency that now dominates our government's foreign policy.

* * *

This article originally appeared in the *Providence Journal.*

America's Compassion in Iraq Is Self-Destructive

Elan Journo and *Yaron Brook* January 12, 2005

The horrific suicide bombing in December of a U.S. mess tent near Mosul and the assassination on January 10 of the deputy chief of Baghdad police—the second Iraqi official murdered in five days—are further indications that the war in Iraq is worsening. Things are going badly not because, as some claim, the United States is arrogant and lacking in humility—but because it is self-effacing and compassionate.

The Bush administration's war in Iraq embraces compassion instead of the rational goal of victory. Such an immoral approach to war wantonly sacrifices the lives of soldiers and emboldens our enemies throughout the Middle East to mount further attacks against us.

Regardless of whether the Iraqi dictatorship should have been our initial target in the war against totalitarian Islam, when in the nation's defense a president sends troops to war, morally he must resolve to soundly defeat the enemy while safeguarding our forces and citizens. But America's attention has been diverted to rebuilding Iraqi hospitals, schools, roads and sewers, and on currying favor with the locals (some U.S. soldiers were even ordered to grow moustaches in token of their respect for Iraqi culture, others are now given cultural sensitivity courses before arriving in Iraq). Since the war began, Islamic militants and Saddam Hussein loyalists have carried out random abductions, devastating ambushes, and catastrophic bombings throughout the country. That attacks on U.S. forces (including those engaged in reconstruction efforts) have gone unpunished has emboldened the enemy.

Early and stark evidence of the enemy's growing audacity came in March 2004 with the grisly murder and mutilation of four American contractors. Following the attack, U.S. forces entered the city of Fallujah vowing to capture the murderers and punish the town that supports them. But such resolve was supplanted by compassion.

In the midst of the fighting, the United States called a unilateral ceasefire to allow humanitarian aid in and to enable the other side to collect and bury its dead. The so-called truce benefited only the enemy. The Iraqis, as one soldier told the Associated Press, were "absolutely taking advantage" of the situation, regrouping and mounting sporadic attacks: as another soldier aptly noted, "It is hard to have a cease-fire when they maneuver against us, they fire at us." As the siege wore on, the goal of capturing the murderers quietly faded—and the enemy's confidence swelled.

Neither the later offensive on Fallujah in November nor any of the subsequent incursions have quelled the insurgents: witness the unending string of car bombings and (roadside) ambushes. Why?

Because in Fallujah and throughout this war the military (under orders from Washington) has been purposely treading lightly. Soldiers have strict orders to avoid the risk of killing civilians—many of whom aid or are themselves militants—even at the cost of imperiling their own lives. Mosques, which have served as hideouts for terrorists, are kept off the list of allowed targets. Military operations have been timed to avoid alienating Muslim pilgrims on holy days.

There is no shortage of aggressors lusting for American blood, and they grow bolder with each display of American compassion.

Consider the shameful tenderness shown toward the Islamic cleric Moktadr al-Sadr, who aspires to be the dictator of an Iranian-style theocracy in Iraq. An admirer of the 9/11 hijackers, Sadr has amassed an armed militia of 10,000 men (right under the noses of our military), and demanded that Coalition forces leave Iraq. On the run for the murder of another cleric, he took refuge with his militia in the holy city of Najaf, which has been surrounded by U.S. troops. Rather than attacking, however, the United States agreed to negotiate. It is as absurd to negotiate with and trust the word of a villain such as Sadr as it would have been to negotiate with Nazis bent on wiping out Allied forces in World War II. It is shockingly dangerous that the United States allowed a mediator from Iran— part of the "Axis of Evil" and Sadr's ideological ally—to assist in the negotiations.

In the end Sadr was allowed to walk away, along with his armed militia; his agreement to disarm them has—predictably—gone unfulfilled.

For the enemies of America, Iraq is like a laboratory where they are testing our mettle, with mounting ferocity. The negotiations with Sadr; the half-hearted raids on Fallujah; our timid response to daily insurrections throughout Iraq; America's outrageously deferential treatment of its enemies—all of these instances of moral weakness reinforce the view of bin Laden and his ilk that America will appease those who seek its destruction.

If we continue to confess doubts about our moral right to defend ourselves, it will only be a matter of time before Islamic militants bring suicide bombings and mass murder (again) to the streets of the United States.

Though Washington may be blinded by the longing to buy the love of Iraqis, our servicemen know all too well that (as one put it): "When you go to fight, it's time to shoot—not to make friends with people." In its might and courage, our military is unequaled; it is the moral responsibility of Washington to issue battle plans that will properly "shock and awe" the enemy. Eschewing self-interest in the name of compassion is immoral. The result is self-destruction.

Bush's Betrayal of America: The Iraqi Elections

Elan Journo January 28, 2005

President Bush claims that holding elections on January 30 will bring Iraq a step closer to freedom, an outcome allegedly vital to America's security. But the Iraqi election will bring neither freedom to Iraq nor security to America.

Consider the beliefs of the Iraqis who will be voting for "freedom" in the upcoming election. Like so many peoples in the Middle East, Iraqis regard themselves as defined by their membership in some larger group, not by their own ideas and goals. Most Iraqis owe their loyalties—and derive their honor from belonging—to their familial clan, tribe or religious sect, to which the individual is subservient. This deep-seated tribalism is reflected in the parties running in the elections: there is a spectrum ranging from advocates of secular collectivist ideologies (communists and Ba'athists) to those defined by bloodlines (such as Kurds and Turkmens) to members of various religious sects.

What will be the result of an election featuring such voters and candidates? Iraqis will merely bring to power some assortment of collectivists and Islamists. Whatever constitution those leaders eventually frame will reflect their desire to arrogate power to their particular group and to settle old scores, such as the longstanding enmity between the Shiite majority and the Sunnis. It may well permit barbaric treatment of individuals, commonly accepted throughout the Islamic world, such as "honor-killings" of women believed to have had sex before marriage, or the banning of "un-Islamic" speech. And in the long term, the new nation may become an active sponsor of Islamic terrorism.

Perhaps the most alarming outcome for U.S. security would be a popularly elected theocracy aligned with or highly sympathetic to Iran's totalitarian regime. Iran is reported to have smuggled nearly one million people into Iraq to vote and has donated millions of dollars to sway the election in favor of a Shiite-led government. Already, Iranian intelligence officials are said to roam the hallways of Iraqi party offices, on whose walls hang pictures of Iran's supreme leader.

That a theocracy may rise to power in Iraq appears to be totally compatible with the president's conception of "freedom." As he told Fox News in October, if Iraq votes in a fundamentalist government, he would "be disappointed. But democracy is democracy.... If that's what the people choose, that's what the people choose."

This certainly is democracy—in its literal sense of unlimited majority rule. But it is not freedom.

Political freedom does not mean the expression of a collective will, nor the granting of power to one pressure group to exploit others. It means the protection of an individual from the initiation of physical force by others. Freedom rests on the idea of individualism: the principle that every man is an independent, sovereign being, that he is not an interchangeable fragment of the tribe; that his life, liberty and possessions are his by right, not by the permission of any group. Democracy (i.e., majority rule) rests on the primacy of the group; if your gang is strong enough, you can get away with whatever you want, sacrificing the life and wealth of whoever stands in your way. This is why America's Founders rejected democracy and created a republican form of government, limited by the inalienable rights of the smallest "minority": the individual. Our system does have elections, of course, but they are only legitimate within a constitutional framework that prohibits the majority from voting away the rights of anyone.

Can freedom be achieved in Iraq? In the near future, no—which is one of many reasons why it is suicidal for Bush to treat Iraqi freedom as the centerpiece of American self-defense. American security does not require that the terrorism-sponsoring nations of the Middle East be free, only that they be non-threatening—a goal that can be achieved by making it clear to the leaders of these nations that any continued sponsorship of terrorism will mean their immediate destruction.

In the long run, if Iraqis or other peoples of the Middle East are to become free—a task that is their responsibility, not America's—they must first recognize that their current ideas and practices are incompatible with freedom. They must recognize that they need to adopt a philosophy of individualism. A good first step toward teaching this lesson would be not granting them the pretense of elections.

The Foreign Policy of Guilt

Onkar Ghate and *Yaron Brook* July 29, 2005

In the aftermath of the [July 7, 2005, suicide] bombings in London, Prime Minister Tony Blair has asked the British people to remain calm and maintain their daily routines; the terrorists win, he says, if one gives in to fear. This, you may remember, was also George W. Bush's response after September 11, when he called on Americans to return to our shopping malls and not be afraid.

But we should be afraid—precisely because of Blair's and Bush's policies.

We face an enemy, Islamic totalitarianism, committed to our deaths. Its agents have shown an eagerness to kill indiscriminately in London, Madrid, New York and elsewhere, even at the cost of their own lives. They continually seek chemical and nuclear weapons; imagine the death toll if such devices had been used in London's subway bombings. In the face of this mounting threat, what is our response?

Do we proudly proclaim our unconditional right to exist? Do we resolutely affirm to eradicate power base after power base of the Islamic totalitarians, until they drop their arms, and foreign governments and civilian populations no longer have the nerve to support them?

No. Blair's response to the London bombings, with Bush and the other members of the G8 by his side, was, in meaning if not in explicit statement, to apologize and do penance for our existence.

Somehow we in the West and not the Palestinians—with their rejection of the freedoms attainable in Israel and their embrace of thugs and killers—are responsible for their degradation. Thus, we must help build them up by supplying the terrorist-sponsoring Palestinian Authority with billions in aid. And somehow we in the West and not the Africans—with their decades of tribal, collectivist and anticapitalist ideas—are responsible for their poverty. Thus we must lift them out of their plight with $50 billion in aid. This, Blair claims, will help us "triumph over terrorism."

The campaigns in Afghanistan and Iraq might be considered exceptions to this orgy of penance, but that would be an error. In neither war was the aim to smash the enemy. Unlike in WWII, when the Allies would flatten cities to achieve victory, the American and British armies, by explicit order, tiptoed in the Middle East. Terrorists and insurgents went free, free to return to kill our young men, because we subordinated the lives of our soldiers to concern for the enemy's well-being and civilian casualties. Our goal was not victory but, as Bush so often tells us, to bestow with our soldiers' blood an unearned gift on these people, "freedom" and "democracy," with the hope that they would then stop killing us.

According to Blair, our duty is to shower the globe with money. According to Bush, our duty is to shower the globe with "democracy." Taken together, the meaning of their foreign policy is clear. The West has no moral right to exist, because it is productive, prosperous and free; materially and spiritually, with its money and its soldiers' lives, the West must buy permission to exist from the rest of the world. But the rest of the world has an unquestionable right to exist, because it is unproductive, poor and unfree.

Until we in the West reject this monstrous moral premise, we will never have cause to feel safe.

What we desperately need is a leader who proclaims that the rational ideals of the West, reason, science, individual rights and capitalism, are good—that we have a moral right to exist for our own sake—that we don't owe the rest of the world anything—and that we should be admired and emulated for our virtues and accomplishments, not denounced. This leader would then demonstrate, in word and deed, that if those opposed to these ideals take up arms against us, they will be crushed.

Support for totalitarian Islam will wither only when the Islamic world is convinced that the West will fight—and fight aggressively. As long as the insurgents continue with their brutal acts in Iraq, unharmed by the mightiest military force in human history, as long as the citizens of London return to "normal" lives with subways exploding all around them, as long as the West continues to negotiate with Iran on nuclear weapons—as long as the West continues to appease its enemies, because it believes it has no moral right to destroy them, totalitarian Islam is emboldened.

It is the West's moral weakness that feeds terrorism and brings it fresh recruits. It is the prospect of success against the West, fueled by the West's apologetic response, that allows totalitarian Islam to thrive.

Bush has said repeatedly, in unguarded moments, that this war is un-winnable. By his foreign policy, it is. But if the British and American people gain the self-esteem to assert our moral right to exist—with everything this entails—victory will be ours.

The Perversity of U.S. Backing for the Gaza Retreat

Elan Journo August 30, 2005

In a step fraught with danger, Israel is uprooting its citizens and withdrawing its military from Gaza and parts of the West Bank. That Palestinian terrorists are rejoicing over this momentous pull-out is hardly shocking. That the United States is also applauding is contemptible. Worse still, America is demanding more concessions of land: Secretary of State Rice has insisted, "It cannot be Gaza only."

Why is America urging Israel to make such perilous concessions? The rationale is that the withdrawal will open an unobstructed path for the "downtrodden" Palestinians toward a self-governed ethnic state. Such a state, Washington hopes, will alleviate their suffering and establish peaceful co-existence between Israel and the Palestinians.

But such a state will intensify the misery of the few genuinely freedom-seeking Palestinians by entrenching a tyrannical regime. The Palestinian Authority, a provisional governing body, has drained the lifeblood out of its citizens, trampled on their rights and, despite receiving billions in foreign aid, kept them in devastating poverty. Under the PA's anarchic reign, rival "security forces" arbitrarily seize property, arrest and jail people without charge, and summarily execute dissidents.

The actual victors of the withdrawal are terrorists and their vast legions of reverent supporters in the Palestinian population. The motto emblazoned on banners throughout Gaza expresses their belief, borne out in practice, that violence works: "Gaza Today. The West Bank and Jerusalem Tomorrow." The withdrawal has strengthened their resolve, not to achieve peace, but to destroy Israel. "We're going to keep our weapons," one terrorist told reporters, "because the battle with the enemy is a long one." A cleric allied to Hamas, which has carried out umpteen suicide bombings in Israel, observed that "when we offer up our children [as 'martyrs'], it is much better than choosing the road of humiliation and negotiations."

As some have observed, with a populace and leadership so hospitable to terrorists, in time the Palestinian territories may succeed Taliban-ruled Afghanistan as a training ground for jihadists, lusting to murder not only in the streets of Jerusalem and Baghdad, but also London and New York.

Israel's retreat from Gaza—rightly celebrated by terrorists—is neither a means of fostering peace, nor a solution for the plight of innocent Palestinians. Why, then, does America support it?

Because Washington holds that Israel has no moral right to assert its interests, but the Palestinians do. Their quest for statehood enjoys Washington's wholehearted support, encouragement and financing as an incontestable entitlement—even if they tyrannize themselves and terrorize Israel. But if Israel pursues its interests, by contrast, Washington considers that a moral transgression. Israel could, and for a time did, easily protect the lives and property of all individuals within its borders and the contested territories, by smashing aggressors and imposing its rule of law on Palestinians (which innocent Palestinians welcomed). But Washington refuses on principle to endorse such assertions of Israeli interests.

Why this double standard? Our leaders believe in altruism: the view that one's highest moral duty is to selflessly serve the needy—and thus that the world's "haves" must sacrifice for the sake of its "have-nots." The productive, on this abhorrent view, have no moral right to pursue their own interests; their only justification for existing is to serve the needy. Because Israel is strong and prosperous, it is thereby forbidden from imposing its will on the destitute Palestinians—even though it is the innocent victim of Palestinian aggression. Because the Palestinians are weak and poor, they may demand anything they wish—including a state with which to terrorize Israel.

It might seem that President Bush is being hypocritical: forbidding an ally, Israel, from fighting terrorism effectively even as U.S. forces wage a "war on terror." But observe that in fact he is being devastatingly consistent. For Bush, Iraqis are entitled to the sanctity of their Mosques—but our troops are forbidden from rooting out insurgents hiding and sniping from within; Iraqis are entitled to textbooks, hospitals, sewers, roads—but, in defending themselves, our troops must place the lives of Iraqi civilians (some of whom are or aid insurgents) above their own. Attesting to the cost of this sacrificial policy is the burgeoning U.S. death toll.

And Washington has refused to impose on Iraq a constitution that would make the new regime non-threatening—as we did in Japan after World War II. In the name of satisfying the poor Iraqis' demand for "self-determination," President Bush has pledged to recognize as sovereign whatever regime the Iraqis vote for—even a militantly hostile Islamic theocracy that, in unison with Iran's mullahs, clamors for "Death to America."

Neither Israel nor the United States can vanquish Islamist terrorism unless it repudiates the corrupt morality of altruism, which enjoins the sacrifice of the successful as an ideal. Victory can only be achieved if one is convinced of one's moral right to live and to act consistently to achieve one's goals. Every self-effacing step that Israel takes—in lockstep with America and with our blessing—encourages the terrorists with the belief that their success is achievable.

* * *

This article originally appeared in *Capitalism Magazine.*

The Advent of Freedom?

Onkar Ghate October 12, 2005

As the world eagerly watches the Iraqi constitutional referendum, the Bush administration and its intellectual supporters herald the occasion as a historic step toward freedom in the Middle East and security for America. This view betrays an appalling ignorance of the nature of freedom and the requirements of our national self-interest.

Politically, as America's Founding Fathers understood, to be free is to possess the ability to exercise one's rights to life, liberty, property and the pursuit of happiness. To be free means that no other men, whatever their number or position, can coercively prevent an individual from taking the steps rationally required to support his life. It means no one can force him to accept beliefs or dogmas, control what he can or cannot say, seize the material wealth he has produced and earned, or dictate the goals he must live for.

A constitution is valuable only if it strictly delimits the power of government to that of protecting each individual's rights. History demonstrates that government is, potentially, the worst violator of man's rights. A proper constitution declares off-limits any governmental action that would trespass on an individual's rights, no matter whether that action is proposed in the name of the king, the common good, God or public morality.

The draft Iraqi constitution, however, grants virtually unlimited power to the state.

As liberals have demanded in America for over a century, private property will be eviscerated. Although the proposed constitution nominally protects property rights, it explicitly allows that private property can be seized by the government "for the public interest." By contrast, public property "is sacrosanct, and its protection is the duty of every citizen." (In practice, this means that if the government takes a citizen's money, business or home, he must stand aside—and then defend with his life what the government has stolen from him.) The state will dictate whether an Iraqi can sell land to foreigners. It will manage the oil. It will provide to its hapless citizens "free" education and health care, "a correct environmental atmosphere," and work "that guarantees them a good life."

23

The government will also, as conservatives have long dreamed for America, enforce religious morality. "Islam," Article 2 declares, "is the official religion of the state and is a basic source of legislation: No law can be passed that contradicts the undisputed rules of Islam." Experts in Islamic law will sit on the Supreme Court. The state will guarantee protection of motherhood and the "ethical and religious value" of the family. Citizens will have freedom of speech, of press, of assembly—so long as no one says or does anything that violates "public morality," i.e., the dogmas of Islam.

And as if to leave no doubt that the state can exert total control over the individual's life, Article 45 adds that the government can restrict or limit "any of the freedoms and liberties stated in the constitution...as long as this restriction or limitation does not undermine the essence of the right or freedom." Of course, part of the essence of any right or freedom is that it is inviolable.

We in America had no reason to expect freedom from the drafters of Iraq's constitution. Like many of our own intellectuals on the left and the right (some of whom were advisers in Iraq), Iraqi intellectuals are either tribal or religious collectivists (or both). Whichever the case, they deny the individual and his rights. The tribalists deny material independence to the individual and seek to control his every economic step. The religionists, more numerous and powerful, deny spiritual independence to the individual and seek to dictate his every conviction and purpose in life. It is no accident that the draft constitution is both "keen to advance Iraqi tribes and clans" and eager to promote Islam. Freedom's intellectual preconditions do not exist in Iraq.

In the long term, whether Iraq's religious collectivists seize the machinery of state by a protracted, bloody civil war or by the ballot box will make no difference to America's security.

Nor did we have any reason to think that our self-defense requires, at the price of our soldiers' lives, "imposing freedom" on Iraq or the Middle East. It is true that free nations pose no threat to us. But neither do semi-barbarous nations when they and their citizens are demoralized—when they know that taking up arms against us guarantees their devastation. This is the lesson America's military should have taught the Islamic totalitarians and their legions of collectivist supporters and sympathizers in the Middle East after 9/11—indeed, after Iran's embassy takeover in 1979. But this is not the lesson conveyed by Operation Iraqi Freedom, which espouses Bush's "calling of our time": selflessly to bring freedom to those hostile to the idea.

Freedom is an intellectual achievement, which requires disavowal of collectivism and embrace of individualism. Sadly, no matter what the referendum's result, this is not what we are witnessing in Iraq.

* * *

This article originally appeared in *Capitalism Magazine*.

Death to "Diplomacy" with Iran

Elan Journo October 27, 2005

The president of Iran—a country believed to be building nuclear weapons—recently demanded that "Israel must be wiped off the map." But European diplomats, who are courting Iran in an attempt to halt its suspected nuclear weapons program, said that such belligerence won't derail their overtures.

The diplomatic effort led by Britain, France and Germany is touted as a reasonable way to settle the dispute over Iran's suspected nuclear weapons program without any losers. By enticing Iran to the negotiating table, we are told, the West can avoid a military confrontation, while Iran gains "economic incentives" that can help build its economy. But this deal—backed also by the Bush administration—can only strengthen Iran and turn it into a greater menace.

The European deal—which is said to include the sale of civilian aircraft and membership for Iran in the World Trade Organization—rests on the notion that no one would put abstract goals or principles ahead of gaining a steady flow of economic loot. And so, if only we could negotiate a deal that gives Iran a sufficiently juicy carrot, it would forgo its ambitions.

But to believe that Iran really hungers for nuclear energy (as it claims) is sheer fantasy. Possessing abundant oil and gas reserves, Iran is the second-largest oil producer in OPEC. To believe that it values prosperity at all is equally fantastic; Iran is a theocracy that systematically violates its citizens' right to political and economic liberty.

What Iran desires is a nuclear weapon—the better to threaten and annihilate the impious in the West and in Iran's neighborhood. Iran declares its anti-Western ambitions stridently. At an official parade in 2004, Iran flaunted a missile draped with a banner declaring: "We will crush America under our feet." (Its leaders, moreover, have for years repeated the demand that "Israel must be wiped off the map.")

A committed enemy of the West, Iran is the ideological wellspring of Islamic terrorism, and the "world's most active sponsor of terrorism" (according to the U.S. government). A totalitarian regime that viciously punishes "un-Islamic" behavior among its own citizens, Iran actively exports its contempt for freedom and human life throughout the infidel world. For years it has been fomenting and underwriting savage attacks on Western and American interests, using such proxies as Hezbollah. Like several of the 9/11 hijackers before them, many senior al-Qaeda leaders, fugitives of the Afghanistan war, have found refuge in Iran. And lately Iran has funneled millions of dollars, arms and ammunition to insurgents in Iraq.

It's absurd to think that by offering Iran rewards to halt its aggression, we will deflect it from its goal.

The only consequence of engaging such a vociferously hostile regime in negotiations is the whitewashing of its crimes and the granting of undeserved legitimacy. The attempt to conciliate Iran with "incentives" further inflames the boldness of Iran's mullahs. What it teaches them is that the West lacks the intellectual self-confidence to name its enemies and deal with them accordingly. It vindicates the mullahs' view that their religious worldview can bring a scientific, technologically advanced West to its knees.

Far from converting Iran into a non-threat, the "incentives" would sustain its economy, prop up its dictatorial government and perpetuate its terrorist war against the West. Whether Iran accepts the European deal or merely prolongs "negotiations" indefinitely, so long as the "diplomatic" approach continues Iran gains time enough to engage in covert nuclear-weapons research. Iran's flouting of a previous agreement to stop enriching uranium (which prompted the current talks) and its documented attempts to acquire nuclear-bomb technology erase any doubts about how it will behave under any future deal.

This approach of diplomacy-with-anyone-at-any-cost necessarily results in nourishing one's enemy and sharpening its fangs. That is what happened under a 1994 deal with communist North Korea. In return for boatloads of aid and oil from the United States, Japan and other nations, North Korea promised not to develop nuclear weapons. Despite U.N. inspections, North Korea flouted the agreement repeatedly. When caught cheating, it promised anew to end its nuclear program in return for more "incentives." In February 2005, North Korea declared (plausibly) that it had succeeded in building nuclear weapons.

Another, older attempt to buy peace by giving "incentives" to an enemy was a cataclysmic failure. In 1938 the Europeans pretended that Hitler's intentions were not really hostile, and insisted that "peace in our time" could be attained by allowing him to walk into Czechoslovakia. Instead, he was emboldened to launch World War II.

Ignoring the lessons of history, the Europeans are advocating a deal with Iran that likewise purchases the reckless pretense of peace today, at the cost of unleashing catastrophic dangers tomorrow.

To protect American (and European) lives, we must learn the life-or-death importance of passing objective moral judgment. We must recognize the character of Iran and act accordingly. By any rational standard, Iran should be condemned and its nuclear ambition thwarted, now. The brazenly amoral European gambit can only aid its quest—and necessitate a future confrontation with a bolder, stronger Iran.

The Twilight of Freedom of Speech

Onkar Ghate February 21, 2006

To fathom our government's contemptible treatment of a hand-ful of unbowed journalists, you must see the roots of that treat-ment in the moral ideal Christianity bequeathed the West.

In the face of the intimidation and murder of European authors, filmmakers and politicians by Islamic militants, a few European newspapers have the courage to defend their freedom of speech: they publish twelve cartoons to test whether it's still pos-sible to criticize Islam. They discover it isn't. Muslims riot, burn embassies, and demand the censorship and death of infidels. The Danish cartoonists go into hiding; if they weren't afraid to speak before, they are now.

How do our leaders respond? Do they declare that an individu-al's freedom of speech is inviolable, no matter who screams offense at his ideas? No. Do they defend our right to life and pledge to hunt down anyone, anywhere, who abets the murder of a Westerner for having had the effrontery to speak? No—as they did not when the fatwah against Rushdie was issued or his translators were attacked and one murdered.

Instead, the U.S. government announces that although free speech is important, the government shares "the offense that Muslims have taken at these images," and even hints that it is dis-respectful to publish them.

Why does a Muslim have a moral right to his dogmas, but we don't to our rational principles? Why, when journalists uphold free speech and Muslims respond with death threats, does the State Department single out the journalists for moral censure? Why the vicious double standard? Why admonish the good to mollify evil?

The answer lies in the West's conception of morality.

Morality, we are told incessantly, by secularists and religion-ists, the left and the right, means sacrifice; give up your values in selfless service to others. "Serve in a cause larger than your wants, larger than yourself," Bush proclaims to a believing nation.

But when you surrender your values, are you to give them up for men you admire, for those you think have earned and deserve

29

them? Obviously not—otherwise yours would be an act of trade, of justice, of self-assertiveness, not self-sacrifice.

You must give to that which you don't admire, to that which you judge to be unworthy, undeserving, irrational. An employee, for instance, must give up his job for a competitor he deems inferior; a businessman must contribute to ideological causes he opposes; a taxpayer must fund modern, unemployed "artists" whose feces-covered works he loathes; the United States must finance the UN, which it knows to be a pack of America-hating dictatorships.

To uphold your rational convictions is the most selfish of acts. To renounce them, to surrender the world to that which you judge to be irrational and evil, is the epitome of sacrifice. When Jesus, the great preacher of self-sacrifice, commanded "Love your enemies, bless them that curse you, do good to them that hate you, and pray for them which despitefully use you, and persecute you," he knew whereof he spoke.

In the left's adaptation of this perverse ideal, selfless surrender to evil translates into a foreign policy of self-loathing and "sensitivity," of spitting in America and the West's face while showing respect for the barbarisms of every gang.

Bill Clinton, for instance, certainly no radical leftist, jumped into the recent fray to castigate us: "None of us are totally free of stereotypes about people of different races, different ethnic groups, and different religions... there was this appalling example in... Denmark... these totally outrageous cartoons against Islam."

In the right's version, selfless surrender to evil translates into a foreign policy of self-effacing service.

Our duty, Bush declares, is to bring the vote to Iraqis and Palestinians, but we dare not tell them what constitution to adopt, or ban the killers they want to vote for. We have no right to assert our principles, because they are rational and good. But the Iraqis and Palestinians have a right to enact their tribal and terrorist beliefs at our expense, because their beliefs are irrational and evil. In the present crisis, the State Department will not defend free speech, because this principle is rationally defensible; to unequivocally assert this value would be selfish. But the department will suggest that we respectfully refrain from publishing cartoons that upset the mental lethargy of self-made slaves to authority; Muslims have a right to their mystical taboos, precisely because the beliefs are mystical.

Tonight, when you turn on the news and see hatred-seething hordes burning the West's flags and torching its embassies, remember that this is the enemy your morality commands you to love and serve—and remember the lonely Danes hiding in fear for their lives. And then, in the ultimate act of self-assertiveness, pledge to renounce the morality of sacrifice and learn its opposite: the morality of rational self-interest. Though the West's twilight has begun, the darkness of suicide has not yet engulfed us. We still have a chance.

Washington's Failed War in Afghanistan

Elan Journo June 8, 2006

America's campaign in Afghanistan was once widely hailed as a success in the "war on terror." We have nothing more to fear from Afghanistan, our policy makers told us, because the war had accomplished its two main goals: al-Qaeda and its sponsoring regime, the Taliban, were supposedly long gone, and a new, pro-Western government had been set up. But as the daily news from Afghanistan shows, in reality the war has been a drastic failure.

Legions of undefeated Taliban and al-Qaeda soldiers have renewed their jihad. Flush with money, amassing recruits, and armed with guns, rockets and explosives, they are fighting to regain power. In recent months, they have mounted a string of deadly suicide bombings and rocket attacks against American and NATO forces; more U.S. troops have died in Afghanistan in the last twenty months than did during the peak of the war.

Taliban forces have effectively besieged several provinces in southern Afghanistan. Local officials estimate that in some provinces the "number of Taliban...is several times more than that of the police and Afghan National Army." Taliban fighters are said to amble through villages fearlessly, brandishing their Kalashnikovs, and collecting zakat (an Islamic tithe) from peasants. With astounding boldness, they have assassinated clerics and judges deemed too friendly to the new government, and fired rockets at a school for using "un-Islamic" books.

The Taliban and al-Qaeda forces are so strong and popular that Senator Bill Frist recently declared that a war against them cannot be won, and instead suggested negotiating with the Islamists.

How is it that five years after the war began—and in the face of America's unsurpassed military strength—Taliban and al-Qaeda fighters are threatening to regain power?

Victory in Afghanistan demanded two things. We had to destroy the Taliban and we had to ensure that a non-threatening, non-Islamic-warrior-breeding regime take its place. But we did not think we had a moral right to do what was necessary to achieve either goal.

Our military was ordered to pursue Taliban fighters only if it simultaneously showed "compassion" to the Afghans. The U.S. military dropped bombs on Afghanistan—but instead of ruthlessly pounding key targets, it was ordered to gingerly avoid hitting holy shrines and mosques (known to be Taliban hideouts) and to shower the country with food packages. The United States deployed ground forces—but instead of focusing exclusively on capturing or killing the enemy, they were also diverted to a host of "reconstruction" projects. The result is that the enemy was not destroyed and crushed in spirit, but merely scattered and left with the moral fortitude to regroup and launch a brazen comeback.

Even with its hands tied, however, the U.S. military succeeded in toppling the Taliban regime—but Washington subverted that achievement, too.

A new Afghan government would be a non-threat to America's interests if it were based on a secular constitution that respects individual rights. The Bush administration, however, declared that we had no right to "impose our beliefs" on the Afghans—and instead endorsed their desire for another regime founded on Islamic law. Already this avowedly Islamic regime has jailed an Afghan magazine editor for "blasphemy"; earlier this year Abdul Rahman, an Afghan convert to Christianity, faced a death sentence for apostasy. The new Afghan regime cannot be counted on to oppose the resurgence of Islamic totalitarianism. Ideologically, it has nothing to say in opposition to the doctrines of the Taliban (two members of the Taliban leadership are in the new government). It is only a matter of time before Afghanistan is once again a haven for anti-American warriors.

The failure in Afghanistan is a result of Washington's foreign policy. Despite lip-service to the goal of protecting America's safety, the "war on terror" has been waged in compliance with the prevailing moral premise that self-interest is evil and self-sacrifice a virtue. Instead of trouncing the enemy for the sake of protecting American lives, our leaders have sacrificed our self-defense for the sake of serving the whims of Afghans.

The half-hearted war in Afghanistan failed to smash the Taliban and al-Qaeda. It failed to render their ideology—Islamic totalitarianism—a lost cause. Instead, at best it demonstrated

Washington's reluctance to fight ruthlessly to defend Americans. How better to stoke the enthusiasm of jihadists?

America cannot win this or any war by embracing selflessness as a virtue. Ultimately, it cannot survive unless Washington abandons its self-sacrificial foreign policy in favor of one that proudly places America's interests as its exclusive moral concern.

The U.S.–Israeli Suicide Pact

Elan Journo July 20, 2006

The Iran-Hamas-Hezbollah axis is fully responsible for initiating the war on Israel, but the Islamists' aggression is the logical product of U.S.-Israeli policy. The longstanding commitment of Israel and America to "diplomatic engagement" with Palestinians and Islamists—a euphemism for appeasement—is suicidal.

For decades America has urged Israel to placate and surrender to our common enemy. The U.S.-endorsed "Road Map to Peace," like the "Peace Process" and sundry initiatives before it, rationalized Palestinian terrorism as the result of a legitimate grievance. If only the Palestinians' wish for a civilized, peaceful state were fulfilled—Washington deluded itself into believing—terrorism would end. And fulfilling this wish requires not smashing their terrorist infrastructure, but showering them with land and loot.

But the majority of Palestinians actually seek the destruction of Israel, and the slaughter of its people. Because they embrace this vicious goal, hordes of Palestinians idolized arch terrorist Yasser Arafat for waging a terrorist war to wipe out Israel and establish a nationalist dictatorship. They abetted Arafat's terrorism and celebrated his atrocities. They served as cheerleaders or recruits for terrorist groups—and when they had the chance, they embraced the even more militant religious zealots of Hamas. It is no surprise that, according to a recent poll, 77 percent of Palestinians support their government's kidnapping of an Israeli soldier and that 60 percent support the continued rocket fire from Gaza into Israel.

But even as Palestinians mounted more attacks, Washington pressed Israel for more concessions—and bolstered the terrorist-sponsoring Palestinian Authority with millions of dollars in aid. The U.S. forbade Israel from laying a finger on Arafat, and extended this tender solicitude to Hamas leaders. Washington actually whitewashed the blood-stained Arafat and his crony Mahmoud Abbas as peace-loving statesmen and invited them to the White House. And when Hezbollah now fires rockets at major cities in northern Israel, President Bush demands that Israel show "restraint."

Depressingly, Israel has continually relented to American pressure to appease our common enemy. It has prostrated itself before the Palestinians, with flamboyantly self-sacrificial offers of land-for-peace; it has withdrawn from southern Lebanon, ceding ground necessary to its self-defense; it has withdrawn from Gaza, leaving its southern cities at the mercy of rocket fire from the Hamas-run territory.

Such U.S.-endorsed appeasement by Israel, across decades, has enabled Hezbollah and Hamas to mount their current attacks. Yet America remains undeterred in its commitment to appeasement.

The U.S. is now trying to woo Iran with endless offers of economic "incentives," if only Iran promises to stop chasing nuclear weapons. Evading Iran's lust to "wipe Israel off the map," evading its funding of Hezbollah and Hamas, evading its avowed enmity to America, evading its decades of fomenting and orchestrating a proxy terror war against American civilians—evading all of this, Washington deludes itself into believing that paying Iran off will, somehow, wipe out its hostility.

Inevitably, this encourages Iran to continue its aggressive support for terrorists and its fervent quest for nuclear weapons. Merely by prolonging the negotiations endlessly, Iran gains time to acquire a weapon to wield against its neighbors, to provide to Hamas and Hezbollah or to other proxies to use against the United States. And were Iran eventually to accept some deal, American aid would merely be sustaining Iran's regime—and, inexorably, a covert nuclear program.

We are teaching the Islamic totalitarians in Gaza, Lebanon and Iran that their goal of destroying us is legitimate; that aggression is practical; that the more aggressive they are, the more we will surrender. U.S.-Israeli policy has demonstrated that we lack the intellectual self-confidence to name, let alone condemn, our enemies—and that we lack the will to deal with threats mercilessly. It vindicates the Islamists' premise that their religious worldview can bring a scientific, technologically advanced West to its knees.

To protect the lives of our citizens, America and Israel must stop evading the nature of the enemy's cause: our complete destruction. We must stop appeasing our common enemy—and embrace self-defense as a matter of intransigent principle. To put an end to the current rocket attacks from Lebanon and Gaza, America should urge Israel to annihilate the annihilators: Hamas and Hezbollah. And to thwart Iran's nuclear ambition, America must use as much military force as is necessary to dispose of that catastrophic threat and the regime responsible for it.

The Indispensable Condition of Peace

Onkar Ghate July 21, 2006

As Israeli soldiers reenter Gaza and bomb Lebanon, and Israeli citizens seek shelter from Hezbollah's missiles, the world despairingly wonders whether peace between Israel and its neighbors can ever take root. It can—but only if America reverses course.

To achieve peace in the Middle East, as in any region, there is a necessary principle that every party must learn: the initiation of force is evil. And the indispensable means of teaching it is to ensure that the initiating side is defeated and punished. Decisive retaliatory force must be wielded against the aggressor. So long as one side has reason to think it will benefit from initiating force against its neighbors, war must result. Yet this is precisely what America's immoral foreign policy gives the Palestinian Authority, Hamas and Hezbollah reason to think.

Israel is a free country, which recognizes the rights of its citizens, whatever their race or religion, and which prospers through business and trade. It has no use for war and no interest in conquest. But for years, Arafat and the Palestinian authorities, with the aid of Iran, Syria, Saudi Arabia and other states, sought not to learn the conditions of freedom, but to annihilate the only free nation in their midst: Israel. Did the United States demand that the Palestinian leadership be destroyed?

No. Clinton invited Arafat to dine at the White House and Bush declared that peace requires Israel to give in to its aggressor's insistence on a state.

Worse still, as part of the "two state solution" announced in 2002, Bush demanded that Israel withdraw to its pre-1967 borders. In 1967 Israel captured the Golan Heights, West Bank and Gaza Strip after yet another attempt by Arab nations to annihilate it. To give back any of this land—as Israel has done in the face of international pressure—teaches the Arabs that they can launch wars against Israel with impunity. If they at first do not succeed militarily, they need only continue issuing threats against Israel and arming more suicide bombers—and eventually the land they lost in a war they initiated will be returned to them. They can then start the process anew, as they have since Israel withdrew from Lebanon and Gaza.

In order to move toward his "two state solution," Bush championed elections in the Palestinian territories and Lebanon, which predictably brought Hamas and Hezbollah into government. Terrorism, Bush is thus teaching the killers, is the means to political power.

The reason peace eludes the Middle East is therefore not difficult to discern. The lesson President Bush is conveying to the Arabs and Islamists—that the initiation of force is practical—is a continuation of the lesson America's foreign policy has been teaching them for decades. The Egyptians seized the Suez canal from the French and British in 1956—and we demanded that the Europeans not retaliate. Israel had the Palestinian terrorists surrounded in Lebanon in 1982—and we brokered their release. Many Arabs idolized a terrorist for hijacking airliners and murdering civilians—and we poured money into his regime, hailed him for winning the Nobel Peace Prize in 1994, and demanded that Israel enter into a protracted "peace process" that consisted of concession after concession. What possible conclusion could the Arab world draw but that the initiation of force is practical? So long as they have grounds to believe that, war is inescapable.

If we truly seek peace, we must reverse this perverse lesson. We must proclaim the objective conditions of peace. This means declaring to Arab nations that Israel, as a free country, has a moral right to exist, that the Arabs and Palestinians are the initiators of the conflict and that aggression on their part is evil and will not be tolerated. And it means encouraging Israel not to negotiate and compromise with its current assailants, but to destroy them.

Only when the initiators of force learn that their actions lead not to world sympathy and political power, but to their own deaths, will peace be possible in the Middle East.

* * *

This article originally appeared in *Ynetnews.com.*

Why We Are Losing Hearts and Minds

Keith Lockitch September 7, 2006

Five years into our "war on terror," the Iraqi insurgency is raging, with no apparent end to the new recruits eager to wage jihad against the West. Support for offensive action has faded among a disheartened American public, while the terrorists are growing in number and in boldness.

Where have our leaders gone wrong? What kind of leadership failure can demoralize a whole nation of honest, productive citizens, while leaving suicide murderers stirred to righteous action?

The power that inspires righteous action—and which, by its absence, breeds discouragement—is the power of moral idealism. What has brought us to our present state is our leaders' moral weakness in response to the jihadists' moral zeal.

Observe that what draws the recruits to terrorist cells is a powerful ideal: the advancement of their religion. The jihadists believe fervently that Islam is the revealed word of Allah, that selfless submission to Allah is the purpose of life, and that all individuals should be subjugated to Islamic law under a theocracy. They believe in spreading the rule of Islam worldwide and killing any "infidels" who stand in their way. They are morally outraged by the American ideal of individual liberty and regard our this-worldly, capitalistic culture as an evil that must be destroyed.

America can only defend itself against such a zealous, militant movement if we have moral confidence in our own ideals—and fight for them. We must repudiate the Islamists' "ideals" of other-worldliness, of blind faith, of renunciation and suffering, of theocracy, and proudly uphold the superior, American ideals of reason, freedom and the pursuit of worldly happiness.

But our leaders have not shown such moral confidence.

When the terrorists of September 11 struck in the name of Islam, President Bush did not identify them as Islamic totalitarians and condemn their murderous ideology and its supporters. Instead, he painted the hijackers as a band of isolated lunatics who had "hijacked a great religion." (Only recently has President Bush even acknowledged that our enemy is Islamic, with his use of the term "Islamic fascism.")

39

In response to Muslim denunciations of America's secularism, our leaders did not defend this attribute of America, but instead stressed Americans' religiosity. A mere two weeks after September 11, with the ruins of the World Trade Towers still smoldering, our planned Afghanistan campaign, "Operation Infinite Justice," was renamed to appease Muslims protesting that only Allah can dispense "infinite justice."

Unable to defend America intellectually, our leaders are unable to defend her militarily.

Have our leaders acted consistently against terrorist regimes? Consider our policy toward Iran, the primary state sponsor of terrorism. Refusing to identify Iran as the fatherland of Islamic totalitarianism, our president initially beseeched its mullahs to join our "war on terror." And he has consistently answered their chants of "Death to America" and their quest for nuclear weapons with negotiation and spineless diplomacy.

Have our leaders asserted that they will use America's formidable military to secure our way of life by whatever means necessary? No. Lacking the moral confidence to defeat our enemies, they have instead squandered our military resources and sacrificed our brave soldiers in a futile quest to spread "democracy" around the globe—as though bringing the vote to Muslim mobs sympathetic to Islamic totalitarianism will somehow end the terrorist threat.

The reason the terrorists and their state sponsors are not demoralized is that our leaders have failed to demoralize them. Our leaders' words and actions have signaled that we are not as morally committed to our lives and freedom as the terrorists are to our destruction.

We must make it clear to the jihadists that we will destroy anyone who takes up arms for Islamic totalitarianism. No one wants to fight and die for a hopeless cause. The jihadists will continue to be emboldened and to attract new recruits until they are convinced their goal is unachievable. They must see that we have the moral confidence to defend our lives—to answer their violence with an overwhelming military response, without pulling punches. They must see us willing to visit such crushing devastation on them that they fear us more than they fear Allah.

It is often said that we must win the "hearts and minds" of supporters of totalitarian Islam. Indeed we must: their hearts must be made to despair at the futility of their cause, and their minds must be convinced that any threat to our lives and freedom will bring them swift and certain doom.

The ideologues of totalitarian Islam have seized the power of moral idealism in the service of our destruction. It is time we reclaimed that power in defense of our freedom.

What Real War Looks Like

Elan Journo December 7, 2006

The Iraq Study Group has issued many specific recommendations, but the options boil down to a maddeningly limited range: pull out or send more troops to do democracy-building and, either way, "engage" the hostile regimes in Iran and Syria. Missing from the list is the one option our self-defense demands: a war to defeat the enemy. If you think we've already tried this option and failed, think again. Washington's campaign in Iraq looks nothing like the war necessary for our self-defense.

What does such a war look like?

America's security depends on identifying precisely the enemy that threatens our lives—and then crushing it, rendering it a non-threat. It depends on proudly defending our right to live free of foreign aggression—by unapologetically killing the killers who want us dead.

Those who say this is a "new kind of conflict" against a "faceless enemy" are wrong. The enemy Washington evasively calls "terrorism" is actually an ideologically inspired political movement: Islamic totalitarianism. It seeks to subjugate the West under a totalitarian Islamic regime by means of terrorism, negotiation, war—anything that will win its jihad. The movement's inspiration, its first triumph, its standard bearer, is the theocracy of Iran. Iran's regime has, for decades, used terrorist proxies to attack America. It openly seeks nuclear weapons and zealously sponsors and harbors jihadists. Without Iran's support, legions of holy warriors would be untrained, unarmed, unmotivated, impotent.

Destroying Islamic totalitarianism requires a punishing military onslaught to end its primary state representative (Iran) and demoralize its supporters. We need to deploy all necessary force to destroy Iran's ability to fight, while minimizing our own casualties. We need a campaign that ruthlessly inflicts the pain of war so intensely that the jihadists renounce their cause as hopeless and fear to take up arms against us. This is how America and its Allies defeated both Nazi Germany and Imperialist Japan.

Victory in World War II required flattening cities, firebombing factories, shops and homes, devastating vast tracts of Germany

42

and Japan. The enemy and its supporters were exhausted materially and crushed in spirit. What our actions demonstrated to them was that any attempt to implement their vicious ideologies would bring them only destruction and death. Since their defeat, Nazism and Japanese imperialism have essentially withered as ideological forces. Victory today requires the same: smashing Iran's totalitarian regime and thus demoralizing the Islamist movement and its many supporters, so that they, too, abandon their cause as futile.

We triumphed over both Japan and Germany in less than four years after Pearl Harbor. Yet more than five years after 9/11, against a far weaker enemy, our soldiers still die daily in Iraq. Why? Because this war is neither assertive nor ruthless—it is a tragically meek pretense at war.

Consider what Washington has done. The Islamist regime in Iran remains untouched, fomenting terrorism. (And now our leaders hope to "engage" Iran diplomatically.)

We went to battle not with theocratic Iran, but with the secular dictatorship of Iraq. And the campaign there was not aimed at crushing whatever threat Hussein's regime posed to us. "Shock and awe" bombing never materialized. Our brave and capable forces were hamstrung: ordered not to bomb key targets such as power plants and to avoid firing into mosques (where insurgents hide) lest we offend Muslim sensibilities. Instead, we sent our troops to lift Iraq out of poverty, open new schools, fix up hospitals, feed the hungry, unclog sewers—a Peace Corps, not an army corps, mission.

U.S. troops were sent, not to crush an enemy threatening America, but (as Bush explained) to "sacrifice for the liberty of strangers," putting the lives of Iraqis above their own. They were prevented from using all necessary force to win or even to protect themselves. No wonder the insurgency has flourished, emboldened by Washington's self-crippling policies. (Perversely, some want even more Americans tossed into this quagmire.)

Bush did all this to bring Iraqis the vote. Any objective assessment of the Middle East would have told one who would win elections, given the widespread popular support for Islamic totalitarianism. Iraqis swept to power a pro-Islamist leadership intimately tied to Iran. The most influential figure in Iraqi politics is now Moktadr al-Sadr, an Islamist warlord lusting after theocratic rule and American blood. When asked whether he would accept just such an outcome from the elections, Bush said that of course he would, because "democracy is democracy."

No war that ushers Islamists into political office has U.S. self-defense as its goal.

This war has been worse than doing nothing, because it has galvanized our enemy to believe its success more likely than ever—even as it has drained Americans' will to fight. Washington's feeble campaign demonstrates the ruinous effects of refusing to assert our self-interest and defend our freedom. It is past time to consider our only moral and practical option: end the senseless sacrifice of our soldiers—and let them go to war.

The Real Disgrace:
Washington's Battlefield "Ethics"

Elan Journo July 3, 2007

Americans rightly admire our troops for their bravery, dedication and integrity. The Marines, for instance, are renowned for abiding by an honorable code—as warriors and as individuals in civilian life. They epitomize the rectitude of America's soldiers. But a recently disclosed Pentagon study—little noted in the media—has seemingly cast a shadow over our troops.

The study of U.S. combat troops in Iraq finds that less than half of the soldiers and Marines surveyed would report a team member for breaches of the military's ethics rules. Military and civilian observers have concluded from the study that more and stricter training in combat ethics is urgently needed.

But instead of reinforcing the military's ethics, we must challenge them. The Pentagon study provides evidence for a searing indictment not of our soldiers but of Washington's rules of engagement.

Consider the waking nightmare of being a U.S. combat soldier in Iraq: imagine that you are thrust into a battlefield—but purposely hamstrung by absurd restrictions. Iraqis throw Molotov cocktails (i.e., gasoline-filled bottles) at your vehicle—but you are prohibited from responding by force. Iraqis, to quote the study, "drop large chunks of concrete blocks from second story buildings or overpasses" as you drive by—but you are not allowed to respond. "Every group of Soldiers and Marines interviewed," the Pentagon study summarizes, "reported that they felt the existing ROE [rules of engagement] tied their hands, preventing them from doing what needed to be done to win the war."

And the soldiers are right. In Iraq Washington's rules have systematically prevented our brave and capable troops from using all necessary force to win, to crush the insurgency—and even to protect themselves. As noted in news articles since the start of the war, American forces are ordered not to bomb key targets such as power plants, and to avoid firing into mosques (where insurgents hide) lest they offend Muslim sensibilities.

Having to follow such self-effacing rules of engagement while confronting sniper fire and ambushes and bombs from every direction, day in and day out, must be utterly demoralizing and unbearable. No one should be surprised at the newly reported willingness of combat troops to defy military ethics, because such defiance is understandable as the natural reaction of warriors made to follow suicidal rules.

When being "ethical" on Washington's terms means martyring yourself and your comrades for the sake of murderous Iraqis, it is understandable that troops are disinclined to report "unethical" behavior. It is understandable that troops should feel anger and anxiety (as many do), because it is horrifically unjust for America to send its personnel into combat, deliberately prevent them from achieving victory—and expect them to die for the sake of the enemy. It would be natural for an individual thrust into the line of fire as a sacrificial offering to rebel with indignation at such a fate.

How can we do this to our soldiers?

The death and misery caused by Washington's self-crippling rules of engagement—rules endorsed by liberals and conservatives alike—are part of the inevitable destruction flowing from a broader evil: the philosophy of "compassionate" war.

This perverse view of war holds that fighting selfishly to defend your own freedom by defeating enemies is wrong; but fighting to selflessly serve the needs of others is virtuous. It was on this premise that U.S. troops were sent to Iraq: Washington's goal was not to defend America against whatever threat Hussein's hostile regime posed to us, as a first step toward defeating our enemies in the region—principally Iran, the arch sponsor of Islamic totalitarianism. Instead the troops were sent (as Bush explained) to "sacrifice for the liberty of strangers"—spilling American blood and spending endless resources on the "compassionate" goal of lifting the hostile and primitive Iraqi people out of poverty, feeding their hungry, unclogging their sewers. The result of this "compassionate" war is thousands of unnecessary American deaths, and the preservation and emboldening of the enemies we most need to defeat: Iran and Saudi Arabia.

We must put an end to the barbarous sacrifice of American troops, now. It is past time to abandon Washington's self-sacrificial rules of engagement, and its broader policy of "compassionate," self-sacrificial warfare. Instead of subjecting troops to more intensive "ethics" training, we should unleash them from the militarily suicidal ethics of self-sacrifice.

* * *

This article originally appeared in *FrontPageMagazine.com.*

The Pakistan Crisis

Elan Journo December 29, 2007

The assassination of Benazir Bhutto has, we're told, upended Washington's foreign policy. "Our foreign policy has relied on her presence as a stabilizing force.... Without her, we will have to regroup," explained Sen. Arlen Specter (R-Pa.) in the *Washington Post*. "It complicates life for the American government."

But in fact U.S. policy was in disarray long before the assassination.

U.S. diplomats have been scrambling for months to do something about the growing power of Islamists in the nuclear-armed nation which Washington hails as a "major non-NATO ally." Having supported President Musharraf's authoritarian regime, Washington helped broker the deal to allow Bhutto back into Pakistan, hoping she might create a pro-U.S. regime, but then decided to push Musharraf to share power with Bhutto, then insisted that he's "indispensable," but also flirted with the idea of backing Bhutto.

All this against the backdrop of the creeping Talibanization of Pakistan. Islamist fighters once "restricted to untamed mountain villages along the [Pakistani-Afghan] border," now "operate relatively freely in cities like Karachi," according to *Newsweek*. The Taliban "now pretty much come and go as they please inside Pakistan." They are easily slipping in and out of neighboring Afghanistan to arm and train their fighters, and foster attacks on the West.

Why has Washington proven so incapable of dealing with this danger to U.S. security? The answer lies in how we embraced Pakistan as an ally.

Pakistan was an improbable ally. In the 1990s its Inter-Services Intelligence agency had helped bring the Taliban to power; Gen. Musharraf's regime, which began in 1999, formally endorsed the Taliban regime; and many in Pakistan support the cause of jihad (taking to the streets to celebrate 9/11). But after 9/11 the Bush administration asserted that we needed Pakistan as an ally, and that the alternatives to Gen. Musharraf's military dictatorship were far worse.

If the administration was right about that (which is doubtful), we could have had an alliance with Pakistan under only one condition—treating this supposedly lesser of two evils as, indeed, evil.

It would have required acknowledging the immorality of Pakistan's past and demanding that it vigorously combat the Islamic totalitarians as proof of repudiating them. Alert to the merest hint of Pakistan's disloyalty, we'd have had to keep the dictatorial regime at arm's length. This would have meant openly declaring that both the regime and the pro-jihadists among Pakistan' people are immoral, that our alliance is delimited to one goal, and that we would welcome and support new, pro-American leaders in Pakistan who actually embrace freedom.

But instead, Washington evaded Pakistan's pro-Islamist past and pretended that this corrupt regime was good. We offered leniency on Pakistan's billion-dollar debts, opened up a fire hose of financial aid, lifted economic sanctions, and blessed the regime simply because it agreed to call itself our ally and pay lip-service to enacting "reforms." After Musharraf pledged his "full support" and "unstinting cooperation," we treated the dictator as if he were some freedom-loving statesman, and effectively whitewashed the regime.

Since we did not demand any fundamental change in Pakistan's behavior as the price of our alliance, we should not have expected any.

Pakistan's "unstinting cooperation" included help with the token arrests of a handful of terrorists—even as the country became a haven for Islamists. Since 2001, Islamists have established a stronghold in the Pakistani-Afghan tribal borderlands (where bin Laden may be hiding). But our "ally" neither eradicated them nor allowed U.S. forces to do so. Instead in 2006, Musharraf reached a truce with them: in return for the Islamists' "promise" not to attack Pakistani soldiers, not to establish their own Taliban-like rule and not to support foreign jihadists—Pakistan backed off and released 165 captured jihadists.

Far from protesting, President Bush endorsed this appeasing deal, saying: "When [Musharraf] looks me in the eye and says" this deal will stop "the Talibanization of the people, and that there won't be a Taliban and won't be al-Qaeda, I believe him."

We have gone on paying Pakistan for its "cooperation," to the tune of $10 billion in aid. The Islamists, who predictably reneged on the truce, now have a new staging area in Pakistan from which to plot attacks on us (perhaps, one day, with Pakistani nukes).

Why did our leaders evade Pakistan's true nature? Faced with the need to do something against the totalitarian threat, it was far easier to pretend that Musharraf was a great ally who will help rid us of our problems if we would only uncritically embrace him. To declare Musharraf's regime evil, albeit the lesser of two evils, would have required a deep moral confidence in the righteousness of our cause. The Bush administration didn't display this confidence in our own fight against the Taliban, allowing the enablers of bin Laden to flee rather than ruthlessly destroying them. Why would it display such confidence in dealing with Pakistan?

But no matter how much one pretends that facts are not facts, eventually they will rear their heads.

This is why we are so unable to deal with the threat of Pakistan. Our blindness is self-induced.

#

POSTSCRIPT

What We Knew About Pakistan, Islamists and bin Laden

Elan Journo March 26, 2014

Osama bin Laden spent nearly six tranquil years hidden in a compound in Abbottabad, Pakistan. Since that came to light in May 2011, the *New York Times*'s reporter Carlotta Gall has been chasing down leads to figure out what Pakistan knew about bin Laden. Gall's article vividly recounts the trail leading to the answer, but reveals more than that.

First, the answer: her search culminates with an unnamed source admitting that the Pakistani intelligence agency, ISI, "actually ran a special desk assigned to handle bin Laden. It was operated independently, led by an officer who made his own decisions and did not report to a superior. He handled only one person: bin

Laden." That may be the closest thing to a smoking gun that you might hope for, given the corruption and opacity of the Pakistani regime. Which brings us to the other revelation.

Pakistan's post-9/11 alliance with the United States was a massive fraud. Pakistan had declared itself "with us" but as Gall points out incidentally (echoing a view others have also expressed): "the strategy that has evolved in Pakistan has been to make a show of cooperation with the American fight against terrorism while covertly abetting and even coordinating Taliban, Kashmiri and foreign Qaeda-linked militants."

> The United States was neither speaking out against Pakistan nor changing its policy toward a government that was exporting terrorism, the [Pakistani] legislator lamented. "How many people have to die before they get it? They are standing by a military that protects, aids and abets people who are going against the U.S. and Western mission in Afghanistan, in Syria, everywhere."

As I argue in *Winning the Unwinnable War*, Washington was a willing enabler of the fraud. The U.S.-Pakistan relationship was predicated on an evasion of the Pakistani regime's character. After 9/11 the Bush administration wanted to believe that this corrupt regime, which had backed the Taliban, could transform itself overnight in to a good regime. So we treated it as if it already were. The U.S. uncritically blessed the regime, while Pakistan paid lip-service to the notion of being allied with us. For the low, low price of $10 billion-plus, we acquired a new "ally" who turned around and betrayed us, repeatedly. (In the book, I describe some of Pakistan's overt betrayals.) We turned a blind eye. And kept doing that. But wishing away facts is futile.

You might recall that the Bush administration was widely critiqued for being (of all things) "moralistic" in its foreign policy. So much for that.

The Price of Bush's Commitment to Palestinian Statehood

Elan Journo March 30, 2008

On his recent visit to the Middle East, Vice President Cheney voiced the Bush administration's belief that a Palestinian state is "long overdue" and vowed to help make that goal a reality. Many conservatives and liberals agree with the administration that America should help fulfill the long-deferred Palestinian aspirations to statehood. The idea is that in doing so we would go a long way toward dousing the flames of Islamist terrorism.

But does U.S. backing for Palestinian statehood advance our security?

Only if you think we're better off fostering a new terrorist state.

That may seem excessively harsh given President Bush's mantra that Palestinians just want "the opportunity to use [their talents and] gifts to better their own lives and build a future for their children." The Bush line we keep hearing is that the terrorists and their supporters are but a fringe element that will be marginalized under the new state, which will coexist "side by side in peace" with Israel and the Western world.

But listen to Palestinian clerics at Friday sermons, calling for violent attacks on Israel. Look at the lurid posters in the homes and shops of ordinary Palestinians, passionately glorifying "martyrs" and terrorist kingpins. Look at their coordinated digging of tunnels to smuggle in weapons and explosives. Look at the popular collusion with Islamist militants and their stream of recruits. Recall the years of ferocious attacks against Israeli towns.

If the mass of Palestinians just want peace and a better life, they would not despise and war against the only state in the region, Israel, that protects individual rights and that offers a standard of living far superior to (even the richest) Arab regimes. They would be far better off, freer and safer, if they put away their rocks, bullets and dynamite belts and sought to live and work in Israel (as some once did).

Instead, they flood the streets to protest negotiations about peaceful co-existence with Israel. Ideologically, their dominant factions are the Islamic totalitarians of Hamas and the nationalist terrorists of Fatah. These differ only in their form of dictatorship—religious or ethnic. Both promise their followers, one way or another, to wipe out Israel.

That hostility to Israel, the only free nation in the Middle East, should make any U.S. president stand firmly against the Palestinian cause. Particularly in a post-9/11 world, Washington should recognize that U.S. security is strengthened by preventing Islamist terrorists from securing another stronghold and training ground.

Given the overwhelming evidence that it would undermine U.S. security, what explains the Bush administration's come-hell-or-high-water promise to do "everything we can" to back a Palestinian state? It is the administration's belief that America has a duty to ease the suffering of the world's wretched, regardless of the cost in lives to us.

That's why, after Palestinians brought Hamas to power in a landslide, Washington responded with "compassion" for their "humanitarian" needs. Of course the U.S. and its European allies felt compelled to "isolate" the Hamas regime by cutting off direct aid to the Palestinian Authority. But they refused to believe the Palestinians themselves should be held responsible for how they voted, because they're already dirt poor. This meant suspending our judgment and absolving Palestinians of culpability for choosing murderers to lead them. So, despite the embargo on aid to the Hamas-led government, in 2006 U.S. aid to Palestinians increased by 17 percent to $468 million, propping up their terrorist proto-state.

This policy's result is to endorse, facilitate and vitalize Palestinian aggression. We've seen the unleashing of a popularly supported Hamas-Hezbollah war against Israel in 2006 and ongoing attacks springing from Gaza. Al-Qaeda has reportedly already set up shop alongside other jihadists in the Palestinian territories. Just imagine the mushrooming of terrorist training camps and explosives factories under a sovereign Palestinian state. Imagine how emboldened jihadists will feel operating under a regime that Washington has created and blessed.

This is the price of a policy based not on furthering U.S. security, but on undeserved pity. This is the price of willfully ignoring the vile nature of Palestinian goals, treating these hostile people as above reproach and rewarding their irrationality.

Isn't it time we demand a policy that puts our security first?

Bush's War Policy:
The Top Campaign Non-Issue?

Elan Journo June 12, 2008

It's staggering to think that as we march toward a seventh year at war, Iraq (let alone Afghanistan) is hardly an issue on the campaign trail. Of course, nobody has forgotten about the war. But there's been no substantive debate on it, either.

John McCain, echoing many conservatives, regularly touts the supposed gains of the "surge." Upon his return from visiting Iraq, he declared, "We're succeeding. I don't care what anybody says. I've seen the facts on the ground." Hillary Clinton and Barak Obama even grudgingly conceded, at one point, that the "surge" was working. And when they do challenge President Bush's war policy, they complain not about its goals, but about the crushing financial cost.

The war's a backburner issue in the campaign because—strange as it may sound—critics and cheerleaders of the president's policy judge it by the same spurious benchmark. They focus myopically on whether insurgents have been kicked out, for the time being, from one street, in some neighborhood of Baghdad. If that's success, then the issue can be pushed out of mind.

But nobody would have bought that as a vision of success, in the devastating aftermath of 9/11. And nobody should buy it now. The only rational benchmark for success is whether Washington's policies have made the lives of Americans safer from the threat of Islamists. Judged by that standard, Bush's war policy is an abject failure.

Bush vowed to "pursue nations that provide aid or safe haven to terrorism," and warned that either "you are with us, or you are with the terrorists." Bush's war policy, however, was not to target the greatest threat, but instead to minister to those in greatest need. It was to show compassion to oppressed Iraqis and Afghans, to raise them out of poverty, to give them elections.

Six-plus years into a "war on terror," Washington has done nothing to counter the spearhead of the global jihadist movement, the Islamic Republic of Iran. The United States has allowed it to grow stronger. Iran races to acquire nuclear weapons; it taunts and threatens our naval vessels; it arms and trains insurgents in Iraq in attacking Americans; it backs jihadists across the region—all with impunity.

What about Iraq? More than 4,000 U.S. troops died so that hostile Iraqis could elect a new gang of anti-Americans to sit in Baghdad's parliament. Iraq's government is still dominated by Islamist groups, which still operate death squads, and it is still deep, deep in Iran's pocket.

Across the Middle East, Washington campaigned for elections in the strongholds of various Islamist groups—such as Hamas and Hezbollah—that it should have worked to destroy. Many people, true to their ideological beliefs, voted to give these groups more political power. Naturally, the jihadists feel encouraged. According to a new study, the Iranian-backed Hamas has amassed at least eighty tons of explosives in Gaza since 2007, and it has also got its hands on anti-tank weapons. So expect another Islamist war emanating from the terrorist proto-state of "Hamas-stan," which Bush's policy helped create.

In Afghanistan and Pakistan, according to the U.S. National Intelligence Director, al-Qaeda is gaining in strength and prepping new recruits who can blend into American society and attack domestic targets. Jihadists are now fighting to reconquer Afghanistan, and to "Talibanize" large patches of Pakistan. The Afghan-Pakistan border, reports the National Intelligence Director, "serves as a staging area for al-Qaeda's attacks in support of the Taliban in Afghanistan as well as a location for training new terrorist operatives, for attacks in Pakistan, the Middle East, Africa, Europe and the United States."

This is what Bush's war policy has achieved: an enemy that has no fear of us, that spits in our face, and that is gearing up to kill more of us.

This is what a "compassionate" war policy, aimed not at defeating our enemies but at serving the welfare of Iraqis and Afghans, had to achieve. It is a policy that put their lack of freedom and lack of wealth, ahead of our moral right to end the threat of Islamist aggression. Bush's policy held that it was our duty to enable these hostile peoples to vote their political conscience—while evading the fact that so many avidly support jihadist goals.

Shame on Republicans for promising to stay the same disastrous course and toss thousands more troops onto the sacrificial pyre of Iraq. Shame on Democrats for squandering the opportunity of a campaign year to offer us a real Plan B—an alternative policy that would actually combat state sponsors of terrorism.

Each of us deserves—and should demand—more of our leaders. We deserve a foreign policy that truly upholds our right to security.

* * *

This article originally appeared in *Capitalism Magazine.*

The Wreckage:
A Look Back at Bush's Democracy Crusade

Elan Journo Fall 2008

A Review of *Mugged by Reality: The Liberation of Iraq and the Failure of Good Intentions*, by John Agresto. New York: Encounter Books, 2007.

The measure of success in the Iraq war has undergone a curious progression. Early on, the Bush administration held up the vision of a peaceful, prosperous, pro-Western Iraq as its benchmark. But the torture chambers of Saddam Hussein were replaced by the horrors of a sadistic sectarian war and a fierce insurgency that consumed thousands of American lives. And the post-invasion Iraqi regime, it turns out, is led by Islamist parties allied with religious militias and intimately tied to the belligerent Iranian regime. The benchmark, if we can call it that, then shrank to the somewhat lesser vision of an Iraqi government that can stand up on its own, so that America can stand down. But that did not materialize, either. So we heard that if only the fractious Sunni and Shiite factions in the Iraqi government could have breathing space to reconcile their differences, and if only we could do more to blunt the force of the insurgency—that would be progress. To that end, in early 2007, the administration ordered a "surge" of tens of thousands more American forces to rein in the chaos in Iraq.

Today, we hear John McCain and legions of conservatives braying that we are, in fact, winning (some go so far as to say we have already won). Why? Because the "surge" has reduced the number of attacks on U.S. troops to the levels seen a few years ago (when the insurgency was raging wildly) and because there has been a momentary dip in the number of Iraqis slaughtering their fellow countrymen. Victory, apparently, requires only clearing out insurgents (for a while) from their perches in some neighborhoods, even though Teheran's influence in the country grows and Islamists carve out Taliban-like fiefdoms in Iraq.

The goals in Iraq "have visibly been getting smaller," observes John Agresto, a once keen but now disillusioned supporter of the campaign (p. 172). Iraq, he argues contra his fellow conservatives, has been a fiasco. "If we call it 'success,' it's only because we've lowered the benchmark to near zero" (p. 191).

Explaining the Iraq fiasco is Agresto's project in *Mugged by Reality: The Liberation of Iraq and the Failure of Good Intentions*. During 2003 and 2004, while the insurgency built momentum, he was a civilian adviser helping revive Iraq's higher education system. The book recounts his dealings with Iraqis and his observations on why a policy he had so passionately endorsed turned into a horrendous tragedy. What makes this book distinctive, and particularly illuminating, is its focus on the fundamental idea driving the war. While other Americans returning from Iraq have offered explanations for the problems in terms of superficialities—for example, the character flaws of specific officials or leaders—Agresto recognizes that the purpose of the Iraq campaign was to enact a specific ideal.

The point of the war, he writes, was not to enrich Big Oil, nor benefit Israel, nor "whatever the view of the month" happens to be. And while the Bush administration "may have had to highlight the issue of WMDs in its presentations before the U.N. and other international bodies…, finding and destroying such weapons was not something I or most of the civilians and soldiers I worked with in Iraq ever thought central to our going" (pp. 5–6). The goal was to fulfill the Bush administration's altruistic mission of lifting Iraqis out of tyranny and poverty and ignorance; it was, in Agresto's words, to "help secure the liberty of others" (p. 9).

By Agresto's own account, the military operations were prosecuted in compliance with the goal of serving Iraqis. He recounts the "surgical" bombing raids that spared much of the country's infrastructure. "The war was fought so precisely, so carefully," he observes, "that the only pictures of military destruction I was able to take while I was there were photos of former Ba'athist government buildings and military or communications facilities. The cities and towns were intact; homes and schools survived" (p. 173).

One of many appalling and little reported facts revealed in Agresto's narrative is that the devastation that "turned a country on the skids into rubble" was the work, not of Americans (as commonly believed), but of Iraqi looters. They marauded through "not just the universities, but all the schools, all hospitals, and virtually all public buildings, and not a few private homes." At Mustansiriya University, for instance, vandals ripped electrical wiring out of the walls and tore out plumbing fixtures; what they couldn't sell or use (e.g., books) they torched (p. 77).

The aftermath of the invasion itself left "no war-ravaged home-less rummaging through garbage cans, killing each other for crusts" (p. 174). On the contrary, he notes, "It would be hard to imagine a war fought, at the start, with greater care or with greater concern for non-combatants than Operation Iraqi Freedom" (p. 173).

Yet this care and concern, Agresto discovered, was not for the latent freedom-lovers he and so many others expected to meet.

In daily conversations with Iraqis from all walks of life, Agresto came to understand the Iraqi mindset. A number of anecdotal por-traits and snatches of conversations reveal the typical Iraqi mind as profoundly infused with pre-modern, tribalist religion. He encoun-tered Sunni Iraqis (including a university professor) who openly voice a hostility akin to racism toward Shiite Iraqis, regarding them as sub-human, degenerate heretics. Agresto tells of a Sunni man that he knew who went on the pilgrimage to Mecca and by chance found himself among a group of Shiite pilgrims. Hearing them sing a hymn expressing their unfavorable view of the archan-gel Gabriel, the Sunni man was deeply revolted. "These people are not real Muslims," he told Agresto, "These people are heretics, all of them. They shouldn't be allowed to sing that." Then the man's voice grew darkly quiet, "They shouldn't be allowed" (p. 53).

Agresto's experiences in post-invasion Iraq disabused him of an article of faith underlying the Bush crusade: the idea that there is a "universal hunger for freedom" innately planted in all mankind. In reality, the prevailing ideological trend in Iraq—as in the Middle East generally—is totalitarian Islam (which he calls radicalized Islam). When Iraq's universities re-opened, Agresto reports, zealous students seized control, beating and murdering "un-Islamic" pro-fessors and other students. The power of Islamists on campuses—as throughout Iraq—grew so fierce that even female Christian students, in self-preservation, took to wearing Islamic headscarves. The Islamist enforcers worked in league with off-campus religious militias loyal to larger jihadist outfits, such as Moktadr al-Sadr's Mahdi Army.

It was not supposed to work this way: On the view of the Bush administration, once Iraqis were given the option, they would rush to embrace liberty. Washington thus gave Iraqis a free hand to draft a new constitution. But the Iraqis enshrined Islamic law as the government's cardinal principle. The Supreme Federal Court of Iraq can overturn a law "not only if it violated the words of the constitution but also if it violates 'the established provisions of Islam.'" This court, Agresto complains, is an imitation of the twelve-member theocratic "Guardians Council" of the totalitarian Islamic regime in Teheran (p. 118).

Iraq, Agresto suggests, is steps away from theocratic rule.

What went wrong? Agresto blames the proponents of the campaign for failing to understand the Iraqi mindset. This step in his compelling argument brings to light important truths that proponents of the administration's policy evade. A telling example: Washington embraced Grand Ayatollah al-Sistani, spiritual leader of Shiites in Iraq, as a friendly, "moderate" political figure, but Agresto dismisses that view as deluded. The hugely influential cleric, it turns out, refused to meet with any Americans, but sat down with any anti-American antagonist. Demanding that all public legislation be based on Islamic law, Sistani condemned an interim Iraqi constitution because it protected the rights of the Kurds and secured property rights to Jews. The "very first time I heard, in all my months there, an anti-Semitic diatribe," recounts Agresto, "it was from the Grand Ayatollah. One word from Sistani might prevent the killing of journalists and Western civilians in Basra, stop the frightened exodus of Christians from all of Southern Iraq, and restrain the imposition of sectarian dogmatism now rolling over Iraq's schools and universities. There is no such word" (p. 101). Sistani, the book suggests, is a theocrat-in-waiting.

Agresto identifies a second factor toward explaining the situation in Iraq: the campaign was premised on a fundamental ideological confusion. He argues, passionately, that "democracy" and freedom are vastly different things. In criticizing the popular equation of democracy and freedom, Agresto observes that "elections are a means, not an end" and that there "is no alchemy in either the word 'elections' or 'democracy'" that transforms genocidal Islamists from bad to good (p. 99). Freedom in American, Agresto rightly points out, depends on the protection of rights. Freedom cannot be achieved, he argues, by unleashing (through elections) murderous Islamic mobs. In doing so, we have "handed Iraq over to exactly the worst elements" (p. 187).

The major value of the book lies in its exploration of how the war's theoreticians failed to understand both the Iraqi people and the American political ideas we were supposed to be enacting. Much of the narrative, however, is colored by Agresto's religious conservative views that man is moved by brutish impulses and that morality demands self-denial. These premises lead him to draw a broader conclusion that is unconvincing and inconsistent with the evidence he presents, and that seems grafted onto an otherwise trenchant analysis.

In keeping with his support of the campaign's selfless ideal, Agresto places blame—unjustly—on the character of the American occupiers: he reproves the U.S. servicemen implementing Washington's policies for caring more about themselves (!) than about the welfare of Iraqis. He concludes that Americans were not "ready to be the kind of liberating occupiers necessary to do the job right" (p. 182).

Taking this line of thinking further, he claims that the root of so much of the debacle can be traced to "a substratum of a baser human nature that Americans, and especially conservatives, seem forever eager to point out in theory, but forget about when confronted with in reality" (p. 182). The war's neoconservative architects "need to listen to more old-fashioned conservatives who know something about the fallenness of our natures," he admonishes (pp. 186–7). The ideal of serving Iraqis is noble, in other words, but it is beyond the ability of fallen, sinful creatures like us to be sufficiently selfless.

Yet the book fails to demonstrate this claim. The bulk of Agresto's narrative characterizes the mission as implementing, not betraying, Washington's ideal. Straining to support his claim, Agresto spends a chapter begrudging how little money the U.S. federal government (and other nations) gave away to pay for rebuilding universities. But given the Iraqi mindset that he describes, there is no reason to conclude that bestowing greater largesse on Iraqi universities would have averted the country's fall into barbarism. And for the same reason, the book does not and cannot explain how greater U.S. sacrifices, whether political, military or financial, could have brought about a peaceful new Iraqi regime.

In spite of the destructive results of America's selfless endeavor in Iraq, Agresto cannot bring himself to question his deepest moral beliefs, and instead he insists that the problem must be our fallen nature. In this respect he resembles the Marxists who explain away the brutality of Communist regimes by condemning humanity as depraved.

But the book's observant account of the early days of the Iraq campaign points toward a different conclusion entirely. It suggests that we should do what Agresto himself refuses to do: challenge the ideal animating Washington's war policy. That ideal, the events of the book indicate, is antithetical to America's self-defense (a point for which Yaron Brook and I have argued at length in "'Forward Strategy' for Failure," *The Objective Standard*, Spring 2007). *Mugged by Reality* presents gripping, vividly detailed—and at times moving—eye-witness testimony that should prompt Americans to call into question the altruistic ideal shaping our foreign policy.

* * *

This article originally appeared in *The Objective Standard*.

PART 2

Learning the Wrong Lessons

Soon after assuming the presidency in 2009, Barack Obama announced a "comprehensive, new strategy" for the worsening situation in Afghanistan. The strategy assumed—mistakenly—that the main problem was insufficient troops and financial aid. Moreover, Obama dismissed the idea of achieving anything like a World War II–style victory.

Diplomatic outreach to Iran over its nuclear program had begun during the Bush administration, but it was Obama—who, like Bush, evaded Iran's nature and its centrality to the Islamist movement—who consummated the deal in 2015.

Obama's Outreach Whitewashes Iran

Elan Journo March 3, 2009

In his address to the joint session of Congress, President Obama said that "We cannot shun the negotiating table" in conducting our foreign policy. He's previously elaborated that "if countries like Iran are willing to unclench their fist, they will find an extended hand from us." And Iran's president Ahmedinijad tentatively welcomes "talks based on mutual respect and in a fair atmosphere."

The shared idea, evidently, is that our conflict with Iran stems largely from a past failure to use so-called diplomacy to settle disputes. Alluding to George W. Bush's supposedly tough policy, Obama has said he wants to restore "the same respect and partnership that America had with the Muslim world as recently as 20 or 30 years" ago.

Really? Thirty years ago this November, followers of Ayatollah Khomeini, who spearheaded Iran's Islamic revolution, stormed the U.S. embassy in Teheran and took the personnel hostage. President Carter gently admonished Iran, but ruled out military retaliation. Instead his advisers spent months dreaming up schemes to bribe Iran into releasing the hostages—while bending over backward to enable the regime to save face. In the end Khomeini's Islamist theocracy collected a handsome payoff for its aggression, and concluded, rightly, that if attacked, America would crumple to its knees.

Was Obama thinking of the 1980s? In April 1983 Iran's jihadist proxies in Lebanon rammed a truck bomb into the U.S. Embassy in Beirut; the Reagan administration responded by doing nothing. Months later, encouraged by Washington's inaction, Teheran issued a kill order—via its ambassador in Syria—to its allied groups in Beirut. Early one morning, an Islamist suicide bomber set off a massive explosion at the barracks where U.S. marines were sleeping and killed 241 of them.

Reagan spouted hot air about not backing down—and soon after ordered the U.S. troops to bug out. The jihadists wanted America out, they slaughtered our troops, and we caved in and gave them what they wanted.

Osama bin Laden, like jihadists in Iran and elsewhere, viewed our response to the Beirut bombings as further proof that their ideologically driven war was a viable cause. And so, inspired by Iranian aggression, the anti-American jihad kept ramping up.

Maybe Obama meant the fabled halcyon days of the 1990s, when President Clinton tried to mend fences with Iran?

In 1996 a team of jihadists—financed and trained by Teheran—blew up the Khobar Towers building in Saudi Arabia, killing nineteen American servicemen. Clinton's administration learned that Iran was behind the attacks. But Washington brushed aside any notion of retaliating against Iran, in order to facilitate a "reconciliation" with that murderous regime. In an eerie parallel with today, Iran expressed its openness to U.S. groveling—an opportunity Clinton seized.

So Clinton attended a speech by Iran's leader at the U.N.; the administration also permitted the sale of much-needed aircraft parts to Iran, among other sweeteners. Granted the cover of respectability, Iran was emboldened to continue fomenting Islamist aggression and avidly pursue its then-embryonic nuclear program.

Obama's appeasing diplomacy re-enacts the disastrous policy of the past. Our policymakers evaded Iran's character as an enemy, and by rewarding its aggression with bribes and conciliation, they encouraged a spiral of further attacks.

No. Bush was no exception to this trend. After 9/11 his administration invited Iran—the leading sponsor of Islamist terrorism—to join an anti-terrorism coalition(!). Talk of an axis of evil was quickly abandoned, and Washington backed the European scheme to bribe Iran to halt its nuclear program. By late last year, there was talk of opening a U.S. Special Interests Section (a step down from an embassy) in Iran. Meanwhile Bush's welfare mission in Iraq negated U.S. security and left Iran untouched to grow more powerful and resolute.

A genuinely new, rational policy toward Iran would turn away from the last thirty years and begin by facing up to Teheran's ongoing proxy war against us.

* * *

This article originally appeared in *Capitalism Magazine*.

Obama's Solution for the Afghanistan-Pakistan Nightmare

Elan Journo April 6, 2009

In a speech announcing his "comprehensive, new strategy" for Afghanistan and Pakistan, Obama warned that "The situation is increasingly perilous. It has been more than seven years since the Taliban was removed from power [in Afghanistan, where they ruled], yet war rages on, and insurgents control parts of Afghanistan and Pakistan. Attacks against our troops, our NATO allies, and the Afghan government have risen steadily. Most painfully, 2008 was the deadliest year of the war for American forces." He may well have been understating the magnitude of the problem, particularly in Pakistan (considering a recent, brazen attack). And while both liberals and some conservatives have commended Obama's strategy (with minor qualifications), I regard it as fundamentally misconceived.

The strategy lays out what Team Obama claims are necessary steps to deal with the resurgent Islamists on both sides of the Afghan-Pakistan border. That action plan is based on certain assumptions about what went wrong. But that diagnosis, in my view, is false.

Let's start with one of the core claims in Obama's speech. What went wrong in the Afghanistan war? A major factor, according to Obama and many others, was the failure to send enough resources—primarily troops and financial aid. Moving forward, on this premise, "America must no longer deny resources to Afghanistan..."; and so Obama's sending 21,000 American soldiers into Afghanistan, and has promised boatloads of aid.

But this misses the underlying problem.

I've argued on other occasions that Washington's war failed because it was hamstrung by self-effacing battle plans. Our military was ordered to pursue Taliban fighters, for example, only if it simultaneously showed "compassion" to the Afghans. The U.S. military dropped bombs—but instead of ruthlessly pounding key targets, it was ordered gingerly to avoid hitting holy shrines and mosques (known to be Taliban hideouts) and to shower the country with food packages. The U.S. deployed ground forces—but instead of focusing exclusively on capturing or killing the enemy, they were also diverted to "reconstruction" projects for the sake of the Afghan population. And this pattern continues today and is likely to intensify. The *New York Times* reported that "vast numbers of public, religious and historic sites make up a computer database of no-strike zones" while Air Force lawyers vet all air strikes.

The war put concern for the welfare of Afghans ahead of the necessary goal of defeating the enemy. Washington did not aim at smashing the Islamists, so instead they were scattered and left free to re-arm and fight another day. Sending 21,000-plus U.S. troops into Afghanistan will be of limited help—unless they are given new battle plans that entail the total defeat of the Islamists.

If only that were the focus of his strategy. But it's not.

Like the Bush administration, Team Obama believes that we must help the Afghans build a strong government. On the conventional analysis, it is the weakness and corruption of the post-Taliban regime that has contributed greatly to the chaos in that country. The idea is that if the Afghan regime were strong, it would serve as a bulwark against the Islamists. "Afghanistan has an elected government," Obama noted, "but it is undermined by corruption and has difficulty delivering basic services to its people."

Remedying this problem is at the center of Obama's strategy: he has promised to send approximately 4,000 U.S. troops to train the Afghan army and police and will exert pressure on the government to clean up its act. But will this really result in a regime that can oppose the Taliban? Sadly, the evidence suggests that what distinguishes the current government from the Islamists ideologically is only a difference in the degree of their fidelity to the principle of rule under Islam.

Consider some of the evidence. My colleague Tom Bowden recently noted the case of Afghans who were sentenced to twenty years in jail for modifying the Koran into Persian while not including the original Arabic text. That was blasphemous, you see. Or recall the fate of Abdul Rahman, an Afghan convert from Islam to Christianity: raging mobs and clerics demanded his execution. He was spared that fate by being spirited out of the country to Europe, but only because an international outcry embarrassed the government in Kabul. Keep in mind that these incidents are hardly isolated cases and that they took place under the supposedly pro-Western, pro-freedom regime—not the Taliban.

Moreover, the current regime has faced internal pressure to bend itself into greater conformity with the same Islamist political ideal—sharia—that the Taliban is fighting to impose by force throughout the country. There's an official council of Islamic clerics who advise Afghanistan's president. Although their advice is nonbinding, they clearly wield tremendous moral clout. About a year ago, for instance, they demanded that President Karzai stop foreign aid groups from (allegedly) proselytizing for Christianity and that the government reintroduce public executions. Remember that the Taliban, when in power, kicked out foreign aid organizations and regularly put to death all who were deemed enemies of Allah (a practice that continues in the areas of the country where the Taliban regained control).

Among the council's other demands? The NYT reports: "The council also urged Mr. Karzai to stop local television stations from showing Indian soap operas and movies, which are enormously popular in Afghanistan but which it said included obscenities and scenes that were immoral."

Recall that the Taliban excelled at shuttering video-rental stores, tearing down satellite dishes, and "executing" TV sets—all in the name of promoting "virtue" and doing away with "immorality."

Take another example: Afghanistan's president recently signed the Shiite Family Law that "negates the need for sexual consent between married couples, tacitly approves child marriage and restricts a woman's right to leave the home." Sounds a lot like life under the Taliban regime, which among other things, of course, prohibited women from leaving home without a male relative. By signing the new law, President Karzai was apparently hoping to appease "conservative" lawmakers who drafted it.

So even if the improbable were to happen, even if Afghanistan's central government had a sufficient police force and military capable of enforcing the law of the land, that law is founded on Islam (according to the nation's constitution). And judging by current trends, there's reason to expect such a regime to veer toward ever more Taliban-esque policies. Ideologically, the regime has nothing to say in opposition to the doctrines of the Taliban, so how can it really oppose the Islamist resurgence? I don't see any grounds to believe that it could.

Obama's Destination? Non-Victory

Elan Journo August 4, 2009

J uly was the worst month for U.S. casualties in Afghanistan—not just in 2009, but since the war began nearly eight years ago. Keep this awful truth in mind as you read the following observation on that war from our nation's commander in chief:

"I'm always worried about using the word 'victory,' because, you know, it invokes this notion of Emperor Hirohito coming down and signing a surrender to MacArthur," Obama told ABC News.

Obama (echoing Bush) wants you to scale back your expectations: He's saying, "Don't expect us to break the enemy's will and compel it to surrender à la Japan in WWII." Whatever else America may be doing in Afghanistan, the goal is not to achieve anything like a genuine victory: i.e., the defeat of the Islamist enemy.

But why? Why might Obama and many other people hold this view?

Two salient reasons come to mind:

(1) Since 9/11 the Bush administration has failed to properly define the enemy in the war. For a while it was "radical Islamists"; then "Islamofascists" for a week or so; "evil-doers" was in use for a while. The view that has stuck is that the enemy is al-Qaeda and the Taliban, a "shadowy," "non-state actor" (as Obama puts it). The conclusion that people draw: there's no enemy nation (à la Japan in WWII) for us to defeat, only scattered "terrorists." This conclusion is false and enormously destructive of our security.

(2) The Bush administration went to war, but it was a turn-the-other-cheek "compassionate" war, badly defined and lacking a clear objective (it should have been victory). The conclusion many have drawn: war was a disaster (look at Iraq! look at Afghanistan!), so forget war—it cannot be the answer. This conclusion is false, and it contributes to the debasing of our concept of what "victory" is, and how it can be achieved.

These two conclusions are part of the insidious legacy of the Bush administration's policy. And they're compounded by Obama's submissive, appeasing foreign policy. Consider what that means in practice: America sends its youth to die on battlefields—in a war that our leaders regard as unwinnable.

Must it be so? Could we triumph over the enemy? I believe victory is within our grasp—improbable as that may seem today.

To achieve a genuine victory requires a fundamental rethinking of how we got here. For a start, we'd have to define the enemy accurately, and then consider how to defeat it. That's a view I've advocated in some of my articles over the last few years. But there's a lot to say on this issue.

The fact that America's response to 9/11 has gone horribly wrong—and that we can, and must, defeat the enemy—was part of the motivation for the book project that I'm now wrapping up. The book, which I edited and contributed chapters to, is titled: *Winning the Unwinnable War: America's Self-Crippled Response to Islamic Totalitarianism*. Apropos of Obama's statement, quoted at the opening of this post, you may be interested to read the final chapter of the book. In it I describe a positive plan for how we could achieve a genuine victory—a victory on the model of World War II. The book is set to come out early this fall.

The Unending War in Afghanistan

Elan Journo October 7, 2009

Today the war in Afghanistan reaches its eight-year mark. To put that into perspective, by now a child born on the day the war began would probably be starting his third year of elementary school. Or to put it in a wider context, only the American Revolution (which lasted about 8 years 4 months) and the Vietnam War (eight years six months) lasted longer. U.S. involvement in World War II was over in just under four years. The *New York Times* has a chart that illustrates these data in graphic terms. The Afghanistan debacle is on track to drag on longer than any of these. (I disagree with the compilers of this chart that the Iraq war is actually over; the recent bombings around that country suggest otherwise.)

Recall what many people agreed should be our (minimum) objective in Afghanistan eight years ago: the rooting out of the Taliban and its Islamist allies. Today a common view holds that we must resign ourselves to a world in which the Islamist menace remains a fixture of our lives—a threat we might mitigate, but never eliminate. Witness the suggestions by mainstream luminaries in foreign policy that we negotiate some sort of settlement with the Taliban, paying them to put down their arms, at least while we keep doling out cash.

That is not the punchline to a grim joke; it is what some consider to be our best option. The fact that this is taken seriously is a measure of how Americans have been demoralized by the failure of Washington to accomplish even the limited objective of eliminating the Taliban/al-Qaeda forces (to say nothing of dealing with the graver threat from Iran).

Iran's Fist, Clenched Tighter

Elan Journo December 3, 2009

"[I]f countries like Iran are willing to unclench their fist, they will find an extended hand from us," Barack Obama suggested, nearly a year ago. Since then the Iranian regime has found itself inundated by the administration's cordial invitations (to a July Fourth barbecue; to talks over its nuclear program) and unctuous affirmations of our good will (see this video[1]). Even after the mass protests in Iran challenging the theocracy's legitimacy, Team Obama declined to lend its support to the protesters and thereby endorsed the regime that was gunning them down in the streets. By the logic of Obama's policy, all this should have induced Tehran put aside its "decades of mistrust" (of us), and halt its nuclear program and its patronage of Islamist terrorism.

So how's this working out?

Iran has just turned down the latest U.S.-backed deal meant to prevent it acquiring nuclear material suitable for a bomb. Instead, Tehran announced plans to build ten additional nuclear facilities on the scale of the one it already has up and running at Natanz. With that added capacity, it has been estimated that the Iranian regime could produce enough nuclear fuel for something like 160 bombs. Per year.

Then, over the weekend, the Iranian parliament passed a law "earmarking $20 million to support militant groups opposing the West." What's significant about this is not the amount of money, nor the fact that the government is officially budgeting for the sponsorship of Islamic terrorism (in the past Iran has spent tens of millions on Hezbollah alone). What's significant here is Iran's self-confidence.

Obama's policy of so-called engagement (read: appeasement) is working as predicted: it bolsters Tehran's militancy.

The Nobel Speech: Obama on "Just War"

Elan Journo December 11, 2009

When accepting his Nobel Peace Prize—a ludicrous, debased award also bestowed on murderers like Yasser Arafat—President Obama spoke about his foreign policy. Pervading his Nobel speech there was a peculiar undertone of contrition. If translated into words, it would go something like this: "Ideally, we would behave like Gandhi, never resorting to the use of force in asserting our rights... but alas, as commander in chief of the United States, I'm duty-bound to protect the lives of Americans, and that now means having to fight. Sorry about that."

This apologetic drift flows naturally from the substance of Obama's foreign policy.

A key point in the speech is that America must uphold—but has lately fallen short of—the standards set by "just war" doctrine. Summarizing this widely held view of morality in war, he explains that a war is justified only "when it meets certain preconditions: if it is waged as a last resort or in self-defense; if the force used is proportional, and if, whenever possible, civilians are spared from violence."

> Where force is necessary, we have a moral and strategic interest in binding ourselves to certain rules of conduct. And even as we confront a vicious adversary that abides by no rules, I believe that the United States of America must remain a standard bearer in the conduct of war. That is what makes us different from those whom we fight. That is a source of our strength. That is why I prohibited torture. That is why I ordered the prison at Guantanamo Bay closed. And that is why I have reaffirmed America's commitment to abide by the Geneva Conventions. We lose ourselves when we compromise the very ideals that we fight to defend. And we honor those ideals by upholding them not just when it is easy, but when it is hard.

The implication is that Bush's policy was too assertive, was callous, and thus it undermined our interests and security. For these failings, Obama and many others believe, America owes the world an apology and a promise (delivered yet again in the Nobel speech) to change its ways.

But this is wrong. Massively wrong.

True: American foreign policy since 9/11 has been a disaster for our security; that's a driving point of my book, *Winning the Unwinnable War.* But the reason lies not in a failure to abide by "just war" doctrine; a significant part of the problem was Washington's devotion to that doctrine. My colleagues Alex Epstein and Yaron Brook demonstrate that point in chapter 4, where they bring to light the inherent incompatibility between "just war" and a victim nation's right of self-defense.

The "just war" doctrine, in modern form, dovetails with what I've characterized as Bush's "compassionate war." On this approach, Washington subordinated the military goal of defeating the enemy to the imperative of protecting civilians and nation-building Afghanistan and Iraq. The argument we present in the book is that this approach—now embraced, with greater dedication, by Obama—is destructive of U.S. interests. Of course warfare should be shaped by moral principles; the problem is that the dominant moral ideas of our culture, reflected in "just war" doctrine, subvert the self-defense of victims and work to the advantage of aggressors.

Obama's rededication to this way of thinking about war is like the logic of an alcoholic who works to solve his drinking problem by going on a binge.

Iran's Strident Defiance

Elan Journo December 17, 2009

President Obama has sought to buy off Iran with concessions and talks, so that Tehran will agree to end its nuclear program. This policy of so-called engagement (in reality, appeasement) has quite predictably shipwrecked (the administration is admitting as much). I have been arguing that Obama's policy of appeasement works to galvanize Tehran in its belligerence, including notably its nuclear program. That appears to be an intensifying trend.

Secretary of State Clinton starts making noises that the time has come to "pressure" Iran with the additional sanctions. Iran scoffs at a bill in Congress that would sanction its fuel supply. And it successfully test fires an enhanced long-range Sejil 2 missile.

Despite many layers of existing sanctions and restrictions on its access to foreign technology, "Iran has nevertheless learned how to make virtually every bolt and switch in a nuclear weapon, according to assessments by U.N. nuclear officials in internal documents" (*Washington Post*). Leaked documents purporting to be official Iranian reports describe "a four-year plan by Iran to develop and test a neutron initiator of a type that weapons experts say has no known civilian use." That initiator is one of the last technical obstacles on the path to developing a warhead.

Gloating in an interview, an Iranian official told the *Post* "that as Iranian engineers conquer the nuclear sciences, they will 'jump hundreds of meters up in a short time,' pulling even with their counterparts from the West."

Iran's nuclear program, however, is only one element in the regime's efforts to export and propagate its militant Islamist goal. Iran's proxies in that venture are jihadist groups. The leader of Hamas paid an official visit to Iran, which reaffirmed support for that group. Lebanese Hezbollah, another group that counts on Iran's patronage, has carried out attacks from Buenos Aires to Beirut, and is thought to have cells worldwide.

Speaking on another occasion, Ali Larijani, Iran's parliament speaker told reporters earlier this year: "We're proud to defend Hamas and Hezbollah," and "We are not trying to hide it."

What these developments illustrate is how the policy of appeasement rewards aggression, resulting over time in progressively more assertive, self-righteous enemies.

War on (Fill In the Misleading Blank)

Elan Journo December 24, 2009

One of the worst foreign policy developments of 2009 was also one of the most underreported—the Obama administration's decision to do away with the official use of the term "global war on terror" in favor of "Overseas Contingency Operation." The term "global war on terror" was awful, to be sure—it named our enemy vaguely and evasively. But instead of correcting that mistake by a clear identification of the enemy that threatens us with terrorism and nuclear attacks, President Obama's new designation denies the existence of any enemy. We went from worse to worser.

Correctly defining the enemy is indispensable in any war. My colleagues Alex Epstein and Yaron Brook write:

> To fulfill the promise to defeat the terrorist enemy that struck on 9/11, our leaders would first have to identify who exactly that enemy is and then be willing to do whatever is necessary to defeat him.
>
> Who is the enemy that attacked on 9/11? It is not "terrorism"—just as our enemy in World War II was not kamikaze strikes or U-boat attacks. Terrorism is a tactic employed by a certain group for a certain cause. That group and, above all, the cause they fight for are our enemy. [Chapter 4, *Winning the Unwinnable War*]

My colleagues and I define the enemy as the Islamic totalitarian movement—funded, inspired and backed by state-sponsors, principally Iran. We show how misidentifying the enemy by (one of) its tactics, terrorism, undercuts our ability to defend ourselves. "Terrorism"—and the host of other superficial definitions of the enemy ("evil doers," "haters," "hijackers of a great religion," etc.)—obscures the fact that the attackers were committed to an ideological movement, seeking the forcible imposition of Islamic law worldwide. The Bush administration's utter failure to properly name the enemy that threatens us is central to understanding why the U.S. response to 9/11 has been a fiasco.

Team Obama took this to a new low.

Apparently, "war on terrorism" retained some vestige of an association in the public mind with Islamist attacks—some faint hint of an ideologically driven state-supported enemy. The solution? "[M] ove away from the politics of fear toward a policy of being prepared for all risks that can occur," explained Janet Napolitano, Secretary of Homeland Defense. In a speech she gave, Napolitano deliberately avoided "the word 'terrorism,' [and instead] referred to 'man-caused' disasters." [Emphasis added.]

This way of classifying mass-casualty acts of war, like 9/11, is an intellectual abomination. It works to dissolve any link between such violent attacks and the specific ideas motivating the killers. While clouding the intelligibility of the atrocities, this approach further underplays the moral culpability of those who carry them out. Moreover, and perhaps worse, it suggests that we ought to resign ourselves to attacks as if they were woven into the fabric of nature: we can no more eradicate the threat than we can eradicate earthquakes or hurricanes.

That defeatism was already becoming part of our culture in the final years of Bush's time in office; now under Obama it is being officially endorsed.

All of which underscores the crucial importance of correctly answering the simple, but momentous, question: Who is the enemy?

Disconnected Dots

Elan Journo January 12, 2010

Last week, President Obama claimed that "our intelligence community failed to connect those dots" signaling a plot to blow up Northwest Airlines Flight 253, en route from Amsterdam to Detroit, on Christmas Day. But ritual flogging of the intelligence community has diverted attention from a larger failure—this one belonging squarely on Obama's shoulders.

Zoom out from the plentiful red flags outlining what we already know about the Christmas Day attack. Now observe the connection between it and two (of many) other "dots": the suicide bombing by a double agent at a U.S. base in Afghanistan; and the (latest) failed assassination attempt on the Danish cartoonist Kurt Westergaard, who drew the Muhammad-with-a-bomb-in-his-turban cartoon.

On the face of it, these have little if anything in common. Unlike the Nigerian bomber on Flight 253, the bomber in Afghanistan used an explosive-packed vest; the assassin in Denmark wielded an ax. The Nigerian was a recent college graduate, scion of a wealthy family; the killer in Afghanistan was a doctor of Jordanian descent; the Danish assassin, an immigrant from Somalia. Not their origin, not their specific targets, not their choice of weapon, not their age or income-level—none of these are the same. Nor is there any evidence that they ever met.

But they do share an ideological bond that underlies—and drives—their militant action. They belong to a movement that is waging a holy war to impose Islam as the supreme governing authority over the totality of people's lives, by force and everywhere.

That's why the bomber sought to put to death a plane full of infidels on Christmas Day—as punishment for failing to embrace Allah and as a gruesome spectacle vaunting the strength of the jihadist cause.

That's why the would-be assassin of Westergaard planned to hack him apart: Westergaard's drawing had flouted Muslim dogma on "blasphemy." So the assassin came to enforce sharia (Islamic law)—on the totalitarian belief that sharia negates any freedom of speech under secular Danish law.

That's why the Jordanian double agent in Afghanistan felt it necessary to slaughter Americans, including seven CIA operatives: they were working to capture leaders of al-Qaeda, one of many groups advancing Islamic totalitarianism.

These are just three "dots" forming part of a larger picture. We face an ideological, militant movement that (I argue) is spearheaded by state-sponsors, chiefly the Islamist regime in Iran.

But it is a picture that the Obama administration refuses to bring into focus. Recall that after the Flight 253 attack, the president dismissed the bomber as an "isolated extremist" (a term perhaps even more evasive than "terrorist"). And observe the prevailing view that we're dealing with a multitude of separate problems—Iran, Afghanistan, random-seeming attacks on planes, etc.—that have to be dealt with piecemeal.

We have already seen how this approach plays out.

This myopic mentality, I argue in chapter 1 of my book *Winning the Unwinnable War*, is precisely the approach that dominated U.S. policy in the decades leading up to 9/11—decades punctuated with numerous Islamist attacks. The attacks were tagged vaguely as "terrorism" and each regarded as a separate crisis. The fact that there was a distinct ideological force behind these attacks went unrecognized and the enemy, undeterred.

Iraq's "Awakening" Re-Awakens Pro-Jihadist. Shocking.

Elan Journo October 20, 2010

Much has certainly changed in Iraq since the nadir of the brutal civil war, but with increasing insurgent attacks, it's fascinating to see the actual consequences of the U.S. policies that were widely credited with delivering us a "success" (defined on a progressively debased standard of what counts as success; see part 1). Take the widely celebrated "awakening" of U.S.-backed Iraqis who turned against some jihadist groups. In my book, I assess that policy and critique it harshly. One problem: it is predicated on appeasement (the bribing of Iraqis to switch sides, so they turn against the jihadsts); another problem: it papers over the nature of conflicts among Iraqi factions and the deep-seated tribal/sectarian enmities. Here's a flavor.

> What happens when the torrent of cash [paid to members of the Awakening, "Sons of Iraq"] dries up? That future problem will sort itself out, we are told, because once stability is achieved, there will be a reconciliation among Iraq's warring ethnic and sectarian factions. The deadly gangland-style shootouts in the streets and ugly wrangling in parliament will cease, or so we have been promised. Washington believed that by arming and empowering the Sunni tribes, who constitute the bulk of the Sons of Iraq, it would pave the road for them to feel included in the nation's politics—which the majority Shiites now hold in a vise grip. Ultimately, the idea is to fold these gangs of former (and current) criminals, supposedly former jihadists, and ordinary Iraqis into the nation's Shiite-dominated police force. Some of that has happened, but the deep-seated, bitter resentment between Sunnis and Shiites in Iraq cannot be wished away. Many Sons of Iraq believe that their real enemy is the Shiite-run government in Baghdad, and with their American-provided arms, they await the day of reckoning.

What did that money buy? Allies who pledge their sacred honor to defeat Islamists? Consider this *New York Times* report from October 16 ("Sunnis in Iraq Allied with U.S. Quitting to Rejoin Rebels"):

BAQUBA, Iraq—Members of United States-allied Awakening Councils have quit or been dismissed from their positions in significant numbers in recent months, prey to an intensive recruitment campaign by the Sunni insurgency, according to government officials, current and former members of the Awakening and insurgents.

Although there are no firm figures, security and political officials say *hundreds of the well-disciplined fighters—many of whom have gained extensive knowledge about the American military—appear to have rejoined al-Qaeda in Mesopotamia. Beyond that, officials say that even many of the Awakening fighters still on the Iraqi government payroll, possibly thousands of them, covertly aid the insurgency.*

The defections have been driven in part by frustration with the Shiite-led government, which Awakening members say is intent on destroying them, as well as by pressure from al-Qaeda. *The exodus has accelerated since Iraq's inconclusive parliamentary elections in March,* which have left Sunnis uncertain of retaining what little political influence they have and which appear to have provided Al-Qaeda new opportunities to lure back fighters.[Emphasis added]

For my fuller critique of what was (and is) so wrong with America's "successful" policy in Iraq—and, broadly, what went wrong in Washington's post-9/11 policy—I encourage you to check out *Winning the Unwinnable War.*

Taliban's Morale

Elan Journo February 24, 2012

The Taliban and Islamist forces in Afghanistan have had their momentum reversed, their will to fight sapped—or so our policymakers would have us believe. But is that an accurate assessment? A new report from NATO, leaked to the *New York Times*, tells a far different story.

"The State of the Taliban" draws on 27,000 interrogations of 4,000 Taliban and other fighters, and it "portrays a Taliban insurgency that is far from vanquished or demoralized even as the United States and its allies enter what they hope will be the final phase of the war." Yes, very far from it: although more Islamist fighters are being killed or captured, many of those captured and interrogated "remain convinced that they are winning the war."

> The report, dated Jan. 6, provided little evidence to believe that this strategy or the increase in the number of troops during the Obama administration had helped spur the nascent peace talks. "Taliban commanders, along with rank and file members, increasingly believe their control of Afghanistan is inevitable," the report said. "Though the Taliban suffered severely in 2011, its strength, motivation, funding and tactical proficiency remains intact."
>
> It added of the insurgents: "While they are weary of war, they see little hope for a negotiated peace. Despite numerous tactical setbacks, surrender is far from their collective mind-set. For the moment, they believe that continuing the fight and expanding Taliban governance are their only viable courses of action."
>
> Recruits and donations for the Taliban increased over the past year, the report said, citing insurgents' accounts.

What's most alarming about the report, if it's accurate, is that the enemy, though materially weak, demonstrates far greater confidence than any enemy deserves to have after a decade of war with the United States, the world's most powerful military force. For a long time, and particularly in *Winning the Unwinnable War*, I've argued that to win a war, it's necessary to crush the enemy's will to fight, to leave the enemy feeling demoralized, convinced that its cause is lost. That's hardly what our campaign has accomplished. Why? A significant part of the answer lies in the way our own foreign policy has crippled our ability to defeat the enemy—and how we've boxed ourselves in so that we have few if any good options for how to proceed.

Is the report accurate? Obviously the captured fighters may be spouting propaganda that's been drilled into them. Even if that's what they're doing, that so many of them (some 4,000) have the confidence and morale to stay on message during interrogations is itself telling.

How the International Laws of War Subvert Self-Defense

Elan Journo November 2012

A Review of *Israel and the Struggle over the International Laws of War*, by Peter Berkowitz. Stanford, CA: Hoover Institution Press, 2012.

Israel is at the crux of a "new struggle over the international laws of war." So argues Peter Berkowitz, a legal scholar at the Hoover Institution, in his new and important book on the subject.

Exhibit A in Berkowitz's case is the United Nations' putative fact-finding mission on the 2008–9 Gaza war—an investigation which culminated in the notorious Goldstone Report. Exhibit B: the furor over the 2010 Gaza flotilla. According to Berkowitz, these and other incidents of maltreatment of Israel and efforts to criminalize the exercise of its right of self-defense "threaten[s] to effect legal transformations that will impair the ability of all liberal democracies to defend themselves."

By exposing what he regards as abuses of the international laws of war, Berkowitz intends to contribute to their defense. The book's evidence, though, renders that hope forlorn.

With lawyerly precision, Berkowitz dissects the Goldstone Report, highlighting the extent to which it is riddled with inaccuracies, half-truths, and Hamas propaganda uncritically reported at face value. For example, the report found that Israel illegitimately destroyed a family home in Gaza. But in reality, Hamas had used that home as a storage facility for weapons and ammunition, including Grad missiles, rendering it a legitimate military target. Moreover, in the eyes of the Goldstone team, Hamas is not a terrorist organization, but merely one of several "Palestinian armed groups." The report downplays the 8,000+ rockets and mortars launched from Gaza, as if they were causally unrelated to Israel's decision to retaliate. Berkowitz deftly argues that the report's application of relevant norms of war is legally unsound, and that its recommendation that the U.N.

Security Council refer the matter to the International Criminal Court is baseless.

Procedurally, Berkowitz contends, the U.N. infringed on Israel's right to apply the norms of war when it prematurely authorized an investigation, before the fighting ended and before Israel could reasonably carry out its own preliminary assessments. Stoking suspicions that the investigation's verdict was a foregone conclusion, the U.N. General Assembly endorsed the Goldstone Report 114-18 (with 44 abstentions)—despite the report's embarrassingly numerous (yet thematically on-message) factual and legal defects. Curiously, nearly a year and a half later, Justice Richard Goldstone, who headed the investigation, retracted some of the most egregious claims; tellingly, however, the other U.N. team members unapologetically rejected the need to revise, let alone retract, the report.

What Berkowitz illustrates is a pattern wherein the international laws of war operate like a fulcrum for shifting blame from terrorists to the states fighting them.

This pattern was manifest in the outcry over the Gaza flotilla. That convoy, posturing as a humanitarian mission yet closely tied to an Islamist group, sought to pierce Israel's naval blockade of Gaza. After Israeli commandos boarded one recalcitrant vessel, the *Mavi Marmara*, a number of flotilla activists attacked them with axes, pipes and knives. Nine activists were killed in the process, and several dozen more were injured. The chorus of condemnation was instant and shrill and one-sided. The call for a U.N. investigation, Berkowitz observes, was intended not "to determine wrongdoing but rather to place an official stamp on Israel's guilt." The U.N. Human Rights Council—which has been notably mute over the years on incontestable violations of rights globally—bestirred itself to issue a resolution singling out Israel as the aggressor.

Critics warped the international laws of war to argue that Israel was forbidden to engage in the blockade, because it remained an occupying power in Gaza—even though Israel withdrew from Gaza completely in 2005, and Hamas violently took over the territory over some two years later. Berkowitz convincingly demonstrates that Israel cannot legally be regarded an occupier, and, piece by piece dismantles the sophistry employed to deny the blockade's legitimacy.

Dismayed at how the international laws of war are deployed to undercut free nations, Berkowitz notes a paradox: no armies in the history of warfare have devoted greater attention than Israel and the United States to complying with laws of war, yet no armies today "come under greater worldwide attack for violating" those laws.

That moral inversion, Berkowitz suggests, could be rectified by clarifying and upholding the international laws of war. But on this point, the case is unconvincing. The laws of war are themselves deeply problematic. Take the idea, of which Berkowitz approves, that military retaliation must be "proportional" to the attack. Arguably, that precept stands at odds with a free nation's moral right to defend its citizens' lives. In the name of proportionality, should the U.S. retaliation for Pearl Harbor have been limited to bombing the same number of Japanese warships, and nothing more? Should Israel's retaliation against Hamas be confined to firing the same primitive, imprecise mortars at Gaza, and nothing more? Berkowitz calls for a "balance" between military necessity and the need to avoid civilian casualties. But surely the fundamental moral imperative must be the military objective, with the culpability for the unwelcome but sometimes inevitable collateral damage falling to the aggressor.

Compounding the problem is that the UN and related bodies enforce these so-called laws of war. It is not the Russias or Chinas or Irans of the world, but the United States, Israel, and a small number of other free nations that strive to comply with these laws, thereby lending them moral credibility. But the UN is dominated by authoritarian and terrorist-sponsoring regimes, making subversion of those laws all but assured.

Berkowitz assumes that the international laws of war are indispensable. The book's two case studies, however, should lead the reader to question that assumption. It is true that soldiers (indeed, all citizens) of a free nation need to have a sense of justice in their military cause. Yet moral guidance in war is the task not of some international organization but of a sovereign nation's foreign policy and moral principles; these should define the objective and appropriate means in a military conflict—just as they should inform decisions on alliances, treaties and international organizations. What Berkowitz advocates—championing the international laws of war but reserving prime responsibility of enforcement to nation states—leaves the moral high ground open for the usual suspects to seize it anew.

With this book, though, Berkowitz has masterfully exposed how the international laws of war have become a favorite bludgeon wielded against Israel. By bringing greater attention to the nature and provisions of those laws, the book serves as an urgent reminder of the need to scrutinize this doctrine and the international institutions that have become its champions.

* * *

This article originally appeared in *The Journal of International Security Affairs*.

How America and Israel Cripple
Their Own Soldiers

Elan Journo October 8, 2015

A horrific news report from Afghanistan brings to light a wider problem afflicting the American, and Israeli, way of war—but, no, it is not what you think.

Washington faces perpetual allegations of "war crimes" for its military conduct in Afghanistan, and Israel, in Gaza. We're asked to believe that U.S. and Israeli forces are overly aggressive, but that picture is perversely warped. The truth is that Israel and the U.S. wage self-crippled wars. To begin to understand that phenomenon, start with that sickening tale out of Afghanistan.

The practice of turning boys into sex slaves is rife in Afghanistan, reports the *New York Times*, "particularly among powerful men, for whom being surrounded by young teenagers can be a mark of social status." But if American soldiers and Marines in Afghanistan encounter that practice, they "have been instructed not to intervene—in some cases, not even when their Afghan allies have abused boys on military bases." Why?

Washington's turning a blind eye "is intended to maintain good relations with the Afghan police and militia units the United States has trained to fight the Taliban. *It also reflects a reluctance to impose cultural values in a country where pederasty is rife.*" (Emphasis added.)

Outraged at Washington's betrayal of individual rights, some American service members pushed back against the policy. But they "have been disciplined or seen their careers ruined because they fought it." (Read the whole story but be warned: it will turn your stomach.)

Such appeasement of an odious Afghan practice fits the pattern of Washington's self-effacing way of war. The proper objective in Afghanistan was to defeat whatever threat the Islamists posed, by crushing them militarily. And it entailed recognizing the unwelcome necessity of civilian casualties (for which the Islamists bear full responsibility). Instead, U.S. leaders waged a supposedly compassionate war that put the needs and welfare of Afghans first—ahead of the military objective. I document how this way of war played out in my book *Winning the Unwinnable War: America's Self-Crippled Response to Islamic Totalitarianism*. The ultra abridged version: It was a disaster. A few illustrations:

Washington's war planners defined lists of targets that were excluded from bombing missions. On these "no-strike" lists were cultural-religious sites, electrical plants—a host of legitimate strategic targets ruled untouchable, for fear of affronting or harming civilians. At the start of the war, American cargo planes dropped 500,000-odd Islam-compliant food packets to feed starving Afghans and, inevitably, jihadists. Bombing raids were often canceled, sacrificing the opportunity to kill Islamist fighters. The no-strike lists grew ever longer, giving the enemy more places to hide in and fight from. While handing the Islamists umpteen advantages, which they exploited, this self-crippled way of war tied the hands of American soldiers in combat zones.

That is how the Afghan war was actually conducted, because ultimately Washington believed we have no moral right to defeat the Islamists in the battlefield: the Afghan people had to come first. On that premise, who are we to assert the objective superiority of our moral values by standing in the way of Afghan men who turn boys into sex slaves?

Now imagine being an American soldier, witnessing an Afghan leader keeping a boy chained to a bed as a sex slave, and having to decide between complying with orders (ignore it) and doing the right thing (at minimum, speaking up). Defying orders could get you kicked out of the military and destroy your career. Contemplate the psychological toll of looking the other way and plugging your ears.

Soldiers face that same impossible choice—but with their own lives on the line—under the self-crippled rules of engagement on the battlefield. Over the last decade, I've met veterans of the Afghan and Iraq wars at my public talks. The insanely restrictive rules of engagement are maddening, they tell me: we were supposed to go after the enemy, risking our lives, but we were made to back off, retreat, and let them fight another day. Listening to them is heartbreaking. The tragic story behind *Lone Survivor*, recently made into a film, is emblematic. The injustice done to them, by the irrational policy of our leaders, has yet to be acknowledged. What must that do to their morale?

Yes, it is astounding that the world's most powerful military force actually pursued a self-crippled way of war.

But it is not alone: Israel, the Middle East's most powerful military force, has adopted essentially the same approach. Peter Berkowitz, a legal scholar, has noted the searing irony: the U.S. and Israel are widely accused of "war crimes" but in fact both "devote untold and unprecedented hours to studying and enforcing" the customary rules of war, which enjoin the avoidance of harming noncombatants.

Look at last year's Gaza war. Israel's paramount responsibility was to defend the lives of its own citizens. Morally, in defending itself, Israel's priority must be eliminating the threat from Hamas. Hamas declares its goal of destroying Israel in no uncertain terms. It is responsible for devastating suicide bombings and, over the years, thousands of rocket attacks from Gaza against towns and cities in Israel. Yet, against this backdrop—and mirroring the U.S. way of war—Israel subordinated the objective of self-defense in the name of safeguarding civilians in a war zone.

Recall, to take just a few examples, how the Israel Defense Force dutifully went far out of its way to warn of impending strikes. It dropped thousands of leaflets in Arabic warning Gazans to avoid certain areas that may be targeted. It phoned and texted people residing in apartment blocks where a rocket is about to hit, giving them time to evacuate. Often it fired "a knock on the roof" warning rocket, before leveling the building. It aborted missions if civilians were spotted nearby the target. Hamas notoriously stashed weapons, ammunition, and missiles in private homes. And it puts rocket launchers in densely populated areas.

Just as America hamstrung its own troops and drew up no-strike lists, handing a tactical gift to Islamists in Afghanistan, so Israel's conduct, shaped by the same premise, benefited Hamas.

Consider another parallel. Earlier this year, members of the Knesset read aloud testimony from Israeli soldiers who fought in the 2014 Gaza war. The aim was to rebut a UN report on supposed Israeli war crimes.

"The [Israel Defense Force] followed all the rules to clear areas of civilians, but Hamas cynically forced some to stay," MK Dani Atar (Zionist Union) said, reading the testimony of a Golani soldier. "[Palestinians] were killed by explosives they didn't know were there that Hamas planted."

"We lost our element of surprise, the best of our sons, to make sure we wouldn't kill civilians that the enemy used as human shields," he added.

...

MK Merav Ben-Ari (Kulanu) read a testimony by Dror Dagan, who was injured while arresting a terrorist, and listened from the visitors' gallery, sitting in his wheelchair.

"When we burst into the house and quickly scanned the rooms, the wife of the terrorist, a senior Hamas member, fainted. As a medic, I did not hesitate and started taking care of her," Dagan wrote. "Not two minutes passed and it turned out that it was a trap. It was all pretend, a trick to gain time so the suspect could get organized."

"I was injured, because I was taught the values of the IDF, to take care of anyone who is injured, even if it is the wife of a terrorist," Dagan added.

The cumulative aim of the statements was to illustrate—as if further evidence were needed—the tragic lengths to which Israel went to avoid harming civilians in the war zone. It's vital that the lies and distortions about Israeli military conduct be exposed and refuted.

But a fundamental problem common to Jerusalem and Washington is the underlying moral idea shaping their conduct of war. It is the idea that America (and Israel) ought to put their own interests last; that they must sacrifice the lives and security of their citizens to the enemies they are combatting. Both strive to conform to that prevailing norm. The more consistently they conform to it, the more they cripple their ability to engage in self-defense—the prime responsibility of a government to its citizens. The conventional norm shaping the conduct of war subverts free societies that abide by it, while enabling their enemies on the battlefield. Surely it is past time to rethink that way of war.

* * *

This article originally appeared in *The Federalist*.

PART 3

The "Arab Spring," Islamist Winter

To protest police harassment, a young Tunisian man set himself on fire in December 2010. The incident set in motion a series of political uprisings and demonstrations well beyond Tunisia. Commonly referred to as the "Arab Spring," these varied upheavals were seen as heralding a new era of freedom in the Middle East.

In January 2011, tens of thousands of protesters took to the streets of Egypt. They demanded that President Hosni Mubarak, an authoritarian who had held power for thirty years, leave office. Other demonstrations took place in Bahrain, Syria, Libya and elsewhere.

The protests in Syria and Libya grew into civil wars. In Egypt, the Islamists of the Muslim Brotherhood gained control of the government, until a coup returned power to the military.

Egypt's Plight: "Moderates" to the Rescue?

Elan Journo February 3, 2011

In the streets of Cairo, tens of thousands are clamoring to get rid of strongman Hosni Mubarak. Ominously the Muslim Brotherhood—the origin of Hamas, al-Qaeda and other jihadist outfits—is maneuvering to assume leadership of the protests. The Brotherhood is our enemy; its success in Egypt means greater peril for us (to put it mildly). But some protesters evidently despise the Brotherhood's totalitarian political ideal. Where does that leave well-meaning Egyptians who want neither Mubarak nor the Brotherhood?

Beware of pinning your hopes on so-called political moderates. There are at least two related problems here.

(1) In the Arab-Muslim world, the slippery term "moderate" encompasses those who are merely anti-Islamist—not necessarily pro-Western. Many Egyptians readily swallow anti-Semitic, anti-Western conspiracy theories (e.g., the Protocols of the Elders of Zion). Moreover, supporting Palestinian "resistance" (read: terrorism) against Israel is a conventional, mainstream, uncontroversial view. Egypt is one of the places where ordinary people matter-of-factly will tell you that America got what it deserved in the 9/11 attacks. Keep all that in mind, when you ponder what it would mean for so-called moderates to be elected to power in Egypt.

(2) The other problem stems from the argument that so-called moderates can be a bulwark against the political power of Islamist groups like the Muslim Brotherhood. In that part of the world, the political spectrum is far narrower than you may think: whereas Islamists want religion to be the all-encompassing principle of government, a typical "moderate" still acknowledges that Islam has some, albeit limited, role in government. True secularists are scarce and marginal. So could "moderates" in government prevent the Islamists from taking over? Ultimately, no. I touch on this in my book, and here's part of the explanation.

The only intelligible meaning of "moderate" advocates of religion are those who try to combine devotion to faith with concessions to reason. They obey the dictates of Islam in some areas and not others, fencing off certain issues or areas of life from the purview of religion. Let us grant the premise that the West can find moderate Muslims and support them in a way that does not discredit them in Muslim eyes as saboteurs conspiring to undermine Islam. Could moderates really steer their culture away from the totalitarian movement?

The holy warriors hold that Islam must shape every last detail of man's life. The moderates accept the ideal of Islam but shy away from the vision of total state. Moderates might agree to allow sharia to govern schools, say, but not commerce; to dictate marriage laws, but not punishments for blasphemy, apostasy, or adultery. Yet in doing so, moderates ultimately advance the agenda of the totalitarians, since even delimited applications of Islam to government constitute an endorsement of it as the proper source of law.

The tension between moderates and the totalitarians is unsustainable. What happens when the totalitarians push for expanding the scope of sharia a bit more? If sharia can govern banking and trade, for example, why not other aspects of life? Why not also institute Islamic punishments, such as beheading apostates? Having accepted in principle the ideal of sharia, moderates have no grounds to reject further means to that end. They can offer no principled opposition to the slaughter of infidels who refuse to submit, or of apostates who claim the freedom to choose their own convictions. In the face of the incremental or rapid advance of the totalitarian goal, the moderates are in the long run impotent. If Islam is the ideal, why practice it in moderation?

One news report tells us that the ostensibly "moderate" Mohamed ElBaradei has talked about setting up a governing coalition with the Muslim Brotherhood.

The plight of Egypt—like that of much of the region—is intellectual. The protesters who genuinely do want a better future face no good options.

What could help Egyptians? To address that fully would take a separate discussion. At minimum, I'd name three things: the embrace of genuinely pro-freedom ideas, secular government and individualism.

Understanding the "Arab Spring":
A Conversation with Yaron Brook and Elan Journo

Journal of Diplomacy Spring 2012

How should the U.S. respond to the events that have gripped the Middle East over the past year? This question has been debated countless times by the media, academics and politicians alike. Will the toppling of authoritarian regimes unleash a wave of democracy and individual freedoms across the region? Or will the power vacuums created allow darker forces to come to the fore? For a unique answer to these questions, the *Journal of Diplomacy and International Relations* looked to Yaron Brook and Elan Journo, both of the Ayn Rand Institute (ARI) in Irvine, California. Founded to promote the philosophy of twentieth-century novelist Ayn Rand—Objectivism—ARI advocates the principles of reason, rational self-interest, individual rights and laissez-faire capitalism. In the 2009 book *Winning the Unwinnable War*, both of these scholars argue for a revised U.S. foreign policy—one based on the principles that Ayn Rand stood for. To examine just what a foreign policy based on Objectivism would mean for the U.S., the *Journal's* Christopher Bartolotta and Jordan McGillis spoke with Yaron Brook and Elan Journo on the Arab Spring, American interests, Iran, China and much more.

Journal of Diplomacy: The uprisings in the Middle East have received a lot of attention over the past year. Do you view these movements as a positive development for the United States and its interests in the region? How do you approach this situation?

Elan Journo: When talking about U.S. interests, in the Middle East or anywhere else, we take a distinctive approach. We define the basic purpose of foreign policy as an extension of the government's proper function: to protect the individual rights of Americans to their life, liberty, and property. Our national interest, then, consists in safeguarding the lives and freedom of Americans in the face of foreign threats.

That stands in contrast to salient approaches in foreign policy—for instance, realism, liberal internationalism, and neoconservatism. Should we purchase the precarious, immoral friendship of some tyrant who tomorrow seeks to stab us in the back? No. Should we serve the world's have-nots with foreign aid, doling out grain, medical supplies, cash? No. Should we go on a crusade to bring ballot boxes to Iraq and elsewhere, à la Bush? No. Such policies, we argue, are at odds with—indeed, subvert—the goal of protecting the lives and freedom of Americans.

But, should we assert our interests—the safeguarding of the freedom of Americans—and should we use the full range of coercive options, including military force, in retaliatory self-defense when facing objective threats? Yes. Should we distinguish morally between our allies and enemies—acting consistently across time to encourage and support our friends, while shunning, ostracizing, and, when necessary, thwarting enemies? Yes. These key elements—the primacy of defending the rights of Americans, and the centrality of moral judgment in foreign-policy thinking—inform our approach.

To sum it up briefly, in our view, "U.S. national interests" reduces to the aggregate interest of American citizens to have their rights defended, to live free from foreign threats and attacks. We base our approach on the moral-political ideas of Ayn Rand, along with the founding principles of America.

Yaron Brook: When I look at the turmoil in the Middle East, the prospects are depressing. We have long been concerned that adherents of Islamic totalitarianism would rise to power. By the term "Islamic totalitarianism," I'm referring to many groups— the Muslim Brotherhood, al-Qaeda, Hamas, Hezbollah, and the Islamist regimes in Iran and Saudi Arabia. Despite their differences, what unites them as an "ism," as an ideological movement, is the ideal of enforcing the rule of Islamic law (sharia)—as an all-encompassing principle—and their ultimate goal (as far-fetched as it might seem to us in the West) of imposing sharia across the world—by force if necessary.

Today, the situation is far, far worse than even I would have projected when the protesters in Tunisia, Egypt, and elsewhere first took to the streets. Tunisia now has Islamists as leaders. Libya is heading in the same direction; the leadership of the anti-Gaddafi forces are Islamists, and they're likely to end up ruling Libya. If or when the Assad regime falls, it's the local chapter of the Muslim Brotherhood that's poised to take over. More dramatic and ominous, though, is the result of the Egyptian elections: the Muslim Brotherhood and the Salafis, combined, won the decisive majority of the votes in the first round.

Whereas for years the Brotherhood has sought an incrementalist strategy—creating a facade to appear less threatening, less fanatical—the Salafis are frank about their goals. They're far more open about what they want—and the Saudi-like, Taliban-esque way they'd like to impose Islamic dictates. They have been known to destroy stores that sell beer and cut off the ear of someone they accuse of committing sinful acts.

What we're seeing now in Egypt, Tunisia, and elsewhere is a swing from one form of tyranny—by a strongman or military clique—toward another form of tyranny, religious rule. For American interests in the region, every kind of dictatorship, whether an Islamist regime or a military-led police state, is inimical. Mubarak and Assad are horrifically evil tyrants; their rule is not in America's interest, nor obviously in the interests of Egyptians or Syrians. However, I strongly believe that the Islamists pose a much more serious threat, because they have an ideological agenda that is explicitly anti-American. Islamists view America, and the West, broadly, as an enemy, an obstacle to the realization of Allah's kingdom across the globe. On 9/11 we saw one Islamist faction, al-Qaeda, bring the holy war to American soil, hatching their plot in Taliban-ruled Afghanistan. Now project what we may face from holy warriors when more regimes in the region come under the sway of Islamist rule. The ascendancy of Islamists is the most important foreign policy threat facing us today.

JD: *The situation that you portray is quite grim, but some would argue that the revolutions are still in their early stages, and the possibility of fundamental political changes, changes for the better, cannot be foreclosed. Do you see room for that kind of change, long term?*

EJ: We should welcome political developments that bring greater freedom, meaning real respect for individual rights, for the people in that part of the world. We are better off when other nations truly move toward the protection of property rights, economic freedom, free speech—all of which are sorely lacking in the Middle East, with the notable exception of Israel. But for these political ideals to take root would require some fundamental changes in the political culture of the region.

What are the prospects for such fundamental changes? Doubtful. A major reason is the extent to which Islam permeates people's thinking and conceptual lexicon. Take Egypt. One explanation for why the Islamists did so well in the elections is that the Muslim Brotherhood was so well established, with a broad network of followers and organizers, and the ability to get out the vote. That's true, but a superficial explanation. It misses the real reason. The Salafis were far less organized politically, yet did remarkably well. Why?

What both groups have as an advantage over the quasi-secular groups is that the Islamists speak in the religious lexicon that all Muslims have been immersed in, even if they themselves are far from devout. Try advocating a separation between state and religion—something unknown through most of Muslim history; when it became known through contact with the West, it was shunned. If you advocate a separation of state and religion, you'll face resistance. If you advocate a secular state, the Islamists easily undercut it by portraying it as Western, and discrediting "secular" by tying it to pseudo-secular dictators, like Mubarak and Assad, who have ruled for decades. The Islamists can easily vilify "secular" as immoral, even repressive. So secular-oriented activists have to talk in vague terms such as "civilian state" lest they appear to advocate an impious society. The sheer fact that you can discredit something by tagging it as Western is revealing.

That illustrates two things. First, it's the religious groups that set the terms of debate, because they couch their arguments in moral terms, terms that resonate with a broad swath of the populace. Second, there's little understanding of what secular society looks like—a fact evidenced in history by the dearth of terminology in Muslim lands to describe and conceptualize it, and in the present by the implicit equation of secular, or non-religious, with immorality. The few marginal, secular-leaning advocates are thus on the defensive, for fear that they be tarred as enemies of virtue and Allah's law. Islam's cultural influence provides a huge advantage to Islamists.

Another factor here is that for the last few decades, the region has seen a trend of increasing religiosity—a trend that Islamists both help to drive and benefit from politically. Many people see themselves first and foremost as Muslims, rather than as individuals, or even citizens of their country. They identify themselves more closely and consistently by their adherence to Islam. More Egyptians go to prayers. More mosques are sprouting up. According to one report I've seen, in 1986 there was one mosque for every 6,000 or so Egyptians. Nineteen years later—and after a doubling of the population—there was one mosque for every 700 or so people. More women are donning the hijab—without being coerced into it by state-run "morality police." Amid an increase in religiosity, it is the ideologues of Islamic totalitarianism, espousing the need for restoring piety, who stand to gain not merely a respectful hearing, but also followers.

Go to a conventional family in Cairo: you'll find that who a son will marry is often a decision the parents, and other members of the clan, will make. What he wants is extraneous. Who a daughter may marry is conventionally the exclusive prerogative of the family, because the family, sometimes the tribe, as a collective, comes first. What the girl wants or doesn't want is irrelevant. Is she sovereign? Clearly not.

What I'm describing here is not a quirk limited to marriage decisions; it's an illustration of a broader cultural reality, namely, the subordination of the individual to the larger family or tribal group. So long as this kind of collectivized outlook is endemic in a culture—and it is in Egypt and across the region—it's hard to imagine the successful advocacy, let alone the enforcement, of new laws to protect the freedom of individuals to act on their own judgment.

The upheavals in the Middle East have toppled dictators, but there's no evidence of a change in the fundamental ideas or outlook of the populations. On the contrary, we've seen an entrenchment of the worst prevailing ideals.

JD: The Obama administration does not seem to have a coherent policy toward these various uprisings, and often has a different policy toward each state—for example, it took a far more active role in Libya than in Egypt. Do you believe that this was a rational policy, to view each uprising independently, or would a coherent strategy have been more beneficial?
EJ: Behind the incoherence is something else, worse and little understood. What we've witnessed is the impact of ideas in morality on the thinking and practice of U.S. foreign policy. Yaron and I have long argued that certain common moral ideas have subverted U.S. policy—that's the theme of my book examining the Bush administration's post-9/11 policy. The Obama administration is likewise

operating under the guidance of certain ideas about morality that lead to bizarre, and destructive, policy decisions. You can see that if you compare the U.S. response to the uprising in Libya with the response to the post-election protests in Iran, a couple of years ago.

Libya under Gaddafi was a trivial threat to our security. Who the protesters were and what political goals they sought—we didn't inquire, but we nonetheless backed them with airstrikes and other forms of military support. We stated no clear purpose for our involvement in enforcing a NATO-led no-fly zone; morally, we took our cue from that infamous club of tyrants, the Arab League; practically, we subordinated ourselves to the Europeans. From top to bottom, no significant U.S. interest was at stake. There was no evidence that our involvement in the mission would advance our interest—and in fact, all the evidence suggests that it has empowered a new, militant Islamist regime. The Libya mission was diametrically opposed to the goal of protecting the rights of Americans.

Now, recall the massive protests in Iran two years ago. The Iranian regime is designated by our State Department as the most active state sponsor of terrorism. Through proxies like Hezbollah, the Islamist regime in Tehran has committed many acts of aggression against the United States and other Western interests. Its Revolutionary Guard Corps helped create and train Hezbollah, which hijacked a TWA airliner and which kidnapped and tortured to death Americans. Iran was behind the 1983 bombings of the U.S. Embassy in Lebanon and later the barracks of U.S. Marines, killing 241. Iran also orchestrated the 1996 car bombing of Khobar Towers in Saudi Arabia, where nineteen U.S. servicemen died. That's just a glancing indication of what should be thought of as a multi-decade proxy war against us.

So, in Libya, we move against a minor, tin-pot dictatorship where we have no real stake, while leaving the fire-breathing Tehran regime in place, implicitly endorsing its rule by neglecting to help the protesters. In Libya, we launch bombing raids, for the sake of civilians and rebels whose goals are at odds with ours, against a regime that's of minor significance to our security. But against a major threat to us, from Iran, we stand mute and idle.

When our interests are in fact at stake—as they were and are in Iran—we hold back and take an accommodating line toward the belligerent regime. When someone else's needs appear to be on the line (the rebels and civilians in Libya), we dutifully scramble jet fighters and put American lives in harm's way, for the sake of serving others. Why? That double standard has its roots in the prevalent moral view that permeates our foreign policy—a view requiring that we put the needs of others ahead of our own goals and interests.

Acting in accordance with that view has been enormously destructive to American security and freedom, across decades. To expand on this a bit, part of what we've argued about post-9/11 foreign policy is that much of it stemmed from the idea of putting the supposed need of impoverished, oppressed Iraqis to have the vote, ahead of our interest in eliminating actual threats to our security (from known enemy regimes, like Iran). We argued that the Bush campaign to bring elections to the Middle East was wrong, morally. There's much more to say about that, but the macro point here is this: underlying the chaos that passes for U.S. foreign policy are commonly held ideas in morality that are at odds with the goal of protecting the lives and freedom of Americans.

JD: You have both written that America's real enemy in the world today is Iran. What is the reasoning behind this statement, and what are the implications for how the United States has been conducting its War on Terror?

EJ: I'm not claiming Iran is our only enemy, but it is a significant one, because Iran is the standard bearer for the Islamic totalitarian movement. The regime in Tehran embodies the totalitarian ideal and actively seeks to expand its dominion, by force. Since the revolution that gave birth to the Islamist rule in Iran, the regime has inspired Islamist groups across the world by exemplifying their political goal.

Inseparable from that is Iran's efforts to export its Islamist revolution—by inspiring, funding, and supporting proxies and affiliates like Hezbollah—and proving that it can attack America (through proxies and directly) and get away with it. By doing that, Iran purports to show that a truly pious regime can best an infidel superpower, America. Earlier we touched on the long record of Iranian-backed attacks on Americans, beginning with the 1979 seizure of the U.S. Embassy in Tehran. I lay this out in detail in my book *Winning the Unwinnable War*.

When assessing the Islamist threat, part of what makes Iran the salient state-sponsor is the fact that it eagerly seeks the mantle of leading the so-called jihad on the West. Given the regime's past aggression and current belligerence, Iran definitely poses a threat to the individual rights of Americans. Though not the exclusive patron of the Islamist movement—Saudi Arabia and Pakistan are a serious problem too—Iran's funding and ideological inspiration for the movement is crucial. Without it, the movement would be largely impotent.

YB: Since 9/11 there's been massive confusion about the nature of the enemy that struck us. The Bush administration failed to properly define the enemy, and compounded the confusion by championing the term "war on terror"—singling out a tactic as our enemy. The enemy in fact is an ideological movement—what we define as Islamic totalitarianism.

You asked about some implications of our view for how America has responded to 9/11. *Winning the Unwinnable War* deals with that at great length, but to offer a snapshot, consider one key point. The failure to properly define the enemy, and thus to grasp Iran's centrality within the Islamist movement, meant that U.S. policy instead focused on other, I believe lesser, threats—notably Iraq—and left Iran, for the last ten-odd years, to continue its proxy war against us. Our policy served only to encourage Iranian belligerence—witness its backing of insurgents in Iraq, its reach into Afghanistan, and of course its nuclear quest.

JD: In light of the November 2011 IAEA [International Atomic Energy Agency] report, the general international consensus is that Iran is building a nuclear weapon. Given that, what should the policy of the United States be?
EJ: We must recognize that Iran's quest for nuclear capability is neither new nor an anomaly from its past goals and actions. It is part of an ideologically driven campaign to export its Islamic revolution and gain the means to inflict harm on what Tehran regards as its enemies. Iran has for decades backed terrorist proxies to carry out attacks using conventional means—guns and bombs. So, even if Iran never acquires nuclear capability, the fundamental problem is the belligerent regime and its ideological agenda.

YB: How should we deal with this situation? The chief complicating factor is that for thirty-odd years we have turned a blind eye or reached out an appeasing hand to Iran after each of its attacks. That has in many ways allowed the regime to grow stronger and encouraged its militancy. The problem has festered for so long that we've passed the point where non-military solutions could be effective. We failed to act early, and we've been paying for it.

The 2009-10 protests in Iran offered the possibility of a non-military way of replacing the regime with one that's less- or non-threatening. But the administration squandered that opportunity. I see no real solution without using military force.

But to be clear: what I'm referring to is nothing like what the United States did in Afghanistan or Iraq. Those campaigns were far from the kind of war necessary to eliminate a threat; as Elan and I write in the book, those campaigns are best characterized as essentially "welfare" missions, where the priority in reality was not to eliminate whatever threat the regime posed, but rather to fix up hospitals, clear sewers, and deliver ballot boxes.

The kind of military action I believe is necessary in the case of Iran is far, far different. The exclusive goal would be to end the threat—not an open-ended nation-building crusade à la Bush. One consequence of Iraq and Afghanistan is that people can scarcely imagine that military action can actually succeed in delivering peace—as it did, for example, in World War II. Lately in the foreign-policy establishment some have argued that a nuclear-capable Iran is something we can live with, something we could cope with through "containment." It worked with the USSR, they tell us, because of the fear of "mutually assured destruction," so we can count on the same approach to checkmate the threat of a nuclear Iran. I disagree.

The analogy with the communists completely breaks down, because the Soviets at least wanted to live on earth; the fear of mutual destruction could deter them. But an essential characteristic of the Islamist regime in Tehran is that its ideology celebrates martyrdom and glorifies the afterlife. Can we trust containment to succeed in the face of that kind of mentality? No. There are other reasons why containment is untenable—among them the risk that neighboring regimes, themselves politically unstable and unfriendly, will immediately seek nuclear capability, too. The bottom line is that Tehran's ideology is the problem—it's the driving force behind Iran's decades of aggression. Ultimately, only changing that regime can eliminate it as a threat. The hope is that there would be enough Iranians who oppose it from within, capable of establishing a successor regime that is at minimum a lesser or non-threat to the United States.

JD: *You mentioned Saudi Arabia as another problem regime. Many have hailed the "special relationship" between the U.S. and Saudi Arabia,* *claiming that the Saudis are a great U.S. ally in a tumultuous region. But is this really the case? Is Saudi Arabia a great ally of the U.S. or is it actually a covert enemy?*

EJ: The Kingdom of Saudi Arabia is regarded as a loyal U.S. ally, but that standing is undeserved. Within its borders, the regime governs by reference to sharia. Its youth are inculcated, in schools, through state-controlled media and mosques, with hatred for Western values such as political freedom. Regime-endorsed religious leaders deliver anti-American diatribes at Friday sermons. Preachers in mosques, online, and on television incite Saudis to engage in jihad. It works: fifteen of the nineteen hijackers on 9/11 were Saudis. Many insurgents in Iraq came from Saudi Arabia. Moreover, many billions of dollars from Saudi Arabia are channeled through the world to proselytize for the regime's Wahhabist strain of totalitarian Islam.

This is a regime that espouses political ideas opposed to ours and in league with those of the Islamic totalitarian movement. The regime tramples on the rights of its own people. And it funds and advances the spread of Islamist ideas globally.

The U.S.-Saudi relationship is emblematic of the kind of problems in U.S. foreign policy that we've already touched on, particularly the need to assess other regimes objectively and deal with them accordingly.

JD: In today's world, oil is a most precious resource, but many would argue that our dependence on foreign oil is actually enriching our enemies in the Middle East. Do you believe that this is the case? And how should the U.S. restructure its energy policy to ensure its national security while at the same time not hurting the purchasing power of its citizens?

YB: To be clear: I'm in favor of our using oil and gaining access to it from the Middle East. But in doing so, we cannot compromise on our own political ideas—chiefly, the principle of individual rights. We cannot pretend that the Saudis are better than they are. We cannot appease them and flatter the regime with undeserved praise.

Yes, obviously petrodollars go toward funding the Islamist movement. But that's not an argument to deprive ourselves of oil, the lifeblood of our modern civilization. Rather, it's an argument to deal with the Islamist threat head on. Even if it were feasible to reduce our use of Middle East oil—which for technical reasons is nontrivial—that's woefully insufficient to stop Islamic totalitarianism. To stop it requires not only uprooting the movement's logistical-operational network, but, more important, demonstrating to its adherents that their cause is lost. That requires far more than a squeeze on their cash flow. It requires crushing the enemy's will to fight. That can be done by instilling in them a fear of acting on their political goals—a fear that if they act, they will face overwhelming retaliation. Part of the problem lies with state-owned natural resources. Properly, they should be privately held—both here in the United States and everywhere else in the world. State ownership of such resources is all the more problematic when the regime is autocratic or dictatorial. In the book, we talk about how we could accomplish our goal of securing access to oil. I'd argue that the ability to purchase oil is important enough to our prosperity that we should not rule out using military coercion to ensure the flow of oil. One of many ways to do that is to lay down a firm ultimatum to Saudi Arabia, that it must halt all backing for Islamists and assure the export for trade of oil, or else face our military might and, say, have all of its oil facilities privatized and overseen by us.

JD: An under-reported issue that seems to have escaped media attention is the fact that U.S. troops are now fighting in Uganda. Coupled with the recent intervention in Libya, what does this say about the way in which the government is now using the military? Are these new conflicts being fought in the interest of the American people?

EJ: The Uganda mission illustrates an earlier point about U.S. foreign policy: how one conceives of U.S. interests determines the kind of policy one advocates. In our view, the guiding principle is the protection of Americans' individual rights. Are those imperiled by the situation in Uganda? Is the Lord's Resistance Army (LRA), the group that our mission aims to help bring down, an objective threat to our lives or property? No, and I've yet to see anything like a decent argument for that.

Our view is that such a mission fails to meet the standard of advancing U.S. interests, i.e., of safeguarding the lives of Americans. What the LRA is doing is abhorrent, without doubt. But I'd argue that it is not our responsibility to intercede in this conflict. Nor is it moral to put U.S. servicemen in harm's way, for the sake of so-called humanitarian missions.

But like similar missions in the past, what motivates it is a common viewpoint that America, because it is strong and wealthy, has a moral duty to serve the weak and poor, to act as a combination global policeman and social worker. If one were to implement this viewpoint consistently, there's no end to the foreign conflicts that we would be obliged to provide help for. How could turning our military into a global social-services organization ensure our security? It cannot. In fact it squanders our means of protecting ourselves. Ultimately, that's a self-sacrificial policy.

JD: *Some scholars have speculated that the Arab Spring will eventually spread to China, where we will see a popular movement against the Communist Party and in favor of democracy. Is it in the interest of the United States to support a democratic movement in China? Would it be possible to do this without antagonizing the Chinese government?*

YB: I would not say that the so-called Arab Spring is spreading to China. First, the term "Arab Spring" packages together dissimilar events, and it's far from obvious that the implied positive evaluation is warranted: were they uniformly or unambiguously pro-freedom? Hardly. Second, pro-freedom activists in China have mounted protests in various forms at least since 1989. Given political developments in China over the last decade, I would not be surprised if there were an increase in such activism in China.

It is proper for our policy to lend moral support to people who seek greater freedom—wherever they are. That means speaking up in defense of those who genuinely fight for their individual rights. America's moral authority is considerable, but we hardly ever pull our weight by making confident, morally unambiguous declarations of support for true freedom activists.

Lending moral support to pro-freedom activists is an underappreciated means of asserting U.S. interests around the world. Talk to people who lived in the former communist bloc, and many will tell you how powerful an inspiration it was to know that the free world was on their side and recognized their plight. The pro-forma utterances from the White House and State Department, which today pass for statements of moral support, are pathetically meek and therefore ineffectual.

Let me add parenthetically that we should only ever provide military support to pro-freedom causes or nations when there is objective evidence that the rights of Americans are directly threatened, such that it becomes a matter of our self-defense.

What would happen if we actually spoke up for genuine pro-freedom activists in China? It would likely antagonize Beijing. But so what? A principled moral stand in favor of freedom will make us safer, long term—whereas the perception of U.S. weakness and our own irrational policies are a considerable threat to our security.

JD: Many people see communist China as the next enemy of the U.S. But China is by far the U.S.'s largest trading partner, and has an enormous impoverished population that could one day grow and enhance that relationship. Should the United States view a rising China as a threat or as an opportunity?

YB: History has taught us that authoritarian governments are potential enemies, because a regime that violates the rights of its own citizens may feel little or no compunction about trampling on the rights of people beyond its borders. But I don't view China today as an enemy of the United States, though it was once, and could become one again. One legitimate fear is that the Chinese economy stalls, and the regime decides that sparking a conflict with the United States would distract the impoverished population from their economic misery. It's important to recognize that what could make China a military threat is the authoritarian character of its government—not the growth of its economy.

Trade with China is not a threat to us, but rather a voluntary exchange of goods and services to mutual advantage—it's a win-win relationship. We benefit enormously from China's economic growth and success. The more they create and trade with us, the better off we are. But China's long-term economic success is unsustainable unless there is greater political freedom for its people—unless the authoritarian system is abolished. On this point both we and the Chinese people have the same long-term interest: to see China's eventual transition to a free and therefore increasingly prosperous country.

JD: The debt crisis in Europe obviously has large implications for the U.S. and the international financial system. What do you see as the root cause of the financial crisis and the current debt crises threatening the West?

YB: There's more to say about this than I can address fully in our conversation. My colleague Don Watkins and I have a forthcoming book that deals with these and related questions at length. Let me touch briefly on a few key aspects.

Ultimately, behind these economic crises is a moral-political issue: What is the proper role of government? Contrary to conventional wisdom, the system of government that prevails in the West is not, strictly speaking, capitalism—meaning a system in which there's a separation of state and economics. Rather, we have an unstable mixture of some freedom with massive—and growing—state intervention and entitlement programs. The prevailing view holds that government must intervene, regulate, centrally control, and provide handouts and bailouts.

What Don and I argue in our book, in our Forbes.com column, and elsewhere is that the regulatory policies of the federal government are the root cause of the financial crisis—from beginning to end. Obviously, it's an involved story, but a key dynamic in the crisis was the interplay of two long-running policies that spanned both Republican and Democratic administrations: we had a destructive combination of artificially low interest rates and a long-standing campaign to encourage as many people as possible to buy homes. There were other factors, and they too stemmed from the distortions in the financial markets that arise only because of regulatory policies and expected state interventions (e.g., "too big to fail").

Europe is facing a crisis born of its welfare-entitlement system. European governments promised welfare benefits, pensions, health care, wages for public employees, etc., that they cannot afford to pay from tax revenues. Until recently the governments borrowed money to cover the shortfall—but that was unsustainable. Markets eventually realized that at current rates of spending, many European governments would never be able to pay their debts.

America's own entitlement programs—Social Security, Medicare, Medicaid—are a massive unfunded liability that constitutes the lion's share of government spending. Unless we dramatically cut spending on entitlements, we too risk suffering a fate like that of Greece. The problem today is what you could describe as an unlimited government that is enmeshed in all aspects of the economy. If we leave that problem unaddressed, the crisis will continue. It will spread across the developed world. And it will become more severe.

What's needed to re-orient the U.S. economy onto the right track? Massive cuts in government spending, the phasing out of entitlements, real deregulation of business—in other words, a fundamental change in how we view government's role. We need to return to a government that does only one thing, but does it well: the protection of our individual rights to life, liberty, property and the pursuit of happiness.

* * *

This interview originally appeared in the *Seton Hall Journal of Diplomacy and International Relations.*

Islamist Winter

Elan Journo November 2013

A Review of *Spring Fever: The Illusion of Islamic Democracy*, by Andrew McCarthy. New York: Encounter, 2013.

Early on, the conventional view on the so-called Arab Spring was euphoric. In a nutshell, it was that the upheavals herald the triumph of freedom. Two-plus years on, however, Islamist groups have gained considerable political power—an ascendancy ominous not only for those subjugated under sharia, but also for American and Israeli security. Searching for silver linings on a darkening horizon, some point to Turkey: here is a regime widely feted as proof that Islamist rule is compatible with political freedom, after all.

Andrew McCarthy roundly refutes that view in *Spring Fever*. Recep Tayyep Erdogan's regime, he contends, serves as a case study of what to expect of ascendant Islamists in the Middle East: more oppression, and more hostility toward the West. "The trend-lines are unmistakable," he writes, "the trajectory of change more certain than its pace."

Turkey's Islamization hinges on the way Erdogan, like his Islamist brothers-in-arms, exploits the West's uncritical embrace of "democracy." McCarthy reports how, four years before his party assumed power, Erdogan explained that "Democracy is just the train we board to reach our destination." The ploy: feign an interest in freedom, then once in power shift toward Islamist rule.

Erdogan's incrementalist campaign aims to remake Turkey's institutions. He prioritized Islamic over secular education, encouraging greater enrollment in religious academies, and seeded the universities and government posts with Islamists. With religious mores—notably public displays of piety and the subservience of women—becoming the new normal, women withdrew from the workforce in droves. The rate at which women are murdered (including "honor killings") has rocketed upward by 1,400 percent. For women aged 15 to 44, "gender-based violence" is now the leading cause of death (far outstripping cancer, traffic accidents, war and malaria).

Erdogan also replaced some 40 percent of Turkey's 9,000 incumbent judges with loyalists who embrace the Islamist agenda of his Justice and Development Party (known by its Turkish acronym, AKP). And, openly subverting rule of law, he selectively refuses to enforce uncongenial judicial rulings. Critics of the regime have found that freedom of speech is largely a mirage. Challenge the regime's authoritarian control, and you risk being intimidated, detained, framed, and jailed. Last year, Ankara earned the horrifying distinction of having imprisoned more journalists than any other country (more than Iran, more than China). (When an Istanbul park became the epicenter for nationwide protests this summer, the major news outlets were conspicuously silent. And in the brutal crackdown on the crowds, the regime's authoritarian essence was on full display.)

It is in Turkey's foreign policy that McCarthy discerns a stark "transition from the Western to the Islamic sphere." Ankara once cultivated strong economic bonds and military cooperation with Israel. That relationship has frayed. Under the ironically labeled "Zero Problems with Neighbors" policy, Erdogan's regime has befriended Hezbollah, embraced Iran's jihadist leadership, and openly supported Tehran's nuclear program (even resisting attempts to impose UN sanctions against it). A particular favorite is the Palestinian jihadist group Hamas. "I don't see Hamas as a terrorist organization," Erdogan insists. "Hamas is a political party." In 2010, the Gaza Freedom Flotilla, aiming to breach Israel's blockade of Gaza, sailed with Ankara's blessing. Erdogan has hosted Hamas leaders as visiting dignitaries, and Turkey has bankrolled the group to the tune of $300 million. Erdogan has taken his country "from NATO ally to terror sponsor."

There are, to be sure, marked differences between Turkey and Egypt, a particular focus of the book, but the Islamists in both countries are working from the same playbook:

- Profess anodyne goals initially, then gradually ratchet up to full-bore Islamist objectives? Check. In Egypt, the Muslim Brotherhood began by promising to contest fewer than 50 percent of the parliamentary seats—then contested nearly 80 percent; it promised not to field a presidential candidate—but eventually did so and handily installed a dyed-in-the-wool Islamist, Mohamed Morsi. Morsi had campaigned to ensure that Egypt's fundamental law would reflect "the sharia, then the sharia, and finally, the sharia."

- Roll out enforcement of sharia norms in daily life? Check. During Ramadan, a religious edict was announced prohibiting Egyptians from eating during daylight hours.
- Openly turn away from America, Israel, the West to embrace the jihadist agenda? Check. The Brotherhood's Supreme Guide issued a call for jihad until "the filth of the Zionists" is cleansed and "Muslim rule throughout our beloved Palestine" is imposed.

McCarthy carefully delimits the scope of his predictive analysis. The Islamization of Turkey was slowed by the military, the designated guardian of the country's explicitly secular character. Egypt, by contrast, has never undergone an enforced secularization campaign, nor is the military's role predictable. (Having published the book well before the military ousting of Morsi, presumably McCarthy would regard the ensuing pro-Morsi demonstrations as evidence of an enduring, potent constituency for Islamist rule.) And the endgame in Egypt appears far off.

The significance of McCarthy's argument is broader than the rise of Islamists in Turkey, post-Mubarak Egypt, and elsewhere. The very notion of "Islamic democracy," he argues, is a dangerous misconception—one that the West fuels and Islamists exploit. Western leaders and intellectuals, he maintains, have failed (some refuse) to grasp the nature and popularity of the Islamist movement, and by advocating "democracy" in the Middle East have encouraged and materially enabled forces hostile to the West.

Islamists, McCarthy ably explains, should be defined not by their tactics but by their animating goal of enforcing rule under the supreme dictates of sharia. Some adopt violent, terrorist means, others the genteel Western forms of political campaigning and advocacy, but their objectives are identical. And McCarthy plausibly contends that in the culture of the Muslim Middle East, obedience to political authority and the totalitarian interpretation of Islam are both well within the mainstream.

McCarthy holds that culture shapes politics and law, and that elections merely reflect popular sentiment. The authentic, Western idea of "democracy," in McCarthy's view, is gutted of its substantive meaning when applied to Islamic politics. More than "just elections and constitution-writing," democracy should be understood as a "shorthand description of a culture based on freedom." But Islamists, he complains, view "democracy" as a "mere vehicle, a procedural path of least resistance" toward a theocratic society bereft of individual freedoms. So, when a culture has been methodically inculcated with the teachings of Islamic totalitarianism, by the likes of the Muslim Brotherhood—when many in the culture have been taught to equate secular government with impiety, and when individual rights are unknown, and controversial speech is deemed blasphemous—what other result could possibly be expected at the ballot box?

The culture-comes-first argument is cogent, but McCarthy's redefinition of "democracy" as identical with the culture of a free society is unconvincing. Perhaps colloquial usage agrees with him, and certainly "democracy" evokes upbeat connotations, but America's founders would be aghast. They knew, from historical evidence and careful reflection, that the essence of democracy is mob rule, and that a government dedicated to protecting individual rights must never submit individual liberties to a popular vote. Unfortunately, recent American policy has arguably encouraged Islamists to embrace the actual meaning of democracy. President George W. Bush told reporters in 2004 that if Iraq, post-Saddam Hussein, were to vote in an Islamist government, he would be disappointed, but "democracy is democracy" adding, "If that's what the people choose, that's what the people choose." McCarthy's point would be better served by framing the issue in clearer terms.

"Where Bush airbrushed Islamic supremacists, Obama embraces them," writes McCarthy, and he goes on to expose how Obama has whitewashed and abetted the Muslim Brotherhood-backed regime that emerged post-Mubarak. But in view of the book's core argument, McCarthy is incongruously lenient toward Bush. When it was crucial to name precisely the nature and goals of the enemy, President Bush proffered designations (evil-doers, hijackers of a great religion, etc.) that deliberately obscured the identity of the Islamist movement, piling confusion upon the public's ignorance. And, considering Bush's signature policy of spreading democracy, it is hard to imagine a figure who did more to prepare the ground for the "spring fever" self-delusion, the view that McCarthy so skillfully demolishes in this book. The reluctance to reach a more critical verdict is a peculiar omission in an otherwise trenchant analysis.

Hard-headed and richly detailed, *Spring Fever* lays bare the facts and trend lines behind the chilling ascendancy of Islamists.

* * *

This article originally appeared in *The Journal of International Security Affairs*.

POSTSCRIPT

What Happened to Egypt's "Arab Spring"?

Elan Journo June 9, 2014

Just over three years ago, Egypt was ruled by Hosni Mubarak's autocratic police-state. During the "Arab Spring," crowds massed in Tahrir Square to protest the Mubarak regime, and he was soon removed from his throne. Then Mohamed Morsi, aligned with the Islamist Muslim Brotherhood, took power. He sought to establish his own kind of tyrannical control. The military toppled him. Now, a new military-backed strongman, Abdel Fattah al-Sisi, heads Egypt. The country seems poised for another Mubarak-esque period. Egypt has swung from one kind of tyranny (dictatorship) to another (Islamist rule)—and back again. Why?

By way of answering that, I'd single out two salient factors. First, the military establishment and the Islamist factions are deeply entrenched, and in effect dominate the political scene. The military wields enormous control over the apparatus of the state. The religious groups, able to couch their positions in moral terms, can set the terms of debate. One result is that the few secular-oriented groups seeking some modicum of freedom are easily marginalized (see "Understanding the 'Arab Spring,'" p. 93). So the prospects for fundamental change—an enormous undertaking that would require many years—were dismal. A second factor is related to that: the better elements among the protesters in Tahrir Square were hamstrung by lacking a well-defined, positive ideological vision. You can see that point emerge in a riveting, poignant documentary, *The Square*. (The film can be watched on Netflix, and it's definitely worthwhile.)

The film tracks a politically diverse group of friends united by outrage, standing together in the massive protests at Tahrir Square. What lends the film its narrative power is that it enables us to listen to them, uncensored by the state. For example, we sit next to them in the living room of an apartment where the friends gather to track the news and make plans and to argue. The fall of Mubarak fills them with elation, the subsequent rise of the

Muslim Brotherhood, gloom. When the military reasserts control in summer 2013—opening fire on crowds with live ammunition and mowing down protesters with armored vans—the sheer brutality is overwhelming.

Dejected and pensive, one of the protesters in the film reflects on the turmoil. Thinking out loud as much as addressing the documentary crew, he points out that the protesters were united against the Mubarak regime, and that enabled them to bring together many different factions at the Square—but what, exactly, were they for? Without that, he muses, how far could they get.

PART 4

The Islamist Cause: Undefeated, Emboldened, Marching On

In June 2014, it was apparent to honest observers that the Iraq war was a failure. A group called the Islamic State declared a "caliphate." It established a quasi-state—equivalent in size to the United Kingdom—subjecting parts of Syria and Iraq to totalitarian sharia law. Galvanized by these events, thousands of Islamists flocked to live, fight and die under the flag of the Islamic State. They came not only from the Middle East but also from Europe, Australia and North America.

In Paris on January 7, 2015, jihadists entered the office of the magazine *Charlie Hebdo* and shot to death members of its staff for blaspheming against Islam and its prophet.

Fighters linked to the Islamic State carried out deadly attacks in Paris, Berlin, Nice, San Bernardino, Istanbul, Orlando, Manchester and London.

Draw Muhammad, Risk Your Life?

Elan Journo October 6, 2010

Molly Norris was a cartoonist for the *Seattle Weekly*, and although she's still alive, she's gone "ghost": leaving her job, moving, changing her name, and essentially erasing any traces of her identity. For fear of her life.

Exercising her right to free speech—and encouraging others to do the same—she promoted "Everybody Draw Muhammed Day." In July, the Islamist cleric Anwar al-Awlaki (who's linked to the Times Square bomber) announced that Norris "should be taken as a prime target of assassination."(!) Now, at the insistence of the FBI, Norris has gone into the equivalent of a witness protection program—on her own dime.

This scandal has been unfolding for a while...so where are the outraged, fire-breathing editorials in our leading newspapers? Where are the impassioned speeches from politicians upholding the inalienable right of Americans to freedom of speech—and specifically, our right to criticize and ridicule ideologies of every stripe? The muted response to Norris's fate, the lack of outrage—particularly from the news media—is horrifying. That our political leaders have pointedly shied away from taking a stand on this is all the more ominous. Government's crucial job is to protect our rights.

Have we sunk so low that drawing Muhammad means risking your life? Is America willing to surrender the fundamental right to freedom of speech in obedience to the dictates of some Islamist cleric?

Jihadist in the Suburbs

Elan Journo October 19, 2010

The headlines can be macabre—"Make a Bomb in the Kitchen of Your Mom"—and the stories (giving advice on how to pack when you leave for jihad) are in colloquial English. *Inspire* magazine is the work of al-Qaeda's affiliate in Yemen. But the editor behind this publication—which has encouraged would-be jihadists to open fire on lunch crowds in D.C., to take out some U.S. government employees—is a Pakistani-American. NPR has a long, unsettling report on that 24-year-old man, Samir Khan.

One point that caught my eye: while still living in his parents' basement, here in the U.S., Khan published a pro-al-Qaeda website—but took pains, even hiring a lawyer to advise him, so as not to run afoul of the law. Someone who knew him tells NPR that that step defied Khan's Islamist creed. "For him to take shade under the Constitution or to go to a disbelieving lawyer and ask for his help contradicts the entire ideological worldview that he has decided to live by."

Really? Islamic totalitarian groups like Hamas have stooped to taking part in representative elections for government power—as a means of advancing their dictatorial agenda. Ditto for Hezbollah. Islamists have shown in the past that they're quite happy to work "within the system" in order to subvert it. In Europe, there are Islamist activists who use lawful means—lobbying, special pleading, lawsuits—to impose their ideology on others. I touch on this topic in my book, *Winning the Unwinable War*. The point here: it's a myth that Islamists use only the tactic of terrorism in pursuit of their ideological goal—far from it.

Freedom of Speech, "Islamophobia," and the Cartoons Crisis

Elan Journo December 18, 2014

Excerpts from an interview with Flemming Rose, author of *The Tyranny of Silence*

Is there a climate of self-censorship regarding Islam? Has fear led artists and writers to avoid discussion and criticism of Islam? So it seemed to the journalists at *Jyllands-Posten*, Denmark's largest daily paper, in the fall of 2005. To assess the situation, the newspaper invited artists to submit cartoons about Islam. The reaction to the twelve cartoons that were published? Protests, boycotts, deadly riots, attacks on Danish embassies. Some 200 people are thought to have died in the protests. The "cartoons crisis" had gone global.

The aftershocks continued. Just two examples: Yale University Press decided to cut every image depicting Muhammad from a new scholarly book analyzing the cartoons crisis. Kurt Westergaard, the Danish cartoonist who depicted Muhammad with a bomb in his turban, was driven into hiding, escaping two attempts on his life.

What is the situation like today? That was one of the questions I put to Flemming Rose, the editor who commissioned and published the cartoons. He has written a perceptive and riveting new book about the crisis, the reaction to it, and the future of free speech. The book's title hints at the direction of the current trend: *The Tyranny of Silence: How One Cartoon Ignited a Global Debate on the Future of Free Speech*.

Our conversation ranged widely. A few of the issues we touched on: what incidents prompted the commissioning of the cartoons, how self-censorship operated under the Soviet regime and the parallels to today, what lies behind the push to outlaw "defamation of religion," and why the invalid term "Islamophobia" is so destructive.

Below is an excerpt from that interview, edited for inclusion in this book. You can listen to the entire interview (and download the MP3) on our website: bit.ly/tyranny-of-silence.

Elan Journo: *I'm delighted to be speaking today with Flemming Rose about his new book* The Tyranny of Silence: How One Cartoon Ignited a Global Debate on the Future of Free Speech. *Welcome to the podcast.*
Flemming Rose: It's really a pleasure.

EJ: What led you to commission the cartoons and then to decide to publish them?
FR: Some people think that these cartoons came out of the blue, that we just decided to publish some cartoons depicting the prophet, to make a statement or to provoke somebody or because of other reasons. But in fact they didn't come out of the blue. They were published as a reaction to a sequence of incidents in Denmark, beginning in the middle of September 2005.

At the time a children's author went public, saying, 'I'm writing a book about the life of the prophet Muhammad, but I have problems finding an illustrator.' Two illustrators had turned down the offer to illustrate the book. Finally, one illustrator said yes, but insisted on anonymity, due to fear for possible consequences. When an artist doesn't want to publish something in his own name, that's a form of self-censorship.

The story was on the front page of my newspaper, and several other newspapers. Following up on the story, we had a discussion at my newspaper. One reporter suggested that we find out if there really was self-censorship among people working in the field of culture in Denmark: The idea was to approach illustrators and cartoonists, and ask them to draw the prophet to see how they react. That idea ended on my desk, and so I wrote a letter to all the members of Denmark's cartoonist association inviting them to draw the prophet as they see him—a very open invitation, and that's the reason why in fact the cartoons are so different. I received twelve cartoons.

EJ: How many people did you approach?
FR: I approached, in fact, forty-two people. But I was told in the middle of the process that, in fact, there were only twenty-five active members of the illustrators' association, so about 50 percent replied. At the newspaper, we had a discussion about whether this was enough in order to go on with the project. But when I was told that it was about 50 percent, we thought that it's fine. But we put off publishing the cartoons for about another two weeks, because

we had just this one source to this story—the children's writer who said that he couldn't find an illustrator.

While we were discussing those issues at the newspaper, several things happened that convinced me and the other editors that we had to publish those cartoons.

First, the illustrator who had originally insisted on anonymity gave an interview to a Danish newspaper. He acknowledged in public that it was true that he insisted on anonymity because he was afraid. He referred to the fate of Theo van Gogh, a Dutch filmmaker, who was killed on the streets of Amsterdam by a young, offended Muslim in November 2004. The illustrator also referred to the fate of Salman Rushdie, the author of *Satanic Verses*, who was subjected to a fatwa by Ayatollah Khamenei, and had to live in hiding for many.

Then, at the Tate gallery, an art museum in London, there was a retrospective by a very famous British avant-garde artist, John Latham. He exhibited an installation called *God is Great*. It's a copy of the Bible, Talmud, and the Koran torn into pieces and laid in a piece of glass. The Tate museum decided to remove this piece of art from the exhibition without asking the artist and without asking the curator. There was a similar case at a museum in Sweden, where an artist exhibited a painting depicting a man and a woman having sex, and on the top of the painting was the first verse from the Koran. Again, the director of the museum removed this painting, without asking the artist or the curator.

Another example of self-censorship related to a book by Ayaan Hirsi Ali, a former Dutch politician now residing in the U.S. She had written a collection of essays critical of Islam. Without consulting her, the publisher of the Finnish edition of the book removed a sentence that was seen as maybe offensive to Muslims. Also: several of the European translators of the book insisted on anonymity. Contrary to the usual practice, they did not want to have their name published on the cover or inside the book.

Yet another incident: A Danish stand-up comedian gave an interview to my newspaper in which he said, "you know, I have no problems mocking the Bible in front of the camera, but I'm afraid of doing the same with the Koran." So he was making a clear difference between the way he would treat Christianity when it comes to satire, and the way he would treat Islam.

And then the prime minister of Denmark met with a group of Danish imams. This was in the aftermath of the London bombings of July 7, 2005. Two of the imams called on him to influence the Danish press in order to get more positive coverage of Islam, which was basically a call for censorship. It was a call to use the tools of state power in order to get a specific point of view into the press. Both of the imams said this in public after the meeting.

So within the course of one or two weeks, you had several cases all speaking to the same problem of self-censorship when it comes to dealing with Islam in the public space in Denmark and in some other European countries. So we decided that this is a legitimate news story.

You know, in journalism you hear about a problem, and then you want to find out if it's true or not. Usually you would call people and they will tell you what they think about this and that. We just pursued another path, basically following a classic journalistic principle, "Don't tell, show it." So [in writing to the Danish illustrators] we had invited them to show through the medium in which they work to express their opinion, their relationship to this problem.

[Alongside the twelve cartoons we published,] I wrote a short article laying out the background, referring to what I knew about the Soviet Union—that you could end up in prison for ten years for telling a joke in Stalin's Soviet Union—and that this kind of intimidation leads to self-censorship and it's a slippery slope. In this case, we didn't know for sure if this was true or not.

But the events that followed, I think, showed that we really hit a hotspot.

To listen to the entire interview (and download the MP3), please visit ARI's website: bit.ly/tyranny-of-silence.

Freedom of Speech: We Will Not Cower

Onkar Ghate January 7, 2015

When foreign governments, religious leaders and their faithful followers threaten and murder individuals for daring to speak, anyone who values his own life and freedom must stand with, and speak for, the victims.

We call on everyone to post and publicize the content that these totalitarians do not want us to see, as we are doing here.

It does not matter whether you agree or disagree with the particular book, cartoon or movie that they seek to silence. We must defend our unconditional right to freedom of thought and freedom of speech.

The totalitarians are counting on self-censorship: that their threats and attacks will leave most of us too scared to speak out and criticize their doctrines. They then have a chance of killing the few individuals brave enough to defy them.

We must end any hope that this strategy will prove effective.

In the wake of the attacks on Sony, many people rightly observed that if *The Interview* were put up on the Internet and made widely available, the attackers' goal of silencing the filmmaker would be unachieved. The same goes for criticism and satire of Islamic doctrine.

If we now all defiantly make the content and images the jihadists wish to ban widely and permanently available across the web, the attackers will have failed. They may have taken the lives of the editor and cartoonists of *Charlie Hebdo*, for which we grieve, but they will not have taken their freedom.

The alternative is to cower and stick our heads in the sand in hope that the issue goes away. But this will not end the threat. It will only make our freedom disappear.

#JeSuisCharlie ... But for How Long?

Elan Journo January 12, 2015

The aftermath of the *Charlie Hebdo* attack has brought an encouraging reaction. You can see it on the streets of Paris and other cities. Last week, tens of thousands of people joined vigils in solidarity for the murdered journalists. Upwards of a million Parisians took to the streets on Sunday. "Je Suis Charlie" read the signs. Online the corresponding hashtag has swept across social media. Some news outlets—more than I expected—have reprinted *Charlie Hebdo* cartoons. But what's more, the outlets that have refused to publish the images (or pixelated them) have been deservedly bashed. They shame themselves by cowering.

We are all Charlie—at least today and next week. But what happens once grief and horror naturally attenuate over time?

For the Je Suis Charlie phenomenon to translate into a strengthening of freedom of speech, a great deal depends on the conclusions people form and act on going forward.

Jeffrey Goldberg at *The Atlantic* admonishes that few fully appreciate what it means to stand up for freedom of speech, or have the courage to do so themselves. I'd add: where was the solidarity nearly a decade ago for *Jyllands-Posten*, Flemming Rose, and the artists who were driven in to hiding after the Muhammad cartoons crisis? And before that, after the murder of filmmaker Theo van Gogh? Or, for *Charlie Hebdo* in 2011 when its offices were firebombed?

By now people have many, many more data points. Now, as in the past, the pattern is blatant. The jihadists seek to extinguish the freedom of speech. At *Charlie Hebdo*, the killers declared that they were avenging the prophet. They voiced a standard battle cry, "Allahu Akbar." They executed the journalists during an editorial meeting.

The future will bring continuing assaults on the freedom of speech. The courage to defend that freedom presupposes a real understanding of it. What's vital now is to champion the freedom of speech, to inform and educate all who will listen. If you value your life and freedom, you should speak up in whatever forum is open to you. Join ARI in our effort to defend the irreplaceable right to the freedom of speech.

Learn about ARI's uncompromising defense of freedom of speech: AynRand.org/freespeech.

Free Speech vs. Religion:
An Interview with Onkar Ghate

The Undercurrent June 23, 2015

Onkar Ghate is a senior fellow and the Chief Content Officer at the Ayn Rand Institute. He has written and lectured extensively on philosophy and serves as dean for the Institute's Objectivist Academic Center in Irvine, California. *The Undercurrent's* Jon Glatfelter had the privilege of interviewing Ghate regarding the May 3, 2015, shooting at the Draw Muhammad cartoon contest in Garland, Texas, as well as religion and free speech, more broadly.

The Undercurrent: *Many of the major U.S. media players, including CNN and FOX, still have not published the cartoon contest's winning piece. Why do you think that is?*
Onkar Ghate: I haven't kept tabs on which outlets have and have not published that cartoon, but there were similar responses in regard to the *Charlie Hebdo* cartoons and, before that, the Danish cartoons in 2005–06. Sometimes a media outlet would try to explain why it is not showing its audience a crucial element of the news story, and I think these explanations have revealed a mixture of motives at work.

Here's a non-exhaustive list: fear, cowardice, appeasement, sympathy. Let me say a word on each. Some media outlets are afraid of violent reprisals and of the ongoing security costs that would be necessary to protect staff. And because the U.S. government refuses to take an unequivocal stand in defense of the right to free speech, the totalitarians are emboldened, which makes violent reprisals more likely. So that's one reason. But despite this legitimate fear, I do think there is often an element of cowardice. The likelihood of an attack can be overstated, and of course if more news outlets publish the cartoons, it is more and more difficult to intimidate and attack them all, and less and less likely that a particular organization will be singled out. Here there is strength in numbers. A third motive is the appeaser's false hope that if he gives in and doesn't publish the cartoons, he will have satisfied the attackers and no further threats or demands will follow. Finally, many are sympathetic: out of deference to the non-rational, faith-based emotions of Muslims, they don't publish the cartoons, even though those cartoons are news. They view the cartoonists and publishers as the troublemakers and villains. (The roots of this sympathy, I think, are complex and often ugly.)

TU: *Some have condemned the contest's organizer, Pamela Geller, and the winning artist, Bosch Fawstin. They say there's a world of difference between good-natured free expression and malicious speech intended solely to antagonize. What do you think?*

OG: I disagree with many things that I've heard Pamela Gellar say, but I refuse to discuss her real or alleged flaws when totalitarians are trying to kill her, as though those flaws, even if real, justify or mitigate the actions of the aspiring killers. The *New York Times* editorial to which you link is a disgrace. After a sanctimonious paragraph saying that we all have the right to publish offensive material and that no matter how offensive that material may be, it does not justify murder, the rest of the editorial goes on to criticize the victim of attempted murder. As my colleague and others have noted, this is like denouncing a rape victim instead of her rapists.

And notice what the editorial glosses over: in the first paragraph stating that offensive material does not justify murder, it concludes with the seemingly innocuous point that "it is incumbent on leaders of all religious faiths to make this clear to their followers."

This is the actual issue. Why don't you similarly have to tell a group of biochemists or historians, when they disagree about a theory, that their disagreements don't justify murdering each other? The answer lies in the difference between reason and faith, as I'm sure we'll discuss, a difference the editorial dares not discuss.

But contra the editorial, the Garland event had a serious purpose. Look at the winning cartoon: it makes a serious point.

Whether we will admit it or not, there exists today a growing number of totalitarians who seek to impose their version of Islam on the world and to dictate what we in the West can and cannot say. A precedent-setting episode was the fatwah against Salman Rushdie. A foreign leader openly calls for the assassination of a Western author and those involved in the publishing of his book, *The Satanic Verses*, and the U.S. and other Western governments do virtually nothing in response, sometimes worse than nothing.

Fast forward a few years and should it be surprising that there exists a climate of self-censorship with respect to Islam? Western writers, artists and cartoonists are afraid to publish things that might be deemed blasphemous by Muslims. To investigate the extent of the self-censorship in regard to illustrations of Muhammad, the Danish newspaper *Jyllands-Posten* runs a cartoon contest in 2005. Worldwide riots and outrage ensue, death threats proliferate, cartoonists and newspaper editors go into hiding, some are later attacked, and the official Western response to all this is again mostly pathetic.

To me this is a serious problem. There are many other episodes that could be mentioned to drive home the extent of the problem, but a simple way to appreciate its extent is to ask yourself whether you can imagine that instead of the sacrilegious *Book of Mormon* winning over audiences and critics on Broadway, it is the equally sacrilegious musical "The Koran." Right now, this isn't even in the realm of the possible. Remember what happened when, in the face of the Danish cartoons crisis, Trey Parker and Matt Stone tried to depict Muhammad on *South Park*?

Now in the face of a totalitarian movement that commands us not to utter blasphemous thoughts and threatens us with death if we do, coupled with our own government's appeasing responses, I think it becomes the responsibility of any self-respecting citizen to refuse to cower and for us as a culture to refuse to collapse into self-censorship. Instead, proudly and defiantly utter the blasphemous thoughts. I think a worthy project during the Rushdie years would have been to raise a fund to make his life in hiding easier, purchase the rights to his book for a generous sum, and then publish and distribute millions of copies for free. Similarly with the *Charlie Hebdo* assassinations, I argued that the forbidden cartoons should be plastered all over the Internet. Let it be seen that the attempt to ban these works achieves the opposite. Make it clear that the totalitarians' goal requires killing us all. Declare that I, too, am Spartacus.

I view the Fawstin cartoon as in this same spirit and thus as making a serious, needed point.

TU: *I have friends who want to stand up for free speech but are worried about being labeled "intolerant" by their friends and acquaintances. How do you think everyday citizens should act?*
OG: I've already indicated part of my answer. The totalitarians' goal is to silence us and make us obey. The current tactic

is assassination of those who dare speak. The hope is that these attacks will create enough fear to produce widespread self-censorship. Unfortunately, that hope is materializing. Defy them. Put up on your Facebook or Instagram pages the forbidden cartoons and explain that you are purposely doing so in the name of free speech and in order to combat the climate of self-censorship. Or put up links to places that do this, such as ARI.

More generally, among some of the best people today in the West, there is a frightening lack of understanding of the right to free speech, why it is vital, who its enemies are at home and abroad, past and present. Educate yourself about this crucial right and its history, and then try to convince your friends and acquaintances of the importance of the issue.

If you get called names in the process, try to use this as a conversation starter and don't become defensive. Ask the person what he means by "intolerance" and if he can state his actual position. Is his view that we should obey every religious taboo? Many Hindus regard cows as sacred and find it offensive that we eat beef. Should we stop eating beef out of tolerance or respect? Or should we stop doing so only if a group of organized Hindus starts assassinating chefs at steakhouses? Won't this encourage religionists to use violence? Or perhaps his view is that we should not criticize religion? Why not? And does he apply this to all religions, or just Islam? If just Islam, why does it warrant special status?

So my advice is that if you are truly talking about friends and acquaintances with whom you have a positive relationship, treat them as open to persuasion even if they begin by dismissing or belittling your position, politely stand your ground, and discuss and argue.

But of course this presupposes that you have some understanding of the issues involved.

TU: In a recent panel with Flemming Rose, author of The Tyranny of Silence, *you said that an individual's right to free speech is one application of a more fundamental right: the right to think. Could you explain that?*
OG: The great battle for freedom in the West was a battle for freedom of thought, including everything this freedom presupposes and everything it leads to. The right to freedom of thought is the right to think for yourself, which means the right to engage in a reasoning process: to gather evidence, logically analyze and weigh it, entertain different arguments, form and follow hypotheses,

perform experiments, pursue various lines of questioning, etc., etc. A reasoning process can have no master other than facts and logic. It cannot be subordinate to the approval of a king, pope, president or fellow citizen, no matter how much they disagree or are offended by what you think. An aspect of this process is to be able to freely discuss and debate ideas with others, and to then present your views and conclusions in an effort to persuade others. Freedom of thought and freedom of speech go together.

Historically, the opponents of freedom of thought and freedom of speech are political authorities operating with the sanction of religion (or some other mystical dogma, like Marxism or Nazism) and religious leaders wielding political power.

TU: *If you view faith and force as intimately linked phenomena, do you see reason and freedom as linked? If so, how has the United States, with its largely Judeo-Christian culture, remained arguably more free than less religious parts of Europe?*
OG: Yes, the connection between faith and force and between reason and freedom is a philosophical issue that some thinkers in the Enlightenment made great strides in identifying and that I think Ayn Rand fully explains.

Very briefly, to extol faith is to extol, in thought and action, blind submission and obedience. As a natural consequence, force will be seen as a means of achieving the good: you can make someone blindly submit and obey by threatening to burn him at the stake or to chop his head off.

But what you cannot achieve by the instruments of terror is rational understanding, knowledge, enlightenment. These require that a person himself initiate and direct a process of reason. And this means that if the goal is rational understanding and knowledge, the individual must have the freedom to think and speak. This is why the Age of Enlightenment became the champion of these freedoms.

To answer the second part of the question, the U.S. is not a Judeo-Christian nation. It is the first nation to consciously separate church from state. It is the last, great accomplishment of the Age of Enlightenment and is built on the Greek-Roman achievements that began to be rediscovered during the Renaissance. Nor is it true that Europe is less faith-based than is America. Yes, Americans are overall more overtly religious, but the faith-based doctrines of nationalism, fascism, socialism and communism swept across Europe in a way that they never did in the U.S. Since the time of the American Revolution and its grounding in the Age of Enlightenment, culturally both Europe and America have moved in the direction of mysticism, but Europe has been more mystical than the U.S. and consequently less free.

For a fuller discussion of these issues, you can watch my talks "Religion vs. Freedom" and "The Morality of Freedom."

TU: In his recent interview with The Undercurrent, *Bosch Fawstin labeled himself "anti-Islam." He described Islam as a fundamentally "totalitarian ideology." Is it different from other religions in this respect?*
OG: There is, in essence, no difference. Any mystical, faith-based doctrine whose leaders are trying to usurp the role of a rational philosophy in human life—as Christians did during the Greek-Roman period, as socialist-Marxists and fascist-Nazis did during the nineteenth and twentieth centuries, and as Islamists are trying to do today—is dictatorial and becomes totalitarian.

Each of these movements is seeking blind submission and obedience to a comprehensive worldview. It should come as no surprise that the daily submission and obedience they desire will eventually be enforced at gunpoint.

This is true of ISIS, of the theocrats in Iran and Saudi Arabia, of the Taliban, of the communists in Russia and China, of Protestants like Calvin and Martin Luther, and of leaders of the Catholic Church.

TU: A widely held view is that Islam, to say nothing of the world's other major religions, is peaceful. In fact, immediately post-9/11, President George W. Bush described Islam as a religion "of peace" that has been "hijacked." Do you agree?
OG: Like much of what comes out of George W. Bush's mouth, this is the opposite of the truth. As I've already indicated, the essence of religion, namely faith, sanctions the use of force. If blind submission and obedience are the goals, coercion is an effective means. A worldview accepted on faith encourages not peace but war. Centuries of religious conflict and warfare are not some inexplicable accident.

Also no accident is that the greatest of America's founding fathers, Jefferson and Madison, deliberately separated church from state. They did so partly in the name of peace. Let us live under principles and laws whose origin is reason, not blind faith, and we can all rationally agree to them and live peacefully together.

TU: It seems that free expression is under assault on a number of fronts today. What does this issue of free speech mean to you personally? Why have you chosen to dedicate a significant portion of your scholarship to defending it?
OG: Because of their viewpoints, many of the Enlightenment's thinkers were on the run from the political and religious authorities. But they eventually won and put an end to such arbitrary power. It is an enormous accomplishment and an enormous gift, not to be surrendered.

I'm an intellectual. My entire career revolves around the reasoned investigation and communication of philosophical ideas and theories, ideas and theories that others often find offensive. If I won't stand up for my right to freedom of thought and speech, and fight for these, I have no business calling myself an intellectual. And I have no business professing admiration for Locke, Jefferson, Madison and other heroes of freedom, if I stand idly by as people try to smash their achievements.

TU: Do you have any recommendations for those who want to explore the topics of free speech and religion in more depth? Can we expect any future projects or events on these issues from you or the Institute?
OG: I've already mentioned a few things of mine and of others at ARI that people can read and watch. Flemming Rose's book, to which you linked, is also definitely worth reading. For those who don't know, he was the editor who published the Danish cartoons; I admire his benevolence and courage.

In a few weeks I will be speaking at OCON, where I will address some of these issues in more detail, including some issues that we did not have time to touch on today. The talk's titled "*Charlie Hebdo,* the West and the Need to Ridicule Religion." I hope to see some of your readers there!

And of course in the months and years to come, look to ARI to continue to uphold and defend the individual's right to freedom of thought and speech.

* * *

This interview originally appeared in *The Undercurrent* (theundercurrent.org).

Iran Nuclear Deal:
The Diplomacy-or-War False Alternative

Elan Journo July 23, 2015

When Obama announced the Iran nuclear deal, he explained the rationale for taking the diplomatic path. There were, he said, three options: negotiate as good a deal as we can get; pull out of the talks; or else take military action against Iran's nuclear facilities, igniting another Middle East war. Turns out these boil down to only two options, really, since pulling out of talks, according to Obama, would also end up leading to military action. So, if the options are diplomacy versus going to war, you can see why Obama's case has swayed some people. But that argument hinges on a tendentious framing of the possibilities.

Obama's either/or argument is a classic example of a false alternative. When the deal was announced, an editorial in the *Wall Street Journal* rightly protested that there was at least one more option: inflicting even stronger economic sanctions to pressure Iran. Fair point: Obama's two alternatives hardly exhaust the possibilities. In my view, the time for considering sanctions, with all of their limitations, passed long ago. But the point stands: Obama's argument hinges on an alternative that's unduly narrow.

Now look at how Obama's argument slants the framing of the two alternatives. Start with the administration's preferred option, a negotiated deal.

Advocates of the deal portray it as requiring inspections so "intrusive" that if the Iranians inched beyond the terms of the deal, "the world would know it." Except that the administration has already started walking back the hyped claim that nuclear inspectors will have "anytime, anyplace" access. The record on monitoring such nuclear deals is pitiful: recall that in 1994 the Clinton administration struck a deal with North Korea over its nuclear program. That deal subjected North Korea to strict nuclear inspections, but the regime has since built and tested nuclear devices and sold some of its technology.

Of course, Iran has cheated at every step so far. The question is not if, but when and in what way(s) Tehran will violate the deal. In theory Iran would face a "snap back" re-imposition of sanctions, if its breach of the deal could ever be detected and if the facts can be agreed upon by a multi-nation committee. Good luck with that.

To imagine that this alternative can reduce the threat of a nuclear Iran is ridiculous. It's like popping two Advil in the expectation of curing a fast-growing cancerous tumor. You delude yourself that you're "doing something" about the problem—Advil is a medicine, after all—even while allowing it to worsen.

The chief selling point for Obama's nuclear deal, however, lies in what the deal is not—it's not military force. And by that, he means we can avoid another Iraq.

The Iraq war was a debacle. And we all recoil from the idea of another quagmire. Is it right, though, to equate military force with a monumentally irrational, disastrous application of such power, the Iraq war? No.

The military is a powerful instrument, but it is our foreign policy that directs it. Clearly military force can be—and, in the past, has been—guided by better policy, and it was effective in advancing our self-defense (World War II comes to mind). What unfolded in Iraq was nothing like the military action necessary for our self-defense. In *Winning the Unwinnable War*, I explain that it was fundamentally a policy, not a military failure: in short, it was a nation-building welfare mission, not a self-interested mission to eliminate threats we faced. The wider point is that it's tendentious to equate the Iraq war (as horrific and disgraceful as it was) with military action in self-defense, and then dismiss that option.

The Iraq war should be taken as discrediting, not military action, but the ideas of our policymakers, who set the battle plans for the military.

What's missing from the debate over Iran is the one option we most need: a fundamentally different approach to our foreign policy, one that properly identifies and eliminates threats to our lives and freedom. For my detailed answer about how to respond to Iran, I point you to my book. Two brief points:

First, we have put ourselves into a situation with Iran that a rational foreign policy would never permit us to get into. We find ourselves here, precisely because Washington for years has followed a perversely short-range and unprincipled foreign policy. At the time of Iran's first act of war against us, three decades ago, we should have retaliated decisively. We didn't. We should have acted after Iran's second, third, fourth, umpteenth act of war. We didn't. For the last decade plus, the evidence of the regime's nuclear program was ineluctable, but we basically allowed it to proceed. For years by letting Iran attack us with impunity, we've encouraged it. By wooing it to the negotiating table—a process that began under Bush—we've signaled that we regard it as a legitimate interlocutor.

Second, we have disarmed ourselves even as the threat from Iran has grown. We ought to recognize that military action—from threats, ultimatums, targeted strikes, and up to war—is sometimes necessary to defend ourselves and (when guided by rational principles) effectual. I have argued that the threat from Iran requires applying military coercion in our self-defense. That would look far different from the self-destructive mission in Iraq. In chapter 7 of my book—which you can read here in PDF—I illustrate the sharp contrast between the policies that begat the nightmare of Iraq and what a rational approach entails.

One of the many pernicious consequences of Bush's foreign policy is that people have come to believe that our military—despite being unrivaled—is ineffectual and, if used, counter-productive. This notion that our self-defense must preclude military action goes a long way to explaining how Obama's nuclear deal is seen as even remotely plausible.

The Iran Nuclear Deal and the Split-Personality Fallacy

Elan Journo August 10, 2015

Why are seemingly sensible people cheering the Iran deal, given the regime's notorious brutality and belligerence? The answer lies in a wonkish affliction that you could call the split-personality fallacy.

Glance at the regime we're talking about. Iran is a horrific theocracy that methodically violates individual rights. Iran's worldwide backing of jihadists last year (according to our own government) was "undiminished." Across the Middle East, Iran vigorously seeks dominion: in Beirut, Damascus, Sanaa, Baghdad and Gaza, it already exerts significant influence, and it has begun outreach to the Taliban. Post-deal, might the mass chants in Iran of "Death to America" end? Might the regime's hostility toward us ("the Great Satan") abate? Whoever cherishes such hopes had them slapped down by Iran's "supreme leader" Ayatollah Khamenei: Our policy toward the "arrogant" U.S. government, he announced after the deal, "won't change at all."

And yet: in a major speech last week at American University, President Obama noted the deal's many backers:

> The United Nations Security Council has unanimously supported it. The majority of arms control and non-proliferation experts support it. Over 100 former ambassadors—who served under Republican and Democratic presidents—support it.

To that tally, add two scholars from the self-described libertarian Cato Institute, who also praised it. They argued that the "agreement must be viewed as a clear success."

How could anyone think that it's a good idea to negotiate with an openly hostile regime that fuels jihadists and seeks our destruction? Enter the split-personality fallacy. The crux of this fallacy is to treat the actions of Iran (or another tyranny we want to engage diplomatically) in isolation, as if carried out by distinct, firewalled personalities that happen to coexist in the same physical regime. Iran's drive for nuclear capability (officially: for civilian purposes!)

reflects one personality. Iran's pervasive violation of individual rights domestically? That's another. How about its ongoing backing of jihadist groups? Still another. What about Iran's quest for regional domination? Yet another, dissociated personality.

The logic of this fractured perspective means that we must handle each personality separately, divorced from any wider context. Thus, many boosters of the Iran deal bless it on the minutely narrow grounds that it might delay Iran's nuclear program. Everything else—the domestic repression, the drive for regional conquest, the backing of jihadists, the hostility toward us—all of that's beyond the deal's scope, and therefore not something we should consider in judging the deal and consequences.

The segmenting out of Iran's nuclear program for piecemeal attention is touted as reflecting a nuanced, hard-headed concern with practicality. But what actually underlies the fractured, ultra-narrow approach toward Iran is a desire to evade the regime's animating ideological character. Observe how we have no concern about nuclear weapons in the hands of the UK or France; but precisely the same weapon in Iran's hands is a grave concern, because of its militant character. Push that out of mind, though, and you can dream up a dealable-with persona, one which (like the UK or France) might actually comply with a pact.

But ignoring Iran's character is policy malpractice. To assess the situation rationally and formulate sound policy, it is crucial that we have a clear understanding of the regime's character. Is it a good idea to negotiate with Iran? Is the nuclear deal signed in Vienna a "clear success"? When you look at the contours of Iran's nature, you see that in truth the answers are: no, and no.

The Iranian regime embodies the idea of Islamic totalitarianism. Its founder and first "supreme leader," Ayatollah Khomeini, brought into reality a theory of clerical rule. Tehran demands from its citizens submission to religious law. Ergo the "morality police" that patrol the streets and harass women for wearing the wrong kind of veil. At the core is the totalitarian ambition to subjugate people. Witness the fate of six Iranian twenty-somethings who videoed themselves singing along to Pharrell's "Happy." Their video went viral. Then they were arrested, tried and found guilty of "participation in the making of a vulgar clip" and "illegitimate relations between members of the group." They may yet escape being flogged or doing jail time (their sentence), but the fact that they were swept up for something so benign perfectly illustrates Tehran's rule-by-intimidation. Insulting the theocratic government and "blasphemy" are crimes. Hashem Shaabani, a poet, was accused of criticizing the regime. The executioner's noose wrung the life out of him. To the Iranian regime, human life is cheap.

This same totalitarian lust for domestic subjugation animates Tehran's aggression beyond its borders. Iran's founding constitution states that the Army and the Revolutionary Guards Corps

> will be responsible not only for guarding and preserving the frontiers of the country, but also for fulfilling the ideological mission of jihad in God's way; that is, extending the sovereignty of God's law throughout the world (this is in accordance with the Koranic verse "Prepare against them whatever force you are able to muster, and strings of horses, striking fear into the enemy of God and your enemy, and others besides them" [8:60]).

Iran has made good on that mission by helping to build and train jihadist groups. Its main proxy force is Hezbollah ("the army of God"). It has carried out attacks from Beirut to Buenos Aries, and it has slaughtered American soldiers and diplomats in Lebanon and in Iraq. Despite being subjected to years of supposedly biting economic sanctions, Iran funneled billions of dollars to support the Assad regime in Syria and to provision Hamas, in the Gaza strip, with weapons and rockets.

But suppose we took the facts of Iran's character seriously. We would be able to formulate a rational approach toward that regime. Here are two key takeaways that ought to shape it.

First, Iran's domestic repression and its imperialist march and its nuclear aspiration are inseparable. They stem from the same causal factor, the regime's declared ideological mission. If Allah's word is the Truth, and Iran's leaders definitely think so, then all mankind must be brought under its purview. How can there be any limits to where the Truth must reign? (Tehran certainly sees no such limits.) How can any means to advance that grandiose vision be precluded? (For Iran, none should be.) Going nuclear would provide Iran with a new means to advance the goal of expanding Allah's dominion.

Second, diplomatic engagement with Iran over the nuclear issue is a disaster in the making. Quite apart from the material "carrots" Iran might pocket and use to fund its jihadist proxies, simply allowing it to pull up a seat at the negotiating table is to confer on the regime an undeserved legitimacy. It implies that Iran, despite all the blood on its hands, is somehow a peace-seeking state; that despite its manifest belligerence, Iran is somehow committed to persuasion. Recall that Iran has engaged in deception at every step; here we're providing that tyranny with moral cover. Far from putting distance between Iran and the bomb, all that this appeasing deal can do is encourage the regime in its malignant campaign.

The split-personality fallacy sabotages policy thinking. Fracturing Iran's character into dissociated shards will not make Iran's character something other than what it clearly is. Blinding ourselves to it just puts great distance between us and the crucial facts needed to resolve the situation. And the nuclear deal promises to land us in graver problems down the road. It strengthens Iran, bringing the regime ever closer to going nuclear. By allowing that to happen, we will multiply the difficulty of using military force to defend ourselves from the Iranian menace. The reality we face is unpleasant and deeply distressing, but ignoring the truth can only subvert our security.

* * *

This article originally appeared in *The Federalist*.

Cheering for the *Charlie Hebdo* Attacks: The Shape of Things to Come?

Elan Journo October 6, 2015

Ten years ago last week, the Danish newspaper *Jyllands-Posten* published twelve cartoons related to Islam. The aim was to gauge a seemingly growing climate of self-censorship in Europe. The ensuing crisis went global.

By looking at the erosion of free speech in Europe, you could see markers of what to expect here. European self-censorship, my colleague Onkar Ghate argued at the time, was coming to America. By the spring of 2006, Borders Books and Waldenbooks announced that they would not stock an upcoming issue of *Free Inquiry* magazine, because it reprinted some of the notorious cartoons.

The fear was pervasive. Major American news outlets refused to reprint the cartoons, even in reports on the rioting and deaths related to the cartoons crisis. Some years later, Yale University Press published a scholarly book analyzing the cartoons crisis—but decided just before going to press to excise every one of the twelve cartoons, along with other images.

In Europe, filmmakers, artists and writers had been threatened, attacked, murdered. Such threats and attacks were occurring here too.

In January 2015: Islamist gunmen massacred journalists at the magazine *Charlie Hebdo* in Paris. In May 2015: Islamists tried to attack a free speech event in Garland, Texas. Writing on *Voices for Reason*, Steve Simpson pointed out that the destruction of freedom of speech succeeds in large part because of the continuing appeasement in the West of those who resort to threats and violence. Steve's post, incidentally, was published five days before the Garland attack.

Although Europe is farther along, the trend is clear. That's what came to mind when I read Brendan O'Neill's account of a debate at the prestigious Trinity College, Dublin, in Ireland, on the right to be offensive. He writes:

> I was on the side of people having the right to say whatever the
> hell they want, no matter whose panties it bunches. The man
> on the other side who implied that *Charlie Hebdo* got what it
> deserved, and that the right to offend is a poisonous, danger-
> ous notion, was one Asghar Bukhari of the Muslim Public
> Affairs Committee.

It is depressing, but not surprising, that Bukhari's view is taken
seriously. What I found bone-chilling is the reaction of students
in the audience. They listened intently to Bukhari's case. Some
cheered.

> This is how screwed-up the culture on Western campuses
> has become [writes O'Neill]: I was jeered for suggesting we
> shouldn't ban pop songs; Bukhari was cheered for suggest-
> ing journalists who mock Muhammad cannot be surprised if
> someone later blows their heads off.

One audience at one debate at one university in one city: obviously that's at most a data point, not a trend. But do the attitudes
of these students—whom O'Neill describes as non-fringe, young
and with-it—reflect broader trends in Europe? Quite possibly.

What does that imply for the future of free speech in Europe—
and here?

San Bernardino and the Metastasizing Jihad

Elan Journo December 8, 2015

From the *Wall Street Journal*, on the butchers who carried out last week's attack in San Bernardino:

> Agents are pursuing "the very real possibility" that Ms. Malik was the catalyst for the violence, said one official. So far her husband "seems like someone who was searching for answers," the official said….
>
> *An initial review of the couple's online activity indicates one or both explored propaganda from al-Qaeda and the Nusra Front, a terror group fighting in Syria,* officials said.
>
> *They also appear to have learned some terrorism tradecraft,* with investigators pointing to their move to smash their cellphones, stockpile thousands of rounds of ammunition and build more than a dozen black-powder pipe bombs.

From my book, *Winning the Unwinnable War: America's Self-Crippled Response to Islamic Totalitarianism* (Lexington Books, 2009):

> Suicide bombing, another tactic heavily practiced in Iraq [during the insurgency], is now rampant in Afghanistan. *The sharing of "best practices" among jihadists is potentially unlimited in its scale and lethal impact. Although person-to-person training may be the traditional mode of transferring combat knowledge, the Web offers Islamists an inexpensive, worldwide communications platform. Through bulletin boards, online videos, and written manuals, they can recruit fighters to their cause and disseminate to them hard-won expertise in mass murder, to be deployed anywhere.*
>
> Nothing that the United States has done in Iraq or Afghanistan has given jihadists reason to abandon their desire for such mass-casualty attacks on the West. Washington's policy has in fact left them stronger than before. *It has made the ideal of Islamic totalitarianism seem ever more viable—both by empowering and blessing Islamist rule, and by betraying its own timidity in the refusal to crush the jihad.* The Islamist equation that fidelity to Islam is the path to existential dominance, while American secularism (read: impiety) means weakness, thus gains added plausibility in their minds.

Emphasis added.

The Other Islamic State, Our Ally

Elan Journo December 19, 2015

Why has Ashraf Fayadh, a poet and artist, been sentenced to death? A court of law found him "guilty on five charges that included spreading atheism, threatening the morals of... society and having illicit relations with women": he has been branded an apostate, for which the penalty is death. Where did this happen?

Maybe Raqqa, the stronghold of ISIS? Good guess, but no; it happened in the Kingdom of Saudi Arabia. Nor, of course, was this horrifying sentence an outlier; on the contrary. By one reckoning, lately the Saudi courts have handed down the "highest recorded number of executions in the kingdom since 1995." Some notable recent cases of Saudi "justice" have included

> the public flogging of a liberal blogger; a death sentence for a protester for offenses committed as a minor; and a sentence of 350 blows for a British man who was arrested with alcohol in his car. (The Briton was released this month after spending more than a year in prison, averting the threatened flogging.)

There are many differences between Saudi Arabia and ISIS. The first is a monarchy, the second believes itself a true "caliphate," or Islamist regime. Saudi Arabia carries out floggings and beheadings without splashy, macabre propaganda videos, unlike ISIS. Saudi Arabia spends hundreds of millions on religious schools and books advancing its strain of Islamic totalitarianism worldwide; ISIS operatives spend a lot of time leveraging social media. The Saudi regime purports to be a U.S. ally; ISIS is at war with the West. These and umpteen other differences are real. They are overwhelmed, however, by the deeper commonality: the shared commitment to the political supremacy of Islamic law, sharia.

That's a fundamental causal factor, from which a great many consequences follow. And that factor would have to inform any serious thinking about our policy toward Saudi Arabia. Yet that regime has enjoyed an underserved standing as our ally, for many years. President George W. Bush embraced the Saudi regime, even hosting a member of the ruling family at his ranch. President

Obama has (literally) bowed in deference to the Saudi king, while viewing the regime as an ally. What explains our irrational approach to Saudi Arabia?

A significant part of the answer lies in a perverse mindset, which Ayn Rand characterized as being "concrete-bound." In foreign policy, that mindset sees only scattered dots, never the trend lines that unite them (such as the decades-long ascent of Islamic totalitarianism across the Middle East); it sees discrete unrelated crises, not a sustained campaign (such as the escalating spiral of jihadist attacks in the years prior to 9/11); it sees only particular superficial features of regimes and Islamist factions, discounting the unifying role of their philosophic ideas (which animate the Islamist movement's diverse factions and state-sponsors). What this fractured mindset avoids is the integration of data into a conceptual perspective. And so, the essential similarity in ideology between Saudi Arabia and ISIS is left unseen, and it is purposely disregarded when inconvenient facts—like a death sentence for a poet—unavoidably intrude.

* * *

This blog post originally appeared in *The Times of Israel.*

Ignoring the Islamist Menace

Elan Journo January 16, 2016

Did you catch those breaking news reports, right after the San Bernardino shooting, suggesting that the attack was workplace violence? You might chalk that up to off-the-cuff speculation. Yet there was a kind of desperation behind the insistence on finding some generic, non-ideological motive. Yet it turned out to be what many expected from the outset, a jihadist attack; one of the murderers had pledged allegiance to Islamic State.

Think back to the mass shooting at Fort Hood in 2009. Officially, it was played down as workplace violence. Yet Nidal Hasan, a psychiatrist serving in the U.S. Army, viewed himself as a "soldier of Allah." When he gunned down thirteen people on the base, he shouted "Allahu Akbar."

Which brings us to the recent murderous ambush of a Philadelphia police officer, while he was sitting in his patrol car. The assailant shot at the officer at close range, inflicting serious injuries. Why?

"This was a criminal with a stolen gun" the mayor of Philadelphia insisted at a press conference. "In no way, shape or form does anybody in this room believe that Islam or the teaching of Islam" is connected with the attack. And yet:

> [I]mmediately after the mayor's pronouncement, the commander of the police department's homicide unit calmly took the microphone. Capt. James Clark reported that the shooter (later identified as 30-year-old Edward Archer) had said, repeatedly, that he followed Allah, that he pledged allegiance to Islamic State and "That is the reason I did what I did."

By now the pattern is familiar. We can see a determined reluctance, flowing into outright refusal, to acknowledge the Islamist menace. Reflecting on this phenomenon, Dorothy Rabinowitz of the *Wall Street Journal* lays the blame at the doorstep of the White House:

> Years of effort by this administration to deny, conceal and sermonize the nation out of its awareness of facts clearly evident

151

to them is the sort of thing that doesn't escape Americans in
this election season, shadowed by the threat of terrorism.

Without question, the current administration has outdone
itself in dodging the issue. I talked about that a while back (see
"War on (Fill In the Misleading Blank)," page 73). But the problem is broader than Obama's policy, and it predates the current
administration.

For years the smear of "Islamophobia" has worked to dampen
serious discussion and critique of the Islamist movement. To find
the intellectuals and scholars and journalists vigorously shouting
down any such discussion, look to the left. Sam Harris has insight-
fully exposed the dishonesty of that smear, and the hypocrisy of
leftist intellectuals who profess to uphold freedom and progress
yet function as apologists for barbarism.

Now, *even Michael Walzer*, an influential left-leaning political
theorist, is tired of this refusal to confront Islamists. Writing in
Dissent, a pillar of the left-wing intellectual establishment, Walzer
admonishes his brothers-in-arms. "I frequently come across
leftists who are more concerned with avoiding accusations of
Islamophobia than they are with condemning Islamist zealotry."
Consequently, many are unable to "consider the very good reasons
for fearing Islamist zealots—and so they have difficulty explaining
what's going on in the world." It says a lot about the gravity of the
problem that Walzer was moved to write this lengthy article. (I hesitate to recommend the article, because although it has some value,
there's much to disagree with.)

At this point, you might form the impression that the refusal to
properly identify and define the Islamist movement (let alone criticize it) is confined to leftist politicians and intellectuals. Not so.

George W. Bush took every opportunity to evade the nature of
Islamic totalitarianism. While the ruins of the World Trade Center
were still blazing, he gave speeches underscoring his belief that "the
terrorists have no home in any faith." On and on he went, hammering at that theme, despite all the evidence to the contrary. For
instance: The 9/11 ringleader had written a note telling his team
how to prepare themselves: "Remember that this is a battle for the
sake of God. As the prophet, peace be upon him, said, 'An action for
the sake of God is better than all of what is in this world.' ... Either
end your life while praying, seconds before the target, or make

your last words: 'There is no God but God, Muhammad is His messenger.'"

For at least the last fifteen years we have lived amid an intellectual smog—combining self-induced mental fog and the pollution of dishonesty. One effect is to hinder our understanding of the character and aims of the Islamic totalitarian movement. Another effect is evident in certain reactions to San Bernardino, Fort Hood, Philadelphia and other attacks. In these we can detect the workings of a kind of political taboo, whose purpose is to discourage us from thinking about the Islamist movement at all.

For how much longer can we allow that taboo to go unchallenged?

* * *

This blog post originally appeared in *The Times of Israel*.

Devaluing Secular Government?

Elan Journo January 23, 2016

The idea of separating religion from state was a major advance in political thought, yet massively undervalued. So much so that many in the West take it for granted. Two recent articles—one about Pakistan, another about France—underscore how that idea deserves greater appreciation and strengthening.

To grasp the importance of secular government, observe its negation in Pakistan. Consider the tragic story of one teenager, Anwar Ali. During a prayer meeting at the neighborhood mosque, he thought the imam asked who loves Muhammad, and naturally he raised his hand. But he had misheard the question; in fact the imam had asked who does not love the prophet. The imam denounced the boy for blasphemy, a crime punishable by death.

The story turns from awful to grisly. In shame the boy went home. He cut off his right hand. And he brought it back to the imam in penance. "What I did," the boy later said, "was for love of the Prophet Muhammad." His father said he felt lucky to have a son so devout. And doubtless the boy and his father really believe all that, but it is also a crucial factor that in allegations of blasphemy, as the *New York Times* reports, it is "nearly impossible for the accused to defend themselves in court. Even publicly repeating details of the accusation is tantamount to blasphemy in its own right."

That incident in Pakistan calls to mind life in Europe long ago, before the Age of Enlightenment, when the dominant religion of the time—then it was Christianity—denounced blasphemers and burned heretics. Politically, with the advent of secular government, we've come a long way since then.

But to grasp why the separation of religion from state must be bolstered within the West, consider an article in *The New Republic*.

Published a year after the attacks at *Charlie Hebdo*, the article pushes back on France's policy of secular government, known as "laicite." Broadly speaking, that policy encompasses freedom of religion, the separation of religion from government, and constraints on religious expression. Laicite was intended to block the influence of the Catholic church on affairs of state. And over all laicite is an admirable policy (though some applications, such as bans on religious attire, arguably infringe on individual freedom).

So, against the backdrop of the jihadist attacks at *Charlie Hebdo* and months later at multiple locations in Paris—attacks intended to punish France for failing to bow in submission; attacks carried out by holy warriors animated by the goal of a totalitarian Islamic society wherein religion and state are inseparable—*The New Republic* floats this outlandish suggestion, "Is it time for France to abandon Laicite?"

The article attempts to defend its proposal for rolling back laicite, but the argument conspicuously ignores the actual character and basic goal of the Islamic totalitarian movement, while harping on the at-best peripheral issue that some Muslims purportedly chafe at the country's secular laws. In the end the proposal boils down to appeasement of the Islamist movement.

It is revealing of our present intellectual climate that a reputable, intellectual magazine—for decades a bastion of American liberalism—has published an article that calls for putting hammer and chisel to the wall separating religion from state as a means of abating the threat from a cause seeking religious totalitarianism.

What's needed now more than ever is wider understanding and an uncompromising defense of the separation of religion from state as a cornerstone of a free society.

Fueling Iran's Hostility

Elan Journo February 2, 2016

The Iran nuclear deal was the centerpiece of Obama's multi-year diplomatic campaign to extend a hand of friendship to Tehran. Six months later, where do things stand? Thanks to the deal, which includes lifting economic sanctions and paying out billions of dollars, Iran has reaped a financial windfall. Quite predictably, Iran has continued funding and arming jihadist groups. But another consequence of the deal—again, in line with predictions—deserves particular emphasis: Iran's swaggering disdain for us.

You can observe that in the words of the regime's president, Hassan Rouhani. While touring around Europe last month to recruit foreign investment, he explained that

> the Americans know very well that when it comes to important regional issues [in the Middle East] they cannot achieve anything without Iran's influence or say.... It's possible that Iran and the United States might have friendly relations. But the key to that is in Washington's hands, not Tehran's.

Though hardly new, this Iranian presumption of holding the moral high ground is amped up. Our diplomatic wooing of the ayatollahs—and the nuclear deal in particular—has fueled it.

Beyond the financial reward, the deal bestowed on Iran an undeserved moral endorsement as a nation that can be dealt with through persuasion, despite its vicious character and goals. Whatever else our diplomats might say, mildly remonstrating with Iran here and there, we've given our affirmation that its theocratic regime is legitimate. A natural result of that was to increase the confidence of a regime that declares itself—and has proven to be—the vanguard of a holy war against the West. Moreover, you can see how our implied endorsement of Tehran would reinforce their view of America as morally bankrupt: economically and militarily, America is the world's most powerful nation, yet it stoops to appease a far weaker adversary. Thus we encourage in them contempt for us and (added) self-righteousness about their jihadist path.

156

The Iran deal has cast a searing light on an obscene spectacle. To adapt in the present context one of Ayn Rand's observations: America has assumed the role of a cringing, bargaining victim, while Iran stands as a self-righteous, resolute aggressor.

* * *

This blog post originally appeared in *The Times of Israel*.

The Mythology of the Iran Nuclear Deal

Elan Journo February 14, 2016

When defending the Iran nuclear deal, the Obama administration and its surrogates made claims that seemed, at least to some people, plausible. For a long time, I've argued that the deal was predicated on evading Iran's jihadist character and malignant goals, and that the deal's selling points were fantastical. Some people felt that "only time will tell"; so let's consider two of the administration's claims.

The nuclear deal, Barack Obama claimed, will "ensur[e] that all pathways to a bomb are cut off." This of course was a central pillar of the case for the deal. Remember the assurances about "anytime, anywhere" inspections of Iran's nuclear facilities? That was a hyped-up talking point that the administration quickly dropped. What about getting a full accounting of Iran's past nuclear research, including its military dimensions (such as warhead design)? No, according to John Kerry, we shouldn't be "fixated" on that, we just have to move on. What about the shutting of "all pathways" to a bomb? Listen to James Clapper, director of national intelligence, who testified before Congress this month: "We do not know whether Iran will eventually decide to build nuclear weapons," adding that if the regime "chooses to," it maintains the "ability to build missile-deliverable nuclear weapons."

Or consider another salient claim: by reintegrating Iran into the global economy, the deal could strengthen (putatively) friendly elements within Iran. Obama told one interviewer: "And then I think there are others inside Iran who think that [opposing the United States, seeking to destroy Israel, causing havoc in the region] is counterproductive. And it is possible that if we sign this nuclear deal, we strengthen the hand of those more moderate forces inside of Iran."

Predictably, the inflow of dollars has gone to Iran's state-owned or semistate-backed industries (the theocracy and its military vanguard dominate the economy). Reiterating what has been known for decades, James Clapper told Congress that the Tehran regime is "the foremost state sponsor of terrorism" and that Iran and its proxy forces "remain a continuing terrorist threat to U.S. interests and partners worldwide." Beyond the financial gains that bolster the regime, what impact has the deal had on Tehran's hostility toward us? It's fueled that hostility, as I argued in an earlier post, a fact that goes underappreciated.

Last week, with something like a "carnival atmosphere," tens of thousands marched in Tehran "chanting 'Death to America and Israel' and waving anti-Western placards," celebrating the "37th anniversary of the country's 1979 Islamic revolution." The regime actively inculcates animosity toward the West. Ponder the outlook of one 22-year-old Iranian who attended the festivities: "I am happy that I was able to come here today, and as an Iranian I can put my fist in America's mouth and say 'Death to America.'"

To revisit major selling points of the Iran nuclear deal is to see just how detached from reality they were.

* * *

This blog post originally appeared in *The Times of Israel*.

The Misunderstood Mullahs

Elan Journo March 31, 2016

A Review of *Iran's Deadly Ambition: The Islamic Republic's Quest for Global Power,* **by Ilan Berman. New York: Encounter Books, 2015.**

"No, Iran Isn't Destabilizing the Middle East." Paul Pillar's article in *The National Interest* a month before the Iran nuclear deal was signed attacked critics of the negotiations. Pillar disputed the "badly mistaken myth" that Tehran is "'destabilizing' the Middle East or seeking to 'dominate' it or exercise 'hegemony' over it, or that it is 'on the march' to take over the region." On the contrary, while we might dislike Iran's conduct—bolstering the Assad regime in Syria, backing Hezbollah in Lebanon, nourishing Hamas in Gaza, dominating what's left of Iraq, funding and training the Taliban in Afghanistan, and arming Islamist rebels in Yemen—Iran is simply reacting to its circumstances as any other state would. Iran's distinctive ideological character and stated goals, in other words, are at best peripheral to understanding and evaluating its conduct.

Pillar spent nearly thirty years as a senior intelligence analyst at the Central Intelligence Agency, and holds impeccable academic credentials. He can hardly be dismissed as a fringe figure. Indeed, the gist of his view—that we shouldn't worry about Iran's distinctive ideological character—informs the Obama administration's approach to Iran. The Obama team acknowledges Iran's pervasive violation of rights domestically, its wholesale backing of Islamist terrorism, and its ominous nuclear program. But these actions have little to do with one another, or with any larger strategic threat. Moreover, despite the weekly "Death to America" chants (merely "rhetorical excess," according to John Kerry) and the stated desire to wipe Israel off the map, Iran's leaders supposedly care chiefly about "regime survival" and the economic aspirations of their citizens—as if a brutal theocracy, deep down, wants what's best for its people. On the unstated premise that everyone in politics has a price, Obama has even suggested that the nuclear deal could entice Iran to improve its conduct while taking on its "rightful role" in the community of nations.

Ilan Berman, however, believes that the derivation of Iran's conduct from its ideology is missing from Washington policy discussions. In *Iran's Deadly Ambition*, Berman argues that the fundamental problem with Iran is not its nuclear quest, but the regime itself: Tehran is animated by "an uncompromising religious worldview that sees itself at war with the West."

> During the tumultuous decade of the 1980s, as [Ayatollah] Khomeini's revolutionaries consolidated power at home, the principle of "exporting the revolution" became a cardinal regime priority. Its importance was demonstrated in the fact that, despite the expense of a bloody, grinding eight-year war with Saddam Hussein's Iraq, the fledgling Islamic Republic sunk colossal resources into becoming a hub of "global resistance."

Three decades later, Tehran remains committed to this vision. Even as we negotiate with Iran over its nuclear program, its leaders are "busy translating their vision of world influence into action."

Berman offers a measured, data-rich survey of Iran's jihadist ambition, an ambition encompassing far more than the nuclear program. The jihadist group Lebanese Hezbollah (literally, "army of Allah") was founded with Tehran's support in the mid 1980s to implement Khomeini's political theory of clerical rule. Hezbollah has become Iran's main proxy force in Syria. Iraq, Europe and Africa. Citing reports compiled by the State Department, Berman shows that Iranian sponsorship of global terrorism continues unabated.

In Iraq, Tehran backed insurgents that undermined and killed American forces. Over time, the new Baghdad government fell under Tehran's dominion. In Afghanistan, Iran lavished millions of dollars to buy the loyalty of government officials: five years ago, Hamid Karzai, the president of Afghanistan at the time, admitted to accepting a $2 million payoff from Tehran. And lately, Iran has bolstered the resurgent Taliban with shipments of arms, ammunition, rocket-propelled grenades, mortars and plastic explosives. In Syria, Iran continued to back the Assad regime, even while Tehran was subject to severe economic sanctions.

Iran advances its agenda, Berman shows, through international enablers, notably China and North Korea. From Pyongyang, which now possesses nuclear weapons, Iran received technological know-how and help procuring materials for its own nuclear program. Beijing relies heavily on Iranian natural gas and petroleum, a trade relationship that has yielded diplomatic benefits for Tehran. China, along with Russia, frequently blocked the imposition of U.N. sanctions on Iran's nuclear program. To circumvent economic sanctions, Iran has found willing allies in Latin America, where its diplomatic footprint has grown. Venezuela, for instance, abetted Tehran in channeling foreign currency through an Iranian-owned local bank.

Berman describes the complex, wide-ranging web of political schemes, diplomatic stratagems, and lethal campaigns, military and terrorist, radiating from Tehran. Examine that web, work through the implications, and it becomes clear that Iran is defined by its ideological vision. Yet, as Berman notes, Washington ignores Tehran's character, resulting in an Iran policy predicated more on "aspiration than reality."

Iran's Deadly Ambition provides a superb, albeit alarming portrait of the Iranian regime. It is alarming, not merely because of the scale of Iran's militant ambition, but also because the prevailing American assessment of the regime is so disconnected from abundant, plainly evident facts. By fixing our attention on Iran's ideological character, this book can help anchor U.S. policy in aspirations that accept rather than deny reality

* * *

This article originally appeared in *The Claremont Review of Books.*

What Unites the Jihadists

Elan Journo April 21, 2016

March 22: suicide bombings at Brussels airport and on the city's metro. March 27: a suicide bombing at a crowded park in Lahore, Pakistan. The differences between these attacks are considerable, and a mainstream perspective would have us focus on that data narrowly. But to understand these attacks—and to assess the jihadist menace—we need to give serious attention to their underlying commonality.

Look at the particulars in each case, and you find umpteen points of difference. Behind each attack, a different group. The Islamic State mounted the Brussels attack; the Pakistani Taliban deployed one of its fighters to the park in Lahore. The capabilities of these groups differ. Clearly ISIS has a reach surpassing the Pakistani Taliban. To this you can add the fact that jihadist groups engage in ferocious infighting. Many factions have different state sponsors that despise each other. The more you dig into these groups, the more dissimilar, the more disconnected, they can appear.

But such a concrete-bound perspective subverts our understanding. It opens the way for pseudo-explanations that have hampered our ability to combat this menace. George W. Bush relied on evasive definitions that whipsawed from the nebulous ("terrorists," "evil doers") to the ultra-narrow (it's al-Qaeda!). The Obama administration reprised the generic label "terrorists" and then emphasized "al-Qaeda" until the rise of ISIS (supposedly the JV team) made that risible; now we're supposed to combat "violent extremism," born of economic privation and lack of political voice.

What this betrays is much more than linguistic confusion. It reveals an underlying conceptual failure: the failure properly to understand and define the nature of the enemy. That's a necessary condition for combatting it effectively, a point confirmed by the policy failures of Bush and of Obama.

Instead we need to recognize what's distinctive—and so dangerous—about the jihadists. No, it's not primarily their use of terrorist means; nor any political or economic hardships. What unites them is their ideological goal. Despite their differences, they do in fact constitute an ideological movement—a movement long inspired and funded by patrons such as Iran, Saudi Arabia and the Gulf states.

Fundamentally, the diverse jihadist factions are united by a common end. They fight to create a society subjugated to religious law (sharia), wherever they can. They seek Islamic totalitarianism. Hearing that, some people balk: Can we really put in one category the Pakistani Taliban, the Afghan Taliban, Islamic State, al-Qaeda, Hezbollah, Hamas, Boko Haram, the Muslim Brotherhood, the Iranian regime, and many others—despite their sectarian, ethnic, regional and language differences?

Yes, because what they strive for is essentially the same. How they seek to realize that goal—strategically and tactically—certainly differs: outright war; terrorism; indoctrination and ballot boxes; some combination of these. But these varied means are geared to the same ultimate end.

And of course they fight against one another, for dominance, for turf, for doctrinal reasons (recall how al-Qaeda disowned ISIS). Such infighting is a feature of ideological movements. For example, there are many varieties of socialists. The British Fabians emphasized education; Lenin was committed to revolution. And there were notorious intra-movement fights: for example, Stalin sent a hit squad to liquidate one rival, Leon Trotsky. The Soviets in Moscow were at odds with the communist rulers in China. The broad common aim, however, was to rid the world of capitalism in the name of imposing state control of the means of production.

With the jihadists, their common theocratic aim is reflected in how they identify their enemies. Their doctrine holds that the path to political supremacy entails a return to piety and the imposition of the "Truth" far and wide, putting to death whoever stands in the way. An enemy is anyone who fails to submit to their religious dogma, including (but not limited to) apostates, heretics (e.g., Muslims of the wrong sect), atheists and assorted unbelievers. For the Muslim Brotherhood in Egypt, a progenitor of the Islamic totalitarian movement, a major focus was on Arab regimes deemed impious. The Islamic State—like al-Qaeda, like the Iranian regime—puts emphasis on the West, with its secular society, man-made laws, and infidel population.

The Lahore bombing underlines just how wrong the prevailing view of the jihadists really is. It's common today to hear how jihadists are moved primarily by economic and political grievances. That would mean that those families lining up for the bumper cars at the fairground in Lahore were slaughtered because they had somehow thwarted the Pakistani Taliban from getting decent jobs and the vote. But in reality the Taliban has it in for Pakistan's Christian minority (who are deemed unbelievers). Many people in the thronged park that day were Christians celebrating Easter.

Moreover, we've heard a great deal about the (relative) poverty of the Molenbeek neighborhood in Brussels, and how some of the "martyrs" who carried out the Paris attacks last November had been petty criminals. Relevant, perhaps; causally fundamental, no. In a "martyrdom video" that ISIS released in January, what do the Paris jihadists themselves tell us? They're at war with us because we're "unbelievers"; they're angry that we oppose the Islamic State in its quest to entrench a totalitarian Islamic society.

Over the last fifteen years, we've witnessed two U.S. administrations evade the responsibility of understanding the Islamic totalitarian movement. And we've witnessed those two administrations fail to defeat it. If we are to succeed at that goal, a crucial first step is to understand the enemy we face. We need to grasp that while Islamic totalitarianism is a multiform movement, it is fundamentally united by its religious doctrine and vicious goal. Only then can we fully understand Brussels and Lahore and Paris and Ankara and San Bernardino and Beirut, and the long, bloody trail of jihad. Only then can we grasp the scope of the Islamist menace and effectively combat it, bringing into focus the need to confront the states that inspire and sponsor it.

* * *

This article originally appeared in *The Federalist*.

After Orlando: Why Trump and Clinton Both Get the Jihadists Wrong

Elan Journo June 15, 2016

What we do know so far about the mass shooting in Orlando: in a 911 call, the killer at the Pulse nightclub pledged allegiance to Islamic State, and he had previously expressed a fervent desire to become a "martyr." In their speeches responding to the massacre, Hillary Clinton and Donald Trump each sought to demonstrate a firmer, clearer grasp of the jihadist menace—and therefore prove themselves best positioned to combat it. Each channeled one of the prevalent views in our culture. Both, however, are profoundly wrong. Both are united, ironically enough, in negating the crucial role of ideas in animating the jihadist cause.

The view Trump put forward, which appeals to many people, is meant to sound like a serious, factual account. "We are importing Radical Islamic Terrorism into the West through a failed immigration system." Because Trump has frequently mouthed the words "radical Islam," some people believe this view constitutes plain-speaking. But instead of conceptualizing the enemy as an ideological movement—one that people join because they choose to embrace particular ideas and doctrines—the account Trump has voiced negates the role of ideas. Essentially, it is a tribalist outlook, dividing the world into us vs. them—America vs. the outsiders

But it turns out that the killer in Orlando was born—like Trump himself—in New York. Revealingly, the blame is put on the fact that the killer's parents were Afghan immigrants: "The bottom line is that the only reason the killer was in America in the first place was because we allowed his family to come here." That applies equally to generations of Americans, the vast majority of whom were law abiding citizens. So for Trump, the blame falls on the killer's outsider bloodline. His parents came from a faraway land, so he is forever an outsider; his beliefs and chosen actions are irrelevant. On this view, the tag "radical Islam" turns out to be vacuous: far from designating a substantive conception of the jihadist cause, in fact it serves as a shorthand for tribalist bigotry against outsiders (which manifests as outright racism when Trump applies it to Hispanics).

You can see that in the depressingly popular "solution" of enacting a sweeping ban on Muslim immigration. Obviously, a rational immigration policy must bar entry to individuals seeking to violate our rights (thus barring anyone with ties to or membership in Islamist groups and organizations), while allowing entry to individuals seeking to live and work peacefully. The proposed ban, however, starts with the opposite, tribalist premise. Outsiders: bad. Maybe some will turn out to be OK, but don't count on it.

Notice how this view wipes out a crucial distinction, one that's necessary for understanding the jihadist cause. While all jihadists are followers of Islam, it is blatantly false that all Muslims are jihadists. It should go without saying, though today it is necessary to say so, that countless Muslims are law-abiding, peaceful, productive Americans. Jihadists, by contrast, are individuals who choose to join an ideological cause, a cause intent on the totalitarian imposition of Islamic religious law. What distinguishes the jihadists is not any inborn tribal identity, but the vicious political-ideological vision they strive to realize. It is this ideological factor that the tribalist view negates.

So does the marginally more sophisticated perspective that Hillary Clinton conveyed in her post-Orlando speech. The killer, she insisted, was a "*madman* filled with hate,...[a] horrible sense of vengeance and vindictiveness in his heart,...rage." [Emphasis added] Here, emotion and above all, some form of madness are taken as fundamental. Therefore, we're instructed, more has to be done to address the persistent "*virus that poisoned his mind*." [Emphasis added.]

Where, then, does his 911 call, swearing fidelity to the caliphate, fit in to this causal narrative? Or his stated wish to become a martyr? Or the reports of him bellowing "Allahu Akbar" as he sprayed bullets into the crowd? These data points reflect a certain ideological outlook. That's precisely what Clinton's view trivializes. And in doing so, it forecloses anything that might resemble a sensible policy for combatting the threat.

The same is true of a variation of the Clintonian narrative, which puts even greater emphasis on mental illness. People who are mentally ill, writes Jeet Heer in *The New Republic*, can be drawn to an "extremist ideology," so, a "mental-health framework has to be a key part of the solution no less than other policy initiatives"—at least on par with everything else. We can agree that many factors are at play in explaining the actions of a given individual. But it is a serious mistake to downgrade ideology as just one factor among many, precisely because of its immense power over people's minds, a fact evident in umpteen jihadist attacks. (Besides, you can make a strong claim that espousing jihadist doctrine is a kind of detachment from reality: for example, what else can it mean to seek "martyrdom"?)

These prevailing views get the jihadists wrong. We need to grasp that fundamentally the jihadists are moved by the ideas they accept and choose to act on. To view this from a wider perspective, note that the communists were moved by their ideal of "from each according to his ability, to each according to his need," erecting dictatorial regimes to put their vision into practice. And that cause attracted some of the worst specimens of humanity, power-lusting thugs, haters of achievement, and psychotics among them. Note that the Founding Fathers, by contrast, upheld the ideals of individualism and reason as the foundation of a free society, creating a constitutional republic to safeguard individual rights. And their cause appealed strongly to productive, independent people seeking a better life. The larger point is that philosophic ideas—whether true or false—are crucial in human life and in understanding cultural-political movements.

That point is lost to many people today, especially the leading presidential candidates. They fail to understand the centrality of philosophic ideas in animating the jihadist cause. The last two administrations failed properly to define the nature of the Islamist movement. Look around—we're living with the consequences of their irrational policies. Fitting within that dismal tradition, Clinton and Trump have put forward views that negate the ideological character of the enemy, and so neither has the understanding necessary to deal effectively with the mounting threat we face.

* * *

This blog post originally appeared in *The Times of Israel*.

PART 5

Confusions, Denials, Taboos

Is religion, specifically Islam, the animating force behind self-identified jihadists? Many of our political and intellectual leaders say no. Some insist that the killers have nothing to do with any faith. Others claim that what truly animates jihadists is some non-religious factor, such as political or economic grievances, and that to suggest otherwise is "Islamophobic."

What really animates the jihadist cause? What confusions, distortions and misconceptions shroud this issue and make rational discussion of Islam almost impossible?

At Free-Speech Event, UCLA Tried to Ban My Book

Elan Journo February 11, 2017

At UCLA Law School last week, a squad of student "thought police" tried to ban my book *Failing to Confront Islamic Totalitarianism: From George W. Bush to Barack Obama and Beyond*. They don't want you to know the book even exists, let alone what's inside it. And the UCLA administration enabled them. This ominous episode underlines how students are learning to be contemptuous of intellectual freedom.

The story of what happened at UCLA is laced with ironies. On February 1, the UCLA chapter of the Federalist Society and the Ayn Rand Institute co-sponsored a panel discussion at UCLA Law School on the vital importance of freedom of speech and the threats to it. My book shows how certain philosophic ideas undercut America's response to the jihadist movement, including notably its attacks on freedom of speech.

Naturally, the book was displayed and offered for sale at a reception prior to the event, which featured Dave Rubin, the contrarian YouTube host; Flemming Rose, the Danish editor who published the now-infamous Muhammad cartoons in 2005 and author of *The Tyranny of Silence*; and Steve Simpson, editor of *Defending Free Speech* (these two books were also displayed).

During the reception, however, a group of UCLA students assembled in front of the book table and objected to mine. Why? Had they read the book, weighed the evidence, and found it lacking? Had they formed a considered evaluation of the book's argument?

No: They felt the book was "offensive" and "insulting." They had "issues" with the views that I and my co-author, Onkar Ghate, put forward. Our views, it seems, were "Islamophobic." Based on what? Apparently, for some of them, it was the book's title.

Yet another irony here is that in the book we disentangle the notion of "Islamophobia." We show that it's an illegitimate term, one that clouds thinking, because it mashes together at least two fundamentally different things. The term blends, on the one hand, serious analysis and critique of the ideas of Islamic totalitarianism, the cause animating the jihadists, which is vitally important (and the purpose of my book); and, on the other hand, racist and tribalist bigotry against people who espouse the religion of Islam. Obviously, racism and bigotry have no place in a civilized society.

Moreover, the book makes clear that while all jihadists are self-identified Muslims, it is blatantly false that all Muslims are jihadists. (It should go without saying, though sadly it must be said, that countless Muslims are law-abiding, peaceful, productive Americans.) Ignorant of the book's full scope and substance, the students felt it had no place on campus.

The students demanded that my book be removed from display. My colleagues who manned the display table declined to remove the book.

So the students enforced their own brand of thought control. They turned their backs to the table, forming a blockade around it, so no one could see or buy the books. Then they started aggressively leaning back on the table, pushing against the book displays. By blocking access to the book, they were essentially trying to ban it.

At this point, you might hope the UCLA administration would step in to re-assert the principle of intellectual freedom that is so crucial to education, a free society, and the advancement of human knowledge. Finally a rep from UCLA did step in—to abet the student protesters. My book was "inflammatory." It had to go.

Thus: *at a panel about freedom of speech and growing threats to it—not least from Islamists—UCLA students and school administrators tried to ban a book that highlights the importance of free speech, the persistent failure to confront Islamic totalitarianism, and that movement's global assaults on free speech.*

This shameful incident reflects a wider phenomenon on American campuses. At university, students should learn to think, to engage with different views, and thus to grow intellectually. But increasingly, students learn to put their feelings above facts. Some students demand to be protected from what they merely believe, without evidence, are uncongenial views. They demand that non-orthodox views be silenced. And such universities as UCLA willingly coddle and appease them.

The universities, observes Steve Simpson in *Defending Free Speech*, are a bellwether of the future of freedom of speech. If today's students are increasingly hostile to intellectual freedom, can we really expect tomorrow's voters, lawyers, judges, politicians to uphold free speech? To champion that principle, you have to value dialogue, knowledge, and, ultimately, the reasoning mind. Yet reason is precisely what those student agitators subordinated to their emotions.

* * *

A version of this article originally appeared at *The Hill*.

POSTSCRIPT

After Banning My Book, UCLA Explains Itself

Two weeks ago, some students and the admin at UCLA School of Law tried to ban my book *Failing to Confront Islamic Totalitarianism* from being displayed at a free-speech panel. (The event was co-sponsored by the Ayn Rand Institute and The Federalist Society; you can read a detailed account in my editorial at *The Hill*.) Appalled by that incident, I wondered whether this was typical of UCLA, whether the university would explain its actions, whether it cared at all about intellectual freedom.

This week, I found out.

In a letter to ARI, the UCLA School of Law issued a formal apology for the incident, and it explained that the decision to ban the book was inconsistent with its vigorous commitment to freedom of speech and respectful debate. Moreover, the school admitted that it had fallen short of its own commitment to apply policies in a content-neutral manner. The administration detailed steps it is taking to prevent such incidents in the future.

I appreciate the university's frank recognition of its error. I applaud the UCLA School of Law's administration for taking the matter so seriously and for reaffirming its commitment to uphold the freedom of speech. When so many universities today are betraying that ideal, UCLA's letter is a heartening contrast.

Today, in innumerable ways the freedom of speech is under assault. At ARI we believe that championing that ideal is mission-critical, because many people in our culture, especially intellectuals and politicians, are indifferent, and even hostile, to intellectual freedom. For decades, we have defended freedom of speech as a matter of principle, and we will continue to do so.

Since the incident at UCLA, people have reached out to me to deplore the university's actions and to express their support for our work at ARI. To all of you, let me say thanks. Thanks for your encouragement. Thanks for getting the word out by posting, sharing and retweeting our work. Thanks, too, for your financial contributions that fuel ARI's progress.

Our recent free-speech panels—at UCLA and Penn State—are part of a wider campaign. We're building on the momentum of those successful events. There's more to come. Stay tuned.

Jihadists: Understanding the Nature of the Enemy

Elan Journo April 16, 2018

A t the peak of its strength, the Islamic State (or ISIS)[2] not only controlled a large swath of territory—an area roughly the size of the United Kingdom—it also proved itself a formidable global menace. It instigated, directed, and inspired attacks from Brussels to San Bernardino, London to Orlando, Paris to Istanbul, Manchester to Barcelona. Now that ISIS has been practically routed from the territory it had once controlled in Iraq and Syria,[3] the natural question is: Will this mean a reduced threat of further attacks?

Perhaps yes, in the near term; but beyond that, no, and we have every reason to expect the problem to persist.

Why? The reason is not just that the Islamic State might linger on, rebuild, or morph and re-emerge in the shape of a new, more deadly faction. That's entirely imaginable. The Islamic State itself began life around 2003 as a member of the al-Qaeda network, later breaking away and eclipsing its former partner in brutality, territorial conquest, and global reach.

Nor is the problem just that future attacks might look different. al-Qaeda made its mark with the intricate September 11 plot to hijack four passenger jets simultaneously and ram them into buildings. But the Islamic State has recruited people to carry out simpler, often unsophisticated, mass murders using knives, guns, and vehicles to mow down their victims.

The reason that we can expect future attacks is that there's far more to the problem than these attacks; more than the Islamic State; more than al-Qaeda. In some vague way, many of us sense that. While people often talk loosely about the "terrorist" threat, it doesn't take much to see that terrorism is a tactic—a means, not an end. And it is a tactic commonly deployed by various groups and organizations (think of the Irish Republican Army, the Basque separatists of ETA, or the Ku Klux Klan), so it's nowhere near a uniquely distinguishing feature of the problem.

What, then, is this cause? Who is the enemy? We should be able to answer these vital questions. Any rational attempt to deal with this threat must begin with a clear conception of the enemy's nature and goals. That's a necessary condition of defining an effective plan for ending the menace. The point holds true in every conflict. Can you imagine America achieving victory in World War II if we had viewed the enemy as "Kamikaze" attacks—the tactic of deploying fighter pilots on suicide missions—rather than imperialist Japan? And yet today, nearly seventeen years since 9/11, we have nothing like clarity on the nature of this enemy.

Notice the semantic breakdancing around the issue of what to call the attackers. For example, after the September 11 attacks, George W. Bush launched a "Global War on Terrorism," referring to our enemy variously as "terrorists," "haters," "evil doers," and "hijackers" of a noble religion. The Bush administration tried out the term "Islamofascism," but quickly dropped it. Barack Obama's team whipsawed between the overly narrow—"al-Qaeda"; then "ISIS"—and the hopelessly broad, favoring the worse than meaningless term "violent extremists." Donald Trump has at times talked of "Radical Islamic terrorism," suggesting some ideological features of the menace, though the administration's own view is less than coherent on that point.

What all this betrays is much more than semantic confusion. It reveals an underlying *conceptual* failure: a major part of the problem is that we haven't properly defined the problem. We see some of the enemy's features, if dimly; we fixate on non-essential or derivative aspects; we play down, ignore, or evade others that are fundamental to it.

That leads to a failure to understand the nature of the enemy. It's a misconception to view the problem as hinging primarily on the most salient faction—whether that's al-Qaeda, or ISIS, or a successor group—or on its preferred tactics. To view the problem so narrowly is to miss what's essential to this enemy, why it predates al-Qaeda and has persisted long after Osama bin Laden's death, why it will outlast the routing of ISIS, what animates it fundamentally—and, thus, what's needed to end it.

We urgently need a clear understanding of the enemy, what ideas animate it, and why. Such clarity is an indispensable condition for combating it effectively, a point confirmed by the failures of American Mideast policy over the last two decades. Let us then step back, take a wider perspective, and bring into focus the nature of this foe.

Confronting Difficult Questions

What's the point of all the slaughter? What's the enemy's end goal? The path to reaching the answers we need is crowded with difficult issues—difficult to untangle, but also difficult emotionally. For example, the killers call themselves jihadists (holy warriors) fighting for the supremacy of Allah's law on earth. While it may be an uncomfortable thought, we must still confront the question: is religion—specifically Islam—the animating force behind the self-identified jihadists?

For many people, particularly our political and intellectual leaders, the answer is a vehement no. The killers, we hear, have nothing to do with any faith, let alone the Muslim faith. We hear that they distort that religion, which is a religion of peace. But is it true that the killers have *nothing* to do with the religion of Islam? It's quite obvious that many, many Muslims repudiate the self-styled jihadists, and that they themselves are peaceful, productive individuals. But does it follow that the agenda of such jihadist groups as al-Qaeda and the Islamic State bears no connection to the religion's commonly recognized teachings?

To ask this question is to risk being accused of prejudice toward Muslims. The worry here is that such a question is meant to imply that the problem is somehow *all* Muslims. That worry stems from a profound distortion and an actual issue in our culture.

There is real prejudice toward Muslims, often manifesting in the United States as xenophobia. Sometimes it manifests as a kind of racism that considers Muslims—whether from Saudi Arabia, Pakistan, or Indonesia—as interchangeably non-white and somehow constituting a race. There's no place for racism, xenophobia, or prejudice in any civilized society.

The distortion is that some people blur together race—which is unchosen—and a religious outlook—which is a chosen set of beliefs. Such blurring leads some to feel an unwarranted, collective hostility toward *all* Muslims. (Partly reacting to that distortion, other people adopt an uncritically positive view of the religion, regarding any analysis of it and of its followers as taboo.) To make sense of the jihadists, however, we must keep the issues of racial identity and religious/ideological outlook sharply differentiated.

Then there's another line of thinking that tells us that what *really* animates jihadists is something non-religious. This view holds that, although these self-styled jihadists quote holy texts and pledge their faith to Allah, fundamentally there are other factors that drive them, notably political or economic grievances. For example, observe that jihadist recruitment videos and talking points hammer on American Mideast policy and the Israeli-Palestinian conflict. What are we to make of such seemingly non-religious factors?

The answers here are not obvious, but they are attainable.

What I intend to convince you of is that the enemy constitutes an ideological movement rooted in Islam. Let me stress key elements of that claim.

It is an *ideological* movement: it's a religious outlook, based on ideas and teachings of Islam, which the followers of the movement *choose* to embrace. It's not about anyone's race, nor is it fundamentally animated by material (political or economic) factors.

It's crucial to see that it is an ideological *movement*: despite murderous enmity, sectarian rifts, splintering, and infighting among its constituent regimes, groups, and factions, what unites them—and defines the movement—is their common end. It is the aim of creating a totalitarian society under similar interpretations of Islamic religious law.

It's an Ideological Movement Deeply Rooted in Islam

Let's start by looking at the evidence of what the jihadists themselves believe and act on. Read the notes left behind by the leader of the 9/11 hijackers, a four-page document with minute guidance on how to prepare for martyrdom. Listen to the courtroom testimony of the man who slaughtered Theo van Gogh, a Dutch filmmaker, proudly admitting his crime in the name of Allah. Notice how the *Charlie Hebdo* attackers—like so many others—screamed "Allahu Akbar!" (God is great!), adding that they were avenging the Prophet Muhammad. Or recall how the shooter at the Pulse nightclub in Orlando, Florida, described himself as a soldier of Allah, pledging his allegiance to the Islamic State. To these examples we can add many more. The commonality is that they see themselves as fighting in the name of Islam.

These holy warriors have been instructed, inspired, and guided by the intellectual leaders of their movement. Prominent among these intellectual leaders are Abu al-Ala al Mawdudi (1903-1979),

Sayyid Qutb (1906–1966), and Ayatollah Ruhollah Khomeini (1902–1989). Many differences separate these three. Mawdudi and Qutb came out of the Sunni sect of Islam; Khomeini, from the Shiite sect. Their arguments are colored by their local political context and concerns. Mawdudi was an Indo-Pakistani thinker, Qutb helped shape the Egyptian Muslim Brotherhood, and Khomeini became the founder and first "Supreme Leader" of Iran's theocracy. Despite these and other differences, several fundamental themes unite them.

First, they see the world around them, and especially the political system, as pervaded with corruption and impiety. Unbelief and godlessness abound across the face of the earth. Islamic religious law, or sharia, no longer governs men's thought and action. Wherever you look, according to Qutb, people's ideas, habits, traditions, culture, art, and laws reflect an ignorance of Allah's will.[4]

Second, they believe that Islamic law, or sharia, must be universal, shaping every facet of society, politics, and the individual's life. Qutb argued that it was necessary to ensure "that the obedience of all people be for God alone," everywhere.[5] The faithful must establish an Islamic dominion, under divine authority, with the ultimate goal of carrying their faith "throughout the earth to the whole of mankind, as the object of this religion is all humanity and its sphere of action is the whole earth."[6]

Third, they hold that it is time for the righteous to solve these problems—the world's deviation from the true path—by imposing religious law as an all-encompassing, total political-social system. In the words of the Muslim Brotherhood, a group that gave rise to al-Qaeda, Hamas, and many other factions, "Islam is the solution."[7] In Khomeini's political vision, realized in the Iranian regime, it is a cleric—one deeply knowledgeable about (religious) law and justice—who must hold ultimate power within society.[8] While Qutb and Mawdudi had their own views of how to structure government, they agreed with Khomeini on the basic solution to the impiety pervading the world: a sharia regime enveloping the totality of human life and society, where religion and the state are one. It is a political system wherein every individual must submit to Allah's will. A fitting description for this vision is Islamic totalitarianism.

Qutb, Mawdudi, and Khomeini also share the belief that jihad is a means for bringing about a truly just world. The term "jihad" is seen as having two meanings—referring both to personal struggle and to a holy war.[9] But what Qutb, Mawdudi, Khomeini, and kindred thinkers call for—and lionize—is the waging of war to expand the dominion of Islam. The Iranian regime was both an embodiment of that totalitarian vision and a self-declared leader in exporting its revolutionary doctrine beyond its own borders. Indeed, the Iranian regime has been not only a galvanizing force for the Islamist movement globally, but also a major leader of it.[10]

It is this political-ideological vision that underlies the jihadist bombings, massacres, and random-seeming violence. The ultimate point of the attacks and killing is to punish unbelievers, compel us to submit in obedience to Allah's law, and enforce sharia law, everywhere. That desire for world domination sounds fanciful and unachievable, but what matters here is that it animates the enemy.

Here's how the Islamic State explained their outlook. Because the statement is particularly clear and emphatic, it's worth quoting at length:

> We hate you, first and foremost, because you are disbelievers; you reject the oneness of Allah—whether you realize it or not—by making partners for Him in worship, you blaspheme against Him, claiming that He has a son, you fabricate lies against His prophets and messengers, and you indulge in all manner of devilish practices. It is for this reason that we were commanded to openly declare our hatred for you and our enmity towards you. "There has already been for you an excellent example in Abraham and those with him, when they said to their people, 'Indeed, we are disassociated from you and from whatever you worship other than Allah. We have rejected you, and there has arisen, between us and you, enmity and hatred forever until you believe in Allah alone'" (Al-Mumtahanah 4). Furthermore, just as your disbelief is the primary reason we hate you, your disbelief is the primary reason we fight you, as we have been commanded to fight the disbelievers until they submit to the authority of Islam, either by becoming Muslims, or by paying jizyah—for those afforded this option—and living in humiliation under the rule of the Muslims. Thus, even if you were to stop fighting us, your best-case scenario in a state of war would be that we would suspend our attacks against you—if we deemed it necessary—in order to focus on the closer and more immediate threats, before eventually resuming our campaigns against you. Apart from the option of a temporary truce, this is the only likely scenario that would bring you fleeting respite from

our attacks. So in the end, you cannot bring an indefinite halt to our war against you. At most, you could only delay it temporarily. "And fight them until there is no fitnah [paganism] and [until] the religion, all of it, is for Allah" (Al-Baqarah 193).[11]

When judged by their words and deeds, what motivates the jihadists is their interpretation of Islam.

Nothing to Do with Islam?

Nonetheless, many people insist that these killers have *nothing* to do with the religion of Islam.

Part of what gives that notion some plausibility is that within the global community of more than one billion Muslims, there are indeed differences on how to understand the Koran and the sayings and deeds attributed to Mohammad. There are rival sects within Islam, and there are also multiple schools of thought on the body of laws known as sharia. But does the outlook of jihadists have *nothing* to do with Islam?

That's the strong claim we hear in many of the post-9/11 speeches of George W. Bush. Bush went so far as to describe them as "traitors to their own faith." The view has persisted. In 2014, after the Islamic State slaughtered an American citizen, President Barack Obama stated that the group's "actions represent no faith, least of all the Muslim faith."

The claim that some interpretation of Islam (or another religion) is a departure from, a perversion, or a "hijacking" of the one true faith relies on a dubious assumption. It counts on the assumption that religious dogma—by definition lacking objective, empirical foundation—lends itself to one definitive interpretation. Conflicting and warring sects may each hold that view, but from the vantage point of the outsider, we see that there is no way to answer which is the true version of, say, Christianity or Islam.

To evaluate whether the Islamist movement is deeply rooted in Islam's teachings and ideas, we need to approach the issue differently. We need to look at whether the movement's views, agenda, and actions constitute an intelligible interpretation of Islamic books and historic doctrines. Put another way, the question to ask is whether the views and injunctions that jihadists take away from their reading of Islamic texts mesh with the religion's commonly recognized teachings—or fly in the face of those religious teachings by denying, for instance, mankind's fundamental duty of submission to religious authority.

The answer we find is that what the leaders of the Islamist movement call for connects to commonly recognized teachings of Islam. Let's compare three key features of the outlook of Islamic totalitarians with commonly identified teachings of the religion of Islam. Take the Islamist demand for (1) submission to Allah's law; (2) the universal scope of sharia law; and (3) expanding the dominion of Islam. For an account of Islam's teachings, let's consult John L. Esposito's college textbook, *Islam: The Straight Path* (Oxford University Press, 3rd ed.). Esposito is a noted scholar of Islam at Georgetown University, and his book is a sympathetic account of the religion.

1. Submission

"Despite the rich diversity in Islamic practice," writes Esposito, "the Five Pillars of Islam remain the core and common denominator, the five essential and obligatory practices all Muslims accept and follow."[12] From Esposito's discussion of the Five Pillars, we can observe that the sum of these supreme duties is to effect and demonstrate the believer's complete submission to authority.

The first pillar is the call upon a Muslim ("one who surrenders") to proclaim: "There is no god but the God [Allah] and Muhammad is the messenger of God." With this acknowledgement, writes Esposito, "a person professes his or her faith and becomes a Muslim."[13]

The second pillar is to reaffirm this commitment through prayer, five times a day.

The third pillar is the obligation of alms-giving (*zakat*): "All adult Muslims who are able to do so are obliged to pay a wealth tax annually"; Esposito goes on to explain: "This is not regarded as charity since it is not really voluntary but instead owed, by those who have received their wealth as a trust from God's bounty, to the poor. The Quran (9:60) and Islamic law stipulate that alms are to be used to support the poor, orphans, and widows, to free slaves and debtors, and to assist in the spread of Islam."[14]

The fourth pillar is the annual fast of Ramadan, when Muslims refrain from eating, drinking, and sex, from dawn to dusk, for a month.

The fifth pillar is the duty to make a pilgrimage (the *Hajj*) to Mecca, incumbent on males.[15]

What do these obligations add up to? We can see that to practice his religion, the believer is duty bound to bow continually before Allah; reaffirm his submission five times a day; cross oceans and continents in pilgrimage to demonstrate unwavering faith; sacrifice worldly values and efface personal desires in the name of devotion to the supernatural master.

All of this hinges on a belief grounded only on faith. To have faith means to believe without evidence (and despite counter-evidence), to suspend one's own perception and rational judgment. The faithful individual is required to put the dictates of religious authority above his or her own grasp of facts. He must learn that he is not a sovereign individual; Allah alone is sovereign, and man must bow to religious authority. What this moral code offers is guidance on how one can achieve the ideal of becoming a servant of Allah.

Islam demands the individual's submission to religious authority. Fundamentally, leaders of the Islamist movement also call for mankind to submit to religious authority. Listen, for example, to Sayyid Qutb:

> The theoretical foundation of Islam, in every period of history, has been to witness *"La ilaha illa Allah"*—"There is no deity except God"—which means to bear witness that the only true deity is God, that He is the Sustainer, that He is the Ruler of the universe, and that He is the Real Sovereign; to believe in Him in one's heart, to worship Him Alone, and to put into practice His laws. Without this complete acceptance of *"La ilaha illa Allah,"* which differentiates the one who says he is a Muslim from a non-Muslim, there cannot be any practical significance to this utterance, nor will it have any weight according to Islamic law.
>
> Theoretically, to establish it means that people should devote their entire lives in submission to God, should not decide any affair on their own, but must refer to God's injunctions concerning it and follow them. We know of God's guidance through only one source, that is, through the Messenger of God—peace be on him. Thus, in the second part of the Islamic creed, we bear witness *"Wa ashhadu anna Muhammadar Rasul Allah"*—"And I bear witness that Muhammad is the Messenger of God."[16]

If the Five Pillars form the core of Islam, is not Qutb's one intelligible interpretation of their meaning and application?

2. Universality of Sharia

Islam provides a body of laws, or sharia, derived mainly from the Koran and interpretations of sayings and deeds attributed to Muhammad.[17] Esposito explains:

> Law in Islam is both universal and egalitarian. The Sharia is believed to be God's law for the entire Islamic community, indeed for all humankind. In the final analysis, God is the sovereign ruler of the world, head of the human community, and its sole legislator. As a result, Islamic law is as much a system of ethics as it is law, for it is concerned with what a Muslim ought to do or ought not to do. All acts are ethically categorized as: (1) obligatory; (2) recommended; (3) indifferent or permissible; (4) reprehensible but not forbidden; or (5) forbidden. To break the law is a transgression against both society and God, a crime and a sin; the guilty are subject to punishment in this life and the next. The idealism of the law can be seen in the fact that ethical categories such as recommended and reprehensible were not subject to civil penalties. Islamic law is also egalitarian; it transcends regional, family, tribal, and ethnic boundaries. It does not recognize social class or caste differences. All Muslims, Arab and non-Arab, rich and poor, black and white, caliph and craftsman, male and female, are bound by Islamic law as members of a single, transnational community or brotherhood of believers.
> The belief that Islamic law was a comprehensive social blueprint was reflected in the organization and content of law.[18]

Notice in Esposito's description how morality and political life are united (the breaking of religious law is both a sin and a crime).

The Islamists agree that Islam's embrace must be universal, and that the Koran answers the needs of mankind. For example, Qutb notes that "The distinctive feature of a Muslim community is this: that in all its affairs it is based on worship of God alone."[19] Islamists argue that Muslims and their rulers have strayed from the requirements of piety by adopting man-made laws, which are morally corrupting, instead of recognizing that sovereignty belongs only to Allah.

For the Islamist movement, the universality of Islam means that it must encompass all of a believer's existence but also the existence of non-believers. It must span all of Allah's creations. Mawdudi, for example, argued that a sharia regime cannot be limited in its scope: "Its approach is universal and all-embracing.

Its sphere of activity is coexistent with the whole of human life."[20] Qutb echoes that theme: Islam, he writes, "addresses itself to the whole of mankind, and its sphere of work is the whole earth. God is the sustainer not merely of the Arabs, nor is His providence limited to those who believe in the faith of Islam. God is the Sustainer of the whole world."[21]

3. Expanding the Dominion of Allah's Law

The call to fight unbelievers in order to expand Islam's earthly dominion flows out of Koranic statements, and it is reflected in the example of the Prophet Muhammad, whose actions are widely seen as embodying the true path. For example, the Koran (9:29) states: "Fight those who believe not in Allah nor the Last Day, nor hold that forbidden which hath been forbidden by Allah and His Messenger, nor acknowledge the religion of Truth, [even if they are] of the People of the Book, until they pay the Jizya with willing submission, and feel themselves subdued."[22]

And in practice, during the last nine years of his life, Muhammad is "recorded as having participated in at least twenty-seven campaigns and deputized some fifty-nine others—an average of no fewer than nine campaigns annually."[23] Islam's vast empire grew under the shadow of the sword. Muhammad's successors marched on.

Fighting unbelievers in order to expand Islam's earthly dominion is precisely what Islamic totalitarians seek to do. That's what the Islamic State sought to do, a point evident in the lengthy passage I quoted earlier. Long before the Islamic State eclipsed al-Qaeda, and before both were household names, the Islamist movement's standard-bearer was, and largely remains, the Iranian regime.

"The Iranian revolution," declared Ayatollah Khomeini, "is not exclusively that of Iran, because Islam does not belong to any particular people…. We will export our revolution throughout the world because it is an Islamic revolution. The struggle will continue until the calls 'there is no god but Allah and Muhammad is the messenger of Allah' are echoed all over the world."[24]

Islamists demand total submission to sharia, they believe sharia's scope to be universal, and their widest aim is to enforce religious tyranny, everywhere. Does that fundamental end, and the idea of fighting to achieve it, fly in the face of Islamic teaching? No.

Does the Islamist movement's interpretation intelligibly flow out of Islam? Yes.

The Islamists constitute an ideological movement deeply rooted in Islam. We should believe jihadists, then, when they tell us that they are Muslims. But while all jihadists are Muslims, it's plainly false that all Muslims are jihadists. Rather, the Islamist movement is a subset within the community of people who profess the religion of Islam. Clearly, even though all Muslims are expected to accept the Koran, only some—the jihadists—hold and practice their interpretation of Islam as a totalitarian ideological-political cause.

To put this point into even sharper focus, let's consider two contrasting views which I brought up earlier in this essay. Each in its own way pushes back on the idea that Islamic ideas are fundamental to the nature and aim of this movement. One blurs ideas and race; the other plays down or negates the role of religious ideas and tells us to look to material factors, such as political or economic issues, as fundamental. Let's take each of these in turn.

It's Not About Heredity; It Is a *Chosen* Religious-Political Worldview

It's true and important that many, many jihadists were born into families and communities that are Muslim. That fact, however, is neither a necessary nor a sufficient condition of becoming a follower of the Islamist movement. It's not about genetic lineage (an unchosen group membership); it's about what is being taught and a recruit's chosen embrace of a religious-political worldview.

You can see that from the cases of individuals who've chosen to join—and from some who reject—the movement. For example, Maajid Nawaz was born in the UK to a Pakistani family. Not particularly religious when he encountered the Islamist movement, he became deeply involved in it and worked for some years as a recruiter for the cause. But he eventually turned his back on the movement and renounced it.[25]

By contrast, John Walker Lindh was raised in Maryland and in Marin County, California; his father is Catholic and his mother, a follower of Buddhism. Having converted to Islam, he went on to read Islamist materials, and made his way to Afghanistan before

9/11, where he trained at an al-Qaeda camp and took up arms alongside the Taliban.

The Islamic State trumpeted the fact that it attracted converts from Christianity who emigrated to live and fight under its black flag. In the July 2016 issue of its magazine *Dabiq*, for example, the Islamic State featured one former Christian from Trinidad, another from Finland.

Yet many people today fail to understand that the Islamist movement is an *ideological* phenomenon—that its followers are fundamentally driven by a set of religious ideas about life, the world, and the good.

No one is born a follower of any religion or ideological cause—whether Islam, Christianity, Judaism, or Marxism. These are belief systems that an individual must come to adopt. An individual may well do so passively, conforming with the flow of the people and culture around them; but it remains the case that they can choose to question that ideological outlook and reject it.

Observe an important implication of this point, which relates to the widespread lack of understanding about the Islamist movement.

Clearly it's essential that we analyze, discuss, criticize and morally judge this ideological movement, just as we must every ideological movement, secular or supernatural. In doing so, we're evaluating a set of ideas and the people who choose to embrace them. That's in sharp contrast with racial, tribal, or xenophobic condemnations of groups of people, which is obviously wrong.

If we recognize this critical distinction, then we should reject the increasingly prevalent idea of "Islamophobia." This deliberately confusing term seeks to shut down critical analysis of the Islamist movement and its ideas by smearing such discussion as inherently prejudiced against Muslims, or worse.

No one seeking to combat prejudice toward Muslims can honestly believe that that problem can be solved by silencing discussion of the Islamist movement and entrenching the cultural ignorance already besetting this issue.

Fundamentally, It's Religious Ideas, Not Political or Economic Factors, that Animate the Islamist Movement

Let's turn now to a contrasting view that would seem to loosen, if not fully sever, the fundamental causal link between jihadists and their religious worldview. The Islamists quote holy texts, but (on this line of thinking) their ideological outlook is not what ultimately motivates them. Instead, we should look to material factors, such as political or economic issues, as fundamental drivers of the movement.[26]

What makes this perspective plausible? Consider two salient points: (1) Some followers are poor, and the Islamist ideologues themselves invoke political grievances in their manifestos and in recruitment propaganda. (2) Some followers of the movement seemingly lack deep knowledge of religious ideas.

Certainly, some jihadists, in some parts of the world, come from desperate poverty. Note, however, that many other people around the world face similar, if not worse, circumstances, but few of them become holy warriors. You can also find eager jihadists who are well-educated, raised in middle-class homes in some of the world's freest, most-advanced countries.[27]

Islamist tracts, recruitment materials, and propaganda videos do invoke various political grievances. For example, bin Laden's infamous 1996 "Declaration of *Jihad*" against America decried the presence of U.S. troops in Saudi Arabia. It also emphasized the issue of "Palestine,"[28] which has been all over various jihadist propaganda, for years.[29] Islamists have leveraged these claims (along with various others) to recruit for their jihad.

But when we take a closer look, it becomes clear that such grievances are effective precisely because of a fundamental religious narrative that frames them. In that story there is a cosmic struggle for a "just" world, one subservient to religious dogma. The crux of that is the striving of the faithful (Islamists) against the unbelievers (impious Muslims, apostates, infidels, atheists; particularly in the West). Within that framework, a great many issues and conflicts can actuate new recruits, who see themselves as part of a global Muslim community (or, "umma").

Here are some emotional-ideological "buttons" that the Islamists have pushed in order to galvanize, recruit, and draw people into the movement. The fight against the Soviet Union in Afghanistan, during the 1980s, attracted a significant influx of foreign holy warriors (Osama bin Laden among them). The Bosnia conflict, during the 1990s, was another trigger because Muslims were targeted.[30] In his memoir Maajid Nawaz recounts how seeing videos of Muslims being slaughtered in the Bosnia conflict inflamed him. The victims were all strangers to him, but they belonged to a global Muslim community, and Nawaz felt impelled to fight for the redemption of his co-religionists.[31] The bond of collective religious solidarity was *that* strong. During the mid-2010s, the rise of Islamic State in Iraq and Syria proved an even more powerful magnet for international jihadists; one of its themes was the sectarian hostility toward non-Sunnis.

The common factor here is the specifically Islamist narrative that frames the worldview of recruits, manipulating their emotions. They are primed to feel a powerful solidarity with co-religionists throughout the world and to regard anything short of an all-encompassing Islamist regime as a metaphysical injustice that they must fight to rectify.

For example, in the case of the "Palestine" issue, the basic concern of Islamists is not any political grievance about Israeli borders, land-use policy, or alleged oppression of particular individuals.[32] They demand not freedom and prosperity for Palestinians (or anyone else), but submission: Islamists seek to enslave the world—including Palestine—under Allah's laws. Only conquering Israel and raising the flag of Islamic totalitarianism over Palestine and Jerusalem could satisfy them.[33]

The same applies to their framing of American foreign policy in the Middle East. The removal of American troops from the region would not pacify the Islamists, nor the cessation of American military strikes in Muslim lands, nor the halting of American backing for some of the region's dictators. U.S Mideast policy is riddled with serious problems (which I've written about at length), but there's no version of American policy in the region, and no genuine problems we might rectify, that Islamists would regard as unproblematic. Their basic objection is that we're unbelievers, everything we do is an affront, and, in the end, it is *they* who should dominate, everywhere, in the name of religious totalitarianism.

Consider how the Islamic State explained this point in its magazine *Dabiq*. Among the reasons for hating and fighting to overthrow the West's secular, liberal societies, the article lists American foreign policy, but stresses how that is a *derivative* factor.

> What's important to understand here is that although some might argue that your foreign policies are the extent of what drives our hatred, this particular reason for hating you is

secondary, hence the reason we addressed it at the end of the above list. The fact is, even if you were to stop bombing us, imprisoning us, torturing us, vilifying us, and usurping our lands, we would continue to hate you because our primary reason for hating you will not cease to exist until you embrace Islam. Even if you were to pay jizyah and live under the authority of Islam in humiliation, we would continue to hate you. No doubt, we would stop fighting you then as we would stop fighting any disbelievers who enter into a covenant with us, but we would not stop hating you. What's equally if not more important to understand is that we fight you, not simply to punish and deter you, but to bring you true freedom in this life and salvation in the Hereafter, freedom from being enslaved to your whims and desires as well as those of your clergy and legislatures, and salvation by worshiping your Creator alone and following His messenger.[34]

What, then, are we to make of the fact that some followers of the Islamist movement appear to lack substantive knowledge of religious doctrine? One anecdote that's taken to illustrate the point: before setting out for the battlefront in Syria, two British would-be jihadists ordered copies of *Islam for Dummies* and *The Koran for Dummies*.

Leaving anecdotes to one side, researchers have found that recruits certainly have varied profiles. Peter Neumann and his colleagues at the International Centre for the Study of Radicalisation at King's College, London, found that recruits bound for the Islamic State fell into three broad categories: "defenders" who were devout and seeking to protect co-religionists; "seekers" attracted to the jihadist counterculture, which met their "need for identity, community, power and a feeling of masculinity"; and "hangers-on" who join because the leader of their social circle decided to.[35]

Should we be surprised if some, many, or most of the tens of thousands of recruits who flocked to join the Islamic State were drawn by the desire for a pseudo self-esteem as heroes for the cause, a source of religiously endorsed self-worth and identity? Should we be surprised that for some the appeal lies in the opportunity to live out a video-game fantasy where they actually get to murder people? None of that should be surprising; it makes sense that such abhorrent specimens of humanity would gravitate to a movement seeking domination.

More broadly, it's a feature of ideological movements that they tend to attract people of varying levels of understanding, from the ardently committed to those whose understanding of the cause is shallow. Was every last warrior for communism a theoretician, or deeply versed in Marxism, or qualified to interpret the sacred theory of dialectical materialism? Clearly, no. What defines the Islamist movement is its over-arching ideological-political end.

Why It Matters That We Grasp the Enemy's Ideological Character

If we are to develop anything like a sensible policy response to the Islamist threat, we need to begin by conceptualizing it as an ideological *movement*. This has at least two major implications.

First, we need to take a wide-angle perspective. There are many Islamist groups, factions, organizations, regimes. Among them, there are differences over doctrine, sect, tactics, even strategic priorities. And they fight among themselves, a lot, and brutally. For example, Saudi Arabia is hostile to the Islamic State, and both revile Iran. They jockey over who is more pious, and who will dominate where. Yet what unites all of them—along with the Muslim Brotherhood, Hezbollah, Hamas, Boko Haram, and still others—is their common ideological goal.

Second, a crucial feature of this movement is that particular regimes—notably Saudi Arabia, the Gulf states, and above all, Iran—are central to it.[36] The Iranian regime has been the movement's spearhead, galvanizing the Islamist cause.

The Muslim Brotherhood, a foundational group in the movement, started in Egypt in the 1920s, but accomplished little. What supercharged the jihadist cause was the 1979 Iranian revolution. That shockwave brought to power in Tehran an Islamic totalitarian regime determined to export its ideological revolution. Iran was such an inspiration because it made the Islamist cause seem achievable. Iran armed, trained, and funded Lebanese Hezbollah, Hamas, Palestinian Islamic Jihad. It has backed insurgent groups in Iraq and Afghanistan.

Meanwhile, in its own way, the Saudi regime has nourished the Islamist cause. The Saudis invested millions of dollars setting up religious schools, distributing books, and proselytizing across the globe for its preferred strain of Islamic totalitarianism. Saudi money funds various jihadist groups, including the Taliban.

And the Gulf states, for their part, have bankrolled their favored jihadist factions. Qatar, for example, is a backer of Hamas.[37]

Absent the inspiration and material backing of these regimes; absent the galvanizing spectacle of real-life, functioning Islamist regimes such as in Iran and elsewhere; the jihadist cause would have amounted to little more than a bunch of seething pamphleteers and ineffectual revolutionaries. Such regimes make the ideal actuating the jihadists appear righteous, potent, practical.

With that understanding, we can define a policy response that directs the full range of our diplomatic and military resources toward eliminating these regimes. Without that understanding? Take a look at the confused mess that has been our Mideast policy for upwards of two decades.

Prior to September 11, American policy was prone to a fragmented, myopic outlook. The 9/11 attacks came as a surprise, but they should not have. Islamists had tried to bring down the Twin Towers before, in 1993, using a truck bomb. Nor was that the only jihadist attack prior to 9/11; in my book *Winning the Unwinnable War*, I describe how the road to 9/11 was punctuated by an escalating sequence of violent attacks. Our policymakers and leaders viewed the threat as a series of crises, to be dealt with in the moment, without wider, ideological context. There were many dots, and we recognized each as a problem, but we failed to connect those many dots to see the bigger picture: the common ideas animating the Islamist movement.

Earlier, I pointed out how George W. Bush continually insisted that jihadists were motivated by something other than religious ideas. Bush's perspective denied the common denominator uniting the Islamist movement. This was a factor in his evasion of the fundamental centrality of Iran and Saudi Arabia to the movement. Despite some of Bush's rhetoric about going after those who harbor and support the "terrorists," recall that Iran and Saudi Arabia were not merely omitted from the "Global War on Terrorism"; Saudi Arabia was affirmed a loyal ally, and, eventually, Bush sought to engage Iran in diplomatic negotiations. After scattering the jihadists in Afghanistan, the focal point of Bush's response became Iraq—a regime that had little to do with the Islamist cause.[38]

The Obama administration, vowing to avoid Bush's failures, reverted to a kind of hyper narrow conception of the threat (our enemy is al-Qaeda! no, it's ISIS!). This conception was drained of ideological substance; a person becomes a "violent extremist," we were told, mainly because of political grievances and economic privation.[39] By playing down the role of ideas, by viewing the problem as consisting of many disparate groups, factions, regimes, rather than a movement united by an ideological outlook, Obama's policy saw no contradiction in seeking to combat "terrorists" while also engaging leading regimes within the movement, chiefly Saudi Arabia and Iran.

The Trump administration has no coherent view of the problem. Trump has at times used the term "radical Islamic terrorism," but he has also implied that the problem is in some sense *all* Muslims (for example, recall the openness to creating a Muslim registry). Furthermore, he's put great emphasis on the fact that certain attackers were "outsiders"—that they did not share his (or, in his view, "our") Anglo-Saxon identity (notice Trump's repeated emphasis on the fact that some attackers were immigrants or the American-born *children* of immigrants).[40] This blurring of ideas and racial identity obscures the crucial fact that we're dealing with an ideological movement, one that individuals must come to embrace by choice (rather than belong to through heredity). Among other things, this means that those who adopt and *advance* this ideology can—and must—be evaluated morally. But notice that, like his predecessors, Trump is not only willing to (re)negotiate with Iran, but is also friendly with Saudi Arabia.

From these sketches of how we've approached the problem, you see that by putting out of focus the nature and goals of the Islamists, we end up with inconsistent, short-term, immoral, and, in the end, ineffectual policy. And it is our persistent failure to confront Islamic totalitarianism that helps explain the durable appeal of this cause. That's reflected not only in the masses who flocked to live under the Islamic State, but also in the ability of that group and of al-Qaeda to actuate independent, so-called lone-wolf jihadists to carry out attacks on their own initiative. Central to that phenomenon is the appeal of furthering a cause that the jihadists continue to see as viable.

For many years now, our approach to the problem has been deeply flawed. We had no clear idea of the nature of the problem, and we persuaded ourselves of explanations that were worse than superficial, fixating on non-essential features.

But it's well within our capability to end this menace. Any sensible response to the jihadist threat requires that we confront not only the salient factions but also, and especially, the regimes at its forefront.

To formulate a workable plan for achieving that goal, we must start by grasping clearly the nature of our enemy.

Trivializing the Islamist Menace

Elan Journo February 6, 2019

How we understand the "terrorist threat" is critical to defining a sound policy for addressing the problem. Yet there's something deeply, dangerously wrong in the way many of us think of the threat. That's manifest not only in the prevailing view, but also, especially, in the outlook of some of its fiercest critics.

The view that has dominated since 9/11 holds that we face a *massive threat*. Hanging in the balance, we are told, is our nation's survival. This outlook shaped the rhetoric and military response of the George W. Bush White House, but it wasn't limited to that administration.[41] For instance, Bruce Riedel, a scholar at the Brookings Institution and an adviser to the Obama administration, contended in 2009 that so long as al-Qaeda maintained its principal stronghold between Afghanistan and Pakistan, it would pose an "existential threat to the United States."[42] And echoes of this assessment can still be heard today from figures associated with the Trump administration.[43] The threat, in this view, is nothing less than "existential."

Take a look at the facts, however, and it's clear the "terrorists" are so vastly outmanned and outgunned that they simply cannot pose an existential threat. For example, when the Islamic State (or ISIS) was at its peak strength, it had some rifles, explosives, and pickup trucks, but no navy, no air force, nothing like the vast, advanced war machine of Nazi Germany or the Soviets. However you tally the material strength of all the jihadists on the face of the globe, they are way, way overshadowed by America's towering military.

The contrasting view, partly a reaction to the "existential threat" outlook, holds that the problem has been *massively overblown*.

Here's how Shikha Dalmia, a columnist for *Reason* magazine, expressed that view. In "What Islamist Terrorist Threat?," Dalmia looked back at the ten years since 9/11 and noted the absence of comparable mass-casualty attacks in that period. She argued that al-Qaeda lacks the skilled operatives and the resources to inflict serious harm on Americans. Apart from 9/11 itself, she suggested, "maybe the Islamists never posed that big a threat to begin with."

Islamist terrorism, she argued, is a minor threat, hardly the kind of thing that would justify a "war." The 9/11 attack warranted "some limited effort to clean out al-Qaeda in Afghanistan" but certainly not trillions of dollars (and counting) on two unending wars and on enhanced homeland security.

Perhaps the scholar who's done the most to advance this line of thinking is John Mueller, a professor at Ohio State University and a senior fellow at the Cato Institute, a libertarian think tank. Back in 2006 he wrote *Overblown: How Politicians and the Terrorism Industry Inflate National Security Threats, and Why We Believe Them*. Along with his frequent collaborator, Mark Stewart, he's written at length, for scholarly and popular outlets, contending that fears of Islamist terrorism—and the policy responses to them—are greatly exaggerated, even "delusional." Mueller's conclusion is built in part on a statistical risk-analysis of terrorist attacks and their cost. One takeaway from his work is that each year more Americans die in the bathtub (from falls and drownings) than from Islamist terrorism. This is a point that President Obama frequently voiced to his staff, underlining America's ability to absorb future attacks.

Much of the appeal of this line of thinking has to do with the disastrous "war on terror." Clearly, no sane person would wish to see the Iraq and Afghanistan debacles repeated—and absolutely not, if we're talking about an enemy that is orders-of-magnitude less powerful militarily. Another Iraq, for a bunch of peasants with rifles? Absurd. Now add in the fact—which Mueller has underscored—that homeland security measures have come at a gargantuan financial cost and, moreover, encroached on the freedom of Americans.

It's true, the "terrorist threat" falls short of being "existential." It is true (as I've also argued at length) that the "war on terror" was a debacle, and I'd argue that the burgeoning footprint of homeland security and mass surveillance is symptomatic of that failure. These are important truths—but granting all of them, there remains a distinct issue: What *is* the scale of the "terrorist threat"? How should we conceive of the Islamist phenomenon?

Is it right, following Mueller and those who share his outlook, that the Islamist threat is really so minor (less deadly than bathtubs!) that we should treat it as an "acceptable," livable-with menace to our lives?

No, that perspective is not only wrong, it's also dangerous. Instead of overstating the problem, it trivializes the threat. It's a hyper-narrow, non-contextual view. It blinds us to an essential feature of the phenomenon that we must understand in order to confront the threat: specifically, that it's *ideas-driven*. It blinds us to the dynamics by which the Islamist menace has grown from a minor, easily extinguishable problem, to something more. It blinds us to the fact that this enemy's agenda is hardly exhausted by inflicting terrorist attacks, and that it has already managed to batter a pillar of free societies, the right of free speech. It blinds us, in short, to the true nature of the threat, and thus it disarms us. Call it the blinkered view.

Missing from the blinkered view is something that's also missing from the "existential threat" outlook. That Bush-era view, in its own way, was willfully blind to the threat's wider context, and that blindness rendered America's policy response to the threat ineffectual. The aim of this essay is to provide an unblinkered, broad-scope perspective on the Islamist threat. By filling in crucial elements of the issue's wider context, which the blinkered view leaves out, I'll try to convince you that the Islamist movement is a serious, worsening menace which—if trivialized—could well become an existential threat.

Terrorists vs. Islamists

Central to the blinkered view is a misconception of the *Islamist* nature of the threat. Let's consider how John Mueller, a major driver of this way of thinking, talks about the Islamists.

To Mueller and many who share his view, Islamists are interchangeable with "terrorists." It just so happens that many of these terrorists have ties to the religion of Islam. That ideological dimension is treated as incidental. The emphasis is on the *means* by which they inflict harm—rather than on their *ends*, the *why* that animates them. If you play down the ideological goals of Islamists, however, you create a blind spot about the nature of the threat.

Perhaps "play down" is an understatement. What makes Islamists distinctive, by their own admission, is their ideological motivation. In the article "Jihadists: Understanding the Nature of the Enemy," I've argued that Islamists constitute a *movement* encompassing regimes such as Iran and Saudi Arabia, along with many rival, infighting factions, notably al-Qaeda, the Islamic State, Hamas, the Muslim Brotherhood and still others. What unites them is the ideological goal they seek to realize: imposing Islamic religious law, sharia, wherever they can. This movement is essentially driven by an ideology deeply rooted in religious ideas. This fact is fundamental to understanding and assessing the threat from Islamists, whether they deploy the tactic of mass-casualty terrorist attacks like 9/11, or other tactics to advance their perverse ideals, such as intimidation and electoral politics (as, for example, the Muslim Brotherhood in Egypt has done in recent years).

So, it's a striking feature of Mueller's conception of the threat that he demurs at seeking an ideological motivation for Islamist attacks. This is doubly bizarre because in arguing against that approach, the evidence he and his co-author (Mark Stewart) present in fact works to stress the centrality of ideas in animating the Islamists.

Mueller and Stewart write that looking to understand the process by which "potential terrorists become 'radicalized'" is unhelpful in understanding the threat, because it "tends to imply an ideological motivation to the violence." In almost all of the cases that Mueller and Stewart documented, the overwhelming driving force did not stem particularly from ideology, but rather from a simmering, and more commonly boiling, outrage at U.S. foreign policy—the wars in Iraq and Afghanistan, in particular, and the country's support for Israel in the Palestinian conflict. Religion was a key part of the consideration for most, but not because they wished to spread sharia law or to establish caliphates. Rather they wanted to protect their religion against what was commonly seen to be a concentrated war upon it in the Middle East by the U.S. government and military.[44]

It is because Mueller and Stewart refuse to take ideas seriously that they fail to properly interpret their own findings. The reported outrage at American foreign policy; the hostility toward U.S. wars in the Middle East and support for Israel; the desire to protect what they feel is an embattled religion—these are manifestations and consequences of an ideological outlook. They reflect the assumption that Islam is the true religion, that it should govern all mankind, and that anyone who opposes or undermines it thereby makes himself an enemy of the faithful.

That's not only consistent with, but in fact reflects, the global strategic vision holding that Islamic religious law (sharia) is the only moral foundation for human society. A particular assailant may only see himself as avenging or retarding the unbelievers' assault on his religion or on his co-religionists overseas (in Iraq, in Afghanistan, in the Palestinian territories), but that's no less an ideological motivation than the wider vision of spreading sharia and establishing a caliphate. Moreover, there is considerable debate among Islamist factions about when, and at what pace, these strategic goals—chiefly, the creation of a caliphate—should be realized; so, it's unsurprising if a foot soldier regards himself as waging a narrower battle in the wider, generations-long war in the path of Allah's law.

In a parenthetical aside, Mueller and Stewart express puzzlement at the attitudes of the would-be attackers they've studied, whom they characterized as essentially non-ideological: "None seems to remember, or perhaps in many cases ever knew, that the United States strongly favored the Muslim side in Bosnia and in Kosovo in the 1990s, as well as, of course, in the Afghan war against the Soviet Union in the 1980s." Ignorance certainly can explain this in some, many, or most cases, but for those who (like Osama bin Laden) are fully aware, it would be irrelevant precisely because from their ideological framework, there's no policy that we unbelievers can pursue that would be acceptable, except for submission and surrender to Islamic law.

Reflecting a common approach, Mueller and Stewart myopically focus on the Islamists' means (the oft-used tactic of terrorism in some form) rather than their ends: "As a result, military installations within the United States were fairly common targets—though not very good ones if one is seeking to do maximum damage and inflict maximum shock."[45] Notice how this observation takes 9/11-scale attacks as something like a defining feature of the Islamist movement; however, Islamist groups view their goals more broadly (more on this later). For example, they've sought to overthrow impious regimes by various means, such as cultural indoctrination, assassinations and wars.

The blinkered view corrupts our understanding of the Islamist threat. A prime example is the meteoric rise of the Islamic State (or ISIS) in the mid-2010s. If we tell ourselves that we're dealing with terrorists-who-happen-to-be-linked-to-Islam, instead of seeing the Islamist phenomenon as fundamentally ideas-driven, there's no compelling explanation for the spectacular, magnetic pull of the Islamist State.

Islamic State, which began as an al-Qaeda splinter group, declared itself a "caliphate" in 2014, seizing control of territory in Iraq and Syria. Having established a totalitarian Islamist regime, ISIS invited the faithful to live and fight under its quasi state. And they came. Tens of thousands of people came. Not only from across the Middle East, but also, remarkably, from the world's freest, most prosperous countries: the United Kingdom, France, Germany, Switzerland, Australia, the United States, Canada, Norway.

While clearly the Islamic State fomented, inspired and directed jihadist attacks globally, what galvanized followers was its ideological vision. The Islamic State presented itself—and was embraced by followers—as the realization of a moral society under Allah's law. Its ideological-political goal was not incidental, but fundamental to its appeal.

There's a disconnect between the blinkered conception of the threat and the reality of the Islamist movement. It stems from an unwillingness to take seriously that the Islamist movement is ideas-driven. To jettison that vital truth is to artificially constrict one's range of vision. It's like fixating on the bark while losing sight of the tree—never mind the forest. This is a self-imposed handicap to understanding the threat and its severity.

To appreciate some of the ramifications of that handicap, let's widen our perspective further to consider, first, how the Islamist movement went from being a piddling nuisance in the decades before 9/11 to becoming a serious menace; and, second, the Islamists' campaign against a pillar of free society, the principle of freedom of speech. A common thread unites these two cases. They illustrate—contra Mueller and others—the destructive results of myopically viewing Islamists as defined by their means rather than their ideological ends. It was our failure to properly conceptualize the nature and goals of the Islamists that opened the door to, indeed encouraged, their aggression.

The Road to 9/11

The 9/11 attacks, Mueller has pointed out, were an "aberration," a "statistical outlier," particularly in the scale of the death toll and the economic destructiveness. No other attack has come close.

True, but that ignores the wider context of how, across decades, the Islamists went from being a puny, largely impotent movement to becoming so daring as to carry out such a massive attack.

The theme of that story is the blinkered, non-ideological view of the problem—in practice. In *Winning the Unwinnable War*, I analyze in detail the major episodes leading up to that fateful day in 2001. Here let me sketch out just the basic pattern. When responding to Islamist attacks, the United States viewed them as scattered, disconnected crises; discounted the ideological character of the threat; and appeased the aggressors—with foreseeable results.

The road to 9/11 began at the gates of the U.S. embassy in Tehran, Iran. One November morning in 1979, amid the revolutionary upheaval in Tehran, an anti-American crowd stormed the embassy grounds and buildings. They took the American diplomats and guards hostage. Invading an embassy is tantamount to invading the sovereign territory of a foreign country. It is an act of war.

The Iran hostage crisis lasted 444 days. More than fifty American hostages endured a living hell. They were, by turns, threatened, beaten, terrorized. Whatever justifications the hostage-takers gave, the cause animating their violence was not outrage at US foreign policy but desire for Islamist theocracy. It's open to question whether the militants invaded the embassy at the explicit command of Ayatollah Khomeini, who was working to solidify Islamist rule. But it's clear Khomeini gave the hostage-takers his blessing and reaped benefits from the crisis.

How did Washington respond to this outrage? You'd expect a nation committed to protecting the lives and freedom of its citizens to have recognized the nature of the crisis—an act of war, initiated by a far weaker adversary—and stood up for itself swiftly. It could have immediately threatened, and if necessary deployed, military force to release the hostages. It could have denounced all forms of religious theocracy. Taking such actions would have affirmed its reputation as a nation that none dare menace. But what America in fact did had the opposite effect.

Jimmy Carter's administration quickly sidelined military options. One fear was that a retaliatory strike might be seen as punitive, rather than simply a means of releasing the hostages (as if punishing such aggression were an illegitimate goal). Another fear was that a US strike might prompt the Iranians to kill the hostages (in fact, not taking that step ended up costing many more

American lives in the following decades). The main thrust of the administration's approach was to tempt Iran with diplomatic "carrots."

The honest name for that policy is appeasement. Iran forcibly kept American citizens hostage, it extorted from Washington a ransom—and we capitulated. The price in dollars paled in comparison to the moral meaning and destructive consequences of Washington's surrender. Iran came away acquitted of any guilt, and Washington, by condescending to negotiate with that theocratic regime, conferred on it undeserved legitimacy.

This turned out to be a milestone on the road to 9/11. Speaking of the hostage crisis, Khomeini famously observed that America cannot do a damn thing. Our capitulation invited further aggression.

In the Islamic Republic of Iran, Khomeini and his followers created what other elements of the Islamist movement in Egypt, Pakistan, and elsewhere had never achieved: an actual regime founded on the principles of Islam as a total state. Take the galvanizing appeal of the Islamic State, and multiply tenfold. The creation of the Islamist regime in Iran supercharged the confidence of Islamist groups far and wide. The new Iran not only inspired hope of future advances, it was committed to hastening them. The Iranian constitution mandated exporting its Islamist revolution, by force. Eager to be seen as the standard-bearer of a global jihad, the Iranian regime was emboldened to escalate from taking Americans hostage to taking American lives.

What followed was a spiral of aggression spearheaded by Iran and its proxies. For example, in April 1983, a jihadist suicide-killer rammed a truck full of explosives into the US embassy in Beirut, Lebanon. The driver belonged to Hezbollah, an Islamist group that Iran helped build, fund, train, and direct. In response the United States did nothing to retaliate.

Six months later there was another explosive-truck attack in Beirut, targeting a barracks housing U.S. marines. The explosion was "the largest non-nuclear explosion that had ever been detonated on the face of the Earth." It claimed the lives of 241 marines. Again, the evidence trail led to Iranian-backed groups: the culpability for the attack rested with the regime in Tehran. The response? Despite some tough rhetoric from President Ronald Reagan, there was no explicit recognition of Iran's central role in the massacre or its role as standard-bearer of the emergent Islamist movement. Eventually, Reagan ordered a redeployment of the marines from Lebanon; it was a retreat.

Years later, Osama bin Laden would gloat about this American retreat, portraying our forces as cowardly, with the implication that stouthearted jihadists could overcome a more powerful enemy.

There were further attacks, not only by Iran and its proxies but also by other jihadist factions. In 1993, there was even an attack on the World Trade Center. The plot was designed to inflict catastrophic harm. The truck-bomb was supposed to topple one of the towers onto its twin, but it failed. The blast did manage to kill six and injure more than a thousand.

Evidence that this was another salvo in a broader jihad against America went unexplored. The dots were left unconnected. The Clinton administration dealt with the bombing as a law-enforcement matter. Then more attacks came, inflicting serious casualties and probing to see how much aggression America would tolerate.

By this time, Osama bin Laden had begun growing the al-Qaeda network, and he had risen to prominence within the Islamist movement. bin Laden famously issued a "declaration of war" against America, spelling out the ideological source of Islamist hostility to America. Few took it seriously, let alone situated al-Qaeda within the wider context of the Islamist movement's rise.

Demonstrating its ambition and ferocity, al-Qaeda in 1998 carried out near-simultaneous bombings targeting US embassies in Kenya and Tanzania, killing more than two hundred people and injuring some five thousand. The Clinton administration launched a toothless retaliation, shelling some al-Qaeda training camps and an empty factory.

This was nowhere near enough to undo the longstanding American pattern of appeasement, sporadic reprisals, and evasion about the nature of the threat. That became tragically clear on 9/11.

The Islamist Assault on Free Speech

The "terrorists," Mueller has observed, seek to inflict "maximum damage and shock," but they rarely succeed, and when they do, their impact is minor—with the exception of 9/11. That's part of why the blinkered view leads to a trivialization of the threat. Few attacks, small impact—so: keep calm and carry on.

But this, again, misconceives the Islamist threat by emphasizing means instead of ends. The tactic of terrorism hardly exhausts the impact that Islamists have sought to achieve in advancing their ideological goal. They want to see their vision of a proper society—one subjugated under Islamic religious law—enforced everywhere. To an astonishing degree, they've made inroads within the West by battering a pillar of free societies—though, on the blinkered view, you'd never connect the dots and see it. That pillar is the secular principle of freedom of speech.

Perhaps even more astonishing—a marker of how the blinkered view can corrupt thinking—is that this Islamist assault on freedom of speech is anything but stealthy. It's blatant, murderous, savage.

For nearly three decades, Islamists have sought to negate freedom of thought by threatening, and actually killing, those who dare criticize their ideas. The pattern goes back to 1989, when Ayatollah Khomeini decreed that the novel *The Satanic Verses*, by the British writer Salman Rushdie, was "blasphemous." Khomeini called upon all pious Muslims, everywhere, to hunt down and kill Rushdie and all those involved in the making of the book, notably including publishers. The Iranian regime offered a bounty for Rushdie's life. Essentially the regime was crowdsourcing a hit squad, globally. Some of the faithful heeded the call. There were firebombs at bookstores, death threats against publishers, and one of Rushdie's translators was killed. Rushdie went into hiding, living under round-the-clock police protection for years.

The point of Khomeini's incitement to execute the "blasphemers" behind *The Satanic Verses* was to elevate Islamic dogma above the secular principle of freedom of speech. Notice the premise of Khomeini's demand: the scope of Islamic law, or sharia, cannot be limited just to the borders of Iran. It must be enforced everywhere, taking precedence over secular laws within Western countries. The basic response of Western governments, responsible for upholding the right to freedom of speech, was pathetic. Washington extended to Iran our "good will." When President George H.W. Bush finally commented publicly on the Iranian death-decree, he said: "However offensive that book may be, inciting murder and offering rewards for its perpetration are deeply offensive to the norms of civilized behavior." With that shameful statement, Bush implied that Khomeini and Rushdie were equally objectionable. He added the pro forma warning that America would hold Iran "accountable" should any action be taken against U.S. interests, a warning no one in Teheran had reason to tremble over.

The Rushdie crisis opened the door to further Islamist assaults, small and large, on the freedom of speech. Then, in 2005 and 2006 came the "cartoons crisis," after a Danish newspaper published twelve cartoons of the prophet Muhammad. The newspaper's editors commissioned those cartoons because they had noticed signs of rampant self-censorship on the subject of Islam in European society, and they wanted to gauge the degree of the problem. What followed: protests, boycotts, deadly riots, and at least two hundred dead. The "cartoons crisis" went global.

Was there a redoubled commitment from our political and intellectual leaders to defend the principle of free speech? No, the prevailing response to the Danish cartoons crisis was shameful. European leaders tripped over themselves in the rush to appease; the George W. Bush administration conveyed that it viewed the cartoons as offensive, and that perhaps they should not have been published in the first place.

The widespread appeasement by Western governments inspired more jihadist aggression. For example: the massacre in 2015 at the Paris office of the magazine *Charlie Hebdo*. The magazine's editors and contributors, having reprinted the Danish cartoons and published various satires on religion, were put to death because they "blasphemed." The executioners were self-identified jihadists. Five months later, there was another jihadist attack on free speech, on American soil, at a cartoon contest in Garland, Texas. Worse, after *Charlie Hebdo* and the Garland attacks, you could hear intellectuals essentially blaming the victims.

The Islamists, enabled by Western appeasement, have altered the culture of the West: to speak up against their ideas can mean risking your life. Ayaan Hirsi Ali, who collaborated on a film mildly critical of Islamic mores, lives under 24-hour security (a jihadist murdered the film's director, Theo Van Gogh, on an Amsterdam street in 2004). She is on an al-Qaeda hit list. So is Flemming Rose, the Danish journalist who commissioned the notorious cartoons. So are two of the cartoonists.

The wider lesson is twofold. First, this assault on the principle of freedom of speech is an integral feature of the Islamist threat, reflecting the essentially ideas-driven nature of the enemy. Second, it's a serious error to assess the scale of the Islamist threat solely, or even primarily, in terms of mass-casualty attacks, which are difficult to carry out. Doing so misses the full context. Islamists have managed to advance their agenda in several ways that have impacted our society.

The climate of self-censorship, well established in Europe a decade ago, has spread. Consider the decision in 2009 by Yale University Press, a prestigious academic publisher, regarding *The Cartoons That Shook the World*. The book is a scholarly analysis of the Danish cartoons controversy; the author, Jytte Klausen, planned to feature images of all twelve of the notorious cartoons along with other illustrations of Muhammad, including a nineteenth-century sketch by Gustave Doré. Yale was initially inclined to publish the images in the book, which are essential to its subject. But in the end Yale decided to omit all the cartoons *and* other images of Muhammad from the book.

Why? Republication of the cartoons, Yale noted in a statement, had "repeatedly resulted in violent incidents, including as recently as 2008," and the academic and security experts that Yale had consulted on the matter "[a]ll confirmed that the republication of the cartoons by the Yale University Press ran a serious risk of instigating violence, and nearly all advised that publishing other illustrations of the Prophet Muhammad in the context of this book about the Danish cartoon controversy raised similar risk."

Or consider Flemming Rose's book, *The Tyranny of Silence: How One Cartoon Ignited a Global Debate on the Future of Free Speech*. It is an illuminating, thoughtful and sober analysis of the "cartoons crisis." Deservedly, *The Economist* named it one of the best books of 2014. But what's startling about the book—providing further evidence of one of its themes—is that it almost never made it into print: *No major U.S. publisher was willing to take the book.* (It finally came out in English, thanks to the Cato Institute.)

Witness the jihadists' veto.

Forty years ago, the Islamist movement was indeed a minor, perhaps even a trivial, threat. But it has grown to become a serious problem over time, because through our evasion, inaction and appeasement, we let it.

A "Solution" That Makes the Problem Worse

Instead of bringing us greater clarity, the blinkered view corrupts our thinking about the Islamist threat. It also distorts how we think about dealing with that threat. What recommendations are we to adopt if our perspective on the issue is encapsulated in the datum that each year more Americans die in bathtubs than at the hands of Islamists?

In his 2006 book *Overblown,* Mueller suggests that a "sensible approach to terrorism would support international policing while seeking to reduce terrorism's principal costs—fear, anxiety, and overreaction—not to aggravate them."[46] It would entail accepting that "some degree of risk is an inevitable fact of life, that the country can, however grimly, absorb just about any damage terrorism can inflict," noting parenthetically that "it now 'absorbs' 40,000 traffic deaths per year."[47] The focus, Mueller writes, should "be on treating terrorism as a *criminal* activity of rather limited importance and on reducing anxieties and avoiding policy overreaction."[48] Neither the Afghanistan War nor the Iraq War, in Mueller's view, was necessary to combat "international terrorism." And in other writings, he and Stewart argue that the counterterrorism measures enacted so far have been vastly cost-ineffective, though the authors grant that "some degree of effort to deal with the terrorism hazard is...certainly appropriate."[49]

Notice how, insofar as it appeals to people, this remedy counts on a number of misconceptions and errors, which leave us ill-equipped to deal with the actual threat.

One is the assumption that only an existential threat warrants retaliatory military force in self-defense. But that's false. The responsibility of a proper government is to protect the lives and freedom of its citizens. If some maniacs went on a spree of stabbing people to death on the New York subway, that rise in the murder rate would be nowhere near an "existential" threat. Yet clearly, we'd expect the police force to find and stop the killers. The same logic applies to the government's responsibility to protect us against foreign threats.

You might object, "What, we need *another* Iraq War to deal with the Islamists? No thanks." Is it right, though, to equate military force with a monumentally irrational, disastrous application of such power, the Iraq War? No, it's a major error.

The military is a powerful instrument, but it is our foreign policy that sets its direction and priorities. Clearly military force can be—and, in the past, has been—guided by better policy, and it was effective in advancing our self-defense (World War II comes to mind). What unfolded in Iraq was nothing like the military action that was necessary for our self-defense in the wake of 9/11. In *Winning the Unwinnable War*, I explain that it was fundamentally a policy failure, not a military failure: in short, it was a nation-building welfare mission, not a self-interested mission to eliminate threats we faced. To demonstrate that conclusion takes a lot of evidence, which I provide in my book; my aim here is not to do that, but just to challenge a false assumption. It's a mistake to equate the Iraq War (as horrific and disgraceful as it was) with military action in self-defense, and then discard that option as ineffectual. To do so is to disarm ourselves in the face of a mounting threat.

Another error, closely related, is evident in the talking point that each year more Americans die in the bathtub (or traffic accidents, or natural disasters, etc.) than at the hands of Islamist attackers. This confuses risks that are fundamentally different in kind. We can distinguish three kinds: natural perils (tornados, lightning), human-initiated accidents (slipping in the bathtub, traffic accidents), and harm deliberately inflicted by people on other people (murders, bombings). The differences matter.

For example, we can mitigate and insure against tornado damage or fail to do so, but our inaction will not lead to more tornados, nor affect their ferocity. We can also refuse to take any steps to lessen the number of accidental deaths in bathtubs, but our inaction will not make bathtubs a growing threat. There's a crucial difference: Neither tornados nor bathtubs are out to kill you, but Islamists are. Inaction in the face of the Islamist menace, therefore, does affect the severity of the threat that they pose and the damage they inflict. And because they're committed to their ideological goal, they'll fight on, and on, and on—unless they're stopped. We've seen that already.

Finally, consider Mueller's recommendation that we view (Islamist) "terrorism as a criminal activity of rather limited importance," something to be dealt with through international policing. This bears a striking resemblance to what was in fact American policy in the decade or so leading up to 9/11—the policy that failed to prevent that catastrophic Islamist attack. For example, the Clinton administration prosecuted the culprits behind the 1993 attack on the World Trade Center. And, recall, Clinton authorized highly limited military action—some missiles—in retaliation against al-Qaeda for the 1998 embassy bombings in Africa, a use of military force notable as a conspicuous exception to the norm.

Reverting to this pattern is no solution at all. Indeed: Trivializing the threat means allowing it to grow worse. If taken seriously, the blinkered view could pave the way for the threat someday actually becoming existential.

The indispensable step to combating this threat is understanding the nature of the Islamist phenomenon. To do that we must turn away from the blinkered view, adopt a broad-scope, integrative perspective, and recognize that, fundamentally, the Islamist movement is ideas-driven.

Sam Harris and Maajid Nawaz in Open Conversation About Islam

Elan Journo March 13, 2019

The new documentary *Islam and the Future of Tolerance* sheds much needed light on an issue engulfed in ignorance, confusion, taboo. The film centers on Sam Harris, an atheist intellectual, and Maajid Nawaz, a former Islamist turned reformer, who engage in a serious, frank, even brave, conversation on Islam, the Islamist threat, and attempts to silence discussion on these issues.

That the documentary was made at all is in itself remarkable. It was funded, not through the backing of any major TV network or well-known production company, but thanks to scores of individuals who chipped in to a Kickstarter campaign. Such campaigns typically offer backers some form of public recognition and thanks. But according to Suzy Jamil, the producer, members of the filmmaking team and some backers "were concerned about privacy and security." A number of contributors asked to have their first, last, or full name withheld from the film's website. And the end credits, which also thank individual funders, list numerous names that are blanked out. It's an eloquent illustration of the climate of fear that surrounds the subject of Islam.

Such fear is understandable in the post–*Charlie Hebdo* era. In a note to supporters on Kickstarter, the filmmakers wrote that, given the documentary's subject matter, "we may end up being targets. That's a risk we are willing to take."

Let's salute them for taking that risk. The documentary makes several important points that help us think more clearly about the Islamist phenomenon, its connection to the religion of Islam, and how discussion of these issues is muzzled.

At the outset, Harris and Nawaz challenge the emerging taboo about discussing Islam. They reject the widely held idea that criticizing Islam is inherently racist or "Islamophobic." Clearly racism against Muslims is a real phenomenon, and it's true that many view Islam as a kind of tribal/racial identity. But there's an essential difference between that and the documentary's purpose: to analyze the religion of Islam as a *set of ideas* and to consider how those ideas shape the actions of its followers.

For thinking about the Islamist menace, Nawaz offers a set of helpful distinctions. Islamists, he says, seek to impose an interpretation of Islam over society. Some of them strive for that end through indoctrination, cultural change, revolution, even electoral politics. A subset of Islamists are jihadists. The jihadists share the same goal, but use violent means, such as terrorist attacks, to advance their vision. These distinctions help unscramble a major confusion in the post–September 11 period. The George W. Bush administration and many others told us the enemy is "terrorism." The illuminating point that emerges from the documentary is that we should understand the Islamist movement as defined fundamentally by its ideological ends, rather than its means.

Distinct from Islamists is a far larger community of Muslims, whose level of religious commitment varies. Many of them, Nawaz argues, should be called "socially conservative Muslims." In contrast to Islamists, they are not seeking to *impose* a political vision defined by religion. But, in line with religious teachings, they share many of the same sentiments of Islamists. Such "socially conservative Muslims" typically believe, for example, that homosexuality is wrong, that criticism of Islam is blasphemous, that women must be subservient to men (it is in such communities that the horrific practice of "honor killings" can be found). Nawaz insists that the views of "socially conservative Muslims" must be challenged. He counts himself a Muslim reformer, a tiny minority group on the margins.

Reformers, he says, recognize openly that there are "troubling passages" in scripture that need nuanced interpretation, and that within Muslim communities there are theocrats who must be challenged. Nawaz believes that Islam can be interpreted to accommodate itself to the principles of a secular, free society. To foster that way of thinking, he started an advocacy organization, Quilliam, and one of its activities is to present reform-minded interpretations of Islamic scripture.

This issue of how to understand religious scripture, particularly the Koran's endorsement of holy war and barbaric punishments, sets the stage for one of the highlights of the documentary. It's one of the points on which Harris and Nawaz differ most acutely (their initial, in-depth exchange on this issue can be found in a 2015 book, which shares the same title as the documentary).

Nawaz takes the position that interpreting a religious text requires a sensitivity to its context, cultural setting, and intent. For example, he considers the Islamic dogma that calls for banning alcohol. He points out that the language in the text uses a term that originally referred not to all forms of alcohol, but just to grape wine. So, the apparently literalist reading of groups like ISIS, which ban all alcohol, ignores the literal meaning of the text in its original context. Or take the Islamic injunction to cut off the hand of the thief, which Nawaz acknowledges is "problematic." Admitting that his approach may seem like an intellectual contortion, he suggests that one has to be sensitive also to the possibility of the metaphorical meaning of a text, which here (presumably) takes "hand" to mean something like a motive or power, rather than an actual hand.

Against that approach, Harris pushes back, and he offers a perspective that gets at something true and important. The problem for "moderates" in any religion and especially in Islam, he argues, is that they're left to read the text selectively, reinterpreting or ignoring the barbarous parts of their scripture, in the light of views that come from outside influences, not the text. By contrast those he calls "fundamentalists" read a text in a more complete, consistent, honest way, neither ignoring any part of it, nor reinterpreting it. Islam has views of martyrdom, jihad, blasphemy, apostasy (leaving the faith), and the moral worth of women, Harris argues, that are deeply inimical to a modern civil society. The problem, he says, is that the doctrines of Islam are not endlessly susceptible to reinterpretations that defy the literal, plausible understanding of the words on the page.

Belief in Islam commits you to its doctrines, and, Harris stresses, your beliefs shape your actions.

To make that point today, however, takes courage, and it invites all manner of dishonest criticism and smears.

Near the end of the documentary, Harris and Nawaz circle back to take a wider perspective on the taboo around discussions of Islam. Both are adamant about the importance of defending freedom of speech and, in particular, discarding that taboo. The "Islamophobia" epithet, Harris argues, is calculated to shut off honest debate, so that the needed analysis of the Islamist phenomenon is pushed to the margins.

Harris goes on to level a trenchant criticism of what he takes to be a "liberal" premise, though it's likely more widespread. It's the premise of discounting the role of ideas—particularly religious belief—in shaping human action. This manifests, for example, in how some people try to explain a Muslim suicide bomber. They imagine that the perpetrator must be the victim of oppression, since only that could drive someone to take such drastic action, and then they go on a hunt for an oppressor. The counterpoint, Harris observes, is that you can find cases of Muslim suicide bombers who were never subjected to oppression. Dropped out of that perspective, Harris notes, is a recognition of the power of belief in human action.

Whereas many in the West fail or refuse to grasp the power of ideas—particularly religious belief—this is precisely what both Harris and Nawaz both appreciate to a remarkable extent. The documentary *Islam and the Future of Tolerance* makes that point emphatically, and perhaps by its example of open, frank engagement with the issue of Islam, the film will exert a salutary impact on the culture.

Why Students Protested Event
Analyzing Islamism

Elan Journo June 17, 2019

When I headed to the University of Rochester to take part in a panel discussion, I had no inkling of the campaign that some students had already launched to shut the event down. The reasons behind their opposition were revealing. In this one incident, concerning one event, at one campus, there's a telling data point about today's intellectual climate.

I went to Rochester to speak on a panel about the ideas behind ISIS, al-Qaeda and the wider Islamist movement in the Middle East. The panel also included Graeme Wood of *The Atlantic* magazine; Faisal Saeed Al Mutar, a secular activist and founder of Ideas Beyond Borders; and Adnan Ahmed, a writer and imam in the Ahmadiyya Muslim community. The event was co-sponsored by the Ayaan Hirsi Ali Foundation, the Ayn Rand Institute, and the campus College Republicans.

Before any of the speakers even arrived on campus, a petition to cancel the event had circulated among students. When the panel was about to begin, several student groups—Students for a Democratic Society among them—showed up to pressure the administration and the organizers to shut down the event.

Fortunately they failed. But they made their presence felt within the hall. Many attended the event, heckling at times; some stood in the back to protest with a sign; and they dominated the question period with mini-speeches and angry objections. Why? Why did they object to the panel? Why did they feel so passionately that this event, and this topic, did not belong on their campus?

You can pick up a few indications from the sometimes strident, sometimes furious questions (watch the entire video on YouTube[50]). But I learned a lot more from my conversations with several of the students after the event, when all four panelists talked with the students at length outside the auditorium.

Initially, it seemed the main objection had to do with timing. The panel happened to be scheduled for March 21, six days after the massacre at two mosques in New Zealand. Several of the Muslim students explained that they were still grieving, and they viewed our panel on the Islamist movement as having been scheduled to make some kind of point, presumably implying an indifference to the New Zealand attack.

Except that our event was months in the planning. It was in early November 2018 that the organizer, Mohamed Ali, a student at Rochester, and I first discussed my taking part in the panel. Moreover, the panel itself began with a moment of silence for the fifty Muslims murdered in New Zealand, and the first topic we discussed was the evil of white supremacy and anti-Muslim bigotry.

Beyond the issue of scheduling, which we addressed during the panel and later, there were other objections. Several students mentioned that the event was co-sponsored by the College Republicans club. None of the speakers, however, is in any way affiliated with the Republican Party or that student club. The issue, it turned out, was that a *former* president of that club had recently been caught distributing white supremacist flyers in a nearby community. But he had left the club the previous school year, the club's current leadership had publicly disavowed him, and all the speakers on the panel were clearly and vocally as opposed to white supremacism as they were to the Islamist movement.

After listening further to the students and probing their views, I took away two core objections of a more substantive nature. Neither is defensible, and both reveal the impact of certain destructive views prevalent on college campuses today.

The first: the protesting students' own campus clubs—including the Arab students association and the Muslim Students' Association—had not been involved or consulted in advance. If they had been, they would have not pushed back on the panel. To understand the views of students, I put aside the implication that these groups were entitled to be involved. OK, I asked one of the club leaders, what kind of involvement or role would they have wanted? How would the panel have been different *with* their involvement? What issues did they want to see discussed?

The event's agenda, she said, would have to explore "U.S. imperialism" in the Middle East and the consequences of America's foreign policy, which she and several other students held to be the main, if not the exclusive, causal factor explaining the Islamist phenomenon. By the time she had finished describing her view of what such a hypothetical event would have looked like, it was clear

there was little room, if any, for an exploration of the *ideas* behind
ISIS, al-Qaeda, and the rest of the Islamist phenomenon. What
she outlined would have been an entirely different event, with the
Islamist issue marginalized if not elided, and the focus squarely
on her interpretation of America's role in the Middle East. (Let me
note that while I'm also critical of U.S. foreign policy in the region,
albeit for different reasons, it's false to view the Islamist phenomenon as essentially motivated by political grievances against
American policy.)

Essentially, the objection was that because the panel focused
on the ideas of the Islamist movement, rather than aligning with
the students' doctrinaire view of American policy, the panel did
not belong on campus. (Later, I learned that these student groups
had indeed been invited to co-sponsor the event, but refused.)

The second core objection turned on the issue of "representation," which came up during the Q&A but more pointedly in the
discussions after the event.

Throughout the event, a number of students in the back of the
room held up a banner that read "You Do Not Represent Us." The
full meaning of that claim became evident in later conversation
with a few students. Mohamed Ali, who had organized and mod-
erated the panel and was listening to this post-event conversation,
has written an illuminating article at Quillette examining what
happened:

> After the event I overheard a student protestor berate one of
> the panelists and complain, *inter alia*, that the event had not
> been organized by an Arab. I interjected to inform her that I
> was the organizer of the event and that I am indeed an Arab.
> "You don't count," she immediately retorted. "We know your
> politics." I subsequently discovered that she is president of the
> Arab student association. I was already aware of this practice
> of "Uncle Tom-ing" members of minorities who challenge
> certain orthodoxies, but this was the first time I had experi-
> enced it firsthand. Such attitudes were evident in many of the
> protesters' objections to the event. Faisal Saeed Al Mutar—an
> Iraqi born secular rights advocate and the only Arab on the
> panel—bore the brunt of these attacks. He was denounced as
> a puppet and a traitor for discussing the role of religion in
> motivating groups like ISIS in his native country.
> Particularly distasteful was the insinuation that race is not
> simply a descriptive category, but that it is thought to require

certain duties of, and impose certain prerogatives upon, the individual. To retain one's status as an "authentic" Arab (or member of any other "marginalized" demographic), one has to believe certain things. Because I had organized this discussion, I was rendered *persona non grata* among those who insist we turn a blind eye towards atrocities committed in the name of Islam. Investigating this matter at all apparently constituted a betrayal of my tribe, the punishment for which is excommunication. I've come to call this attitude "prescriptive racialism"—the notion that racial identity should determine how people act and what they believe. To be accepted as an Arab, I must adopt the same politics as all other Arabs.

Ali goes on to point out incisively that this racial/tribal mindset also pervades the outlook of white supremacists. His article is well worth reading in full.

The upshot of this "representation" objection is that our panel discussion was fundamentally illegitimate because it didn't include acceptable racial/tribal "representatives." The non-"representative" organizer and non-"representative" speakers had no standing to engage with these issues, a standing possible only to relevant tribal members. Therefore, the ideas and views we panelists put forward that night must be silenced.

Both of these objections reflect aspects of a tribalist mindset. The one treats views opposed to its dogmas as illegitimate; the other stresses collective identity as defining one's views. Both are fundamentally anti-intellectual. Such an outlook is pernicious, especially so on a college campus, where students come to learn about and explore new ideas. And it is this anti-intellectual outlook that students are encouraged to adopt.

From one perspective, though, the incident at Rochester reinforced the importance and value of the panel discussion, which brought out important points for understanding the Islamist movement as an *ideas-driven* phenomenon.

A Blind Spot Obscuring the
Islamist Menace

Elan Journo October 23, 2019

Well before the Islamic State declared itself a "caliphate," its leaders announced their aim plainly. But few took them seriously.

"Our objective," stated one of its spokesmen, "is the formation of an Islamic state on the prophetic model that acknowledges no boundaries, distinguishes not between Arab and non-Arab, easterner and westerner, but on the basis of piety. Its loyalty is exclusively to God: it relies on only Him and fears Him alone."

Having promised to establish such a caliphate—a society on "the prophetic model," ruled by sharia, or religious law, a society indifferent to ethnicity and nationality, united only by faith—the Islamic State did exactly that on conquered territory, with its capital in the city of Raqqa (previously in Syria).

Having promised to "acknowledge no boundaries," ISIS worked globally to spread its vision of a political-social order defined by sharia, leveraging social media and disseminating highly produced propaganda articles, magazines, videos.

Having promised loyalty "exclusively to God," the group took the fight to the enemy: unbelievers. It inspired, fomented, and directed deadly attacks on infidels in London, in Manchester, in Brussels, in Ankara, in San Bernardino, California, in Orlando, Florida. Hit especially hard was Paris. In January 2015, jihadists massacred journalists at *Charlie Hebdo* and carried out a deadly siege at a kosher supermarket. Then in November, a squad of jihadists shot up sidewalk cafes and set off suicide bombs outside a soccer stadium and at a music venue, killing 130.

But the reaction of many intellectuals and politicians was denial. A common mantra held that the Islamic State has "nothing to do with Islam"—an echo of the Bush administration's assurance that the 9/11 attackers had hijacked a noble religion. The repetition of this phrase seemed to imply that wishing would make it so.

Graeme Wood, a journalist trying to understand ISIS, recounts talking to scholars who insisted on the non-Islamic character of

Islamic State, without taking the trouble to read the group's statements or religious rulings. Such ignorance, he writes, is "as appalling as if a scholar of Marxism declared the Soviet Union 'not Marxist' and turned out to be unfamiliar with the name Trotsky or Lenin, or the title of anything either of them wrote." He observes: "The Islamic State's self-presentation is suffused with religious language, tropes, and pomp—but when I asked experts on religion for their opinion on the group's religious foundations, they typically denied any meaningful link and instead changed the subject to American foreign policy, neo-Baathist power politics, abnormal psychology, or secular grievance."

While jihadists were blowing themselves up on the streets of Paris and murdering people at a gay nightclub in Orlando, the prevailing notion was that the Islamic State was animated by something other than—*anything* but—an Islamic vision for society.

Pushing back against such self-delusion and denial, two incisive books challenge that conventional outlook. Graeme Wood's *The Way of the Strangers* is an exploration of the Islamic State phenomenon. Contrary to commonly held views, Wood shows that the Islamic State's beliefs, its magnetic appeal for tens of thousands of followers, and the group's social-political aims are all deeply rooted in Islamic ideas. Gilles Kepel's *Terror in France* examines how Islamist ideas came to be "firmly implanted in France." What's especially illuminating in Kepel's account is his analysis of a distinctive jihadist strategy focused on Europe. In contrast to previous strategies, it entails fostering among Muslims within France a primarily religious identity and pitting them against secular society.

Taken together, these two books cast a bright light on the essentially religious motivation that unites Islamists.

Islamic State's Deeply Religious Character

Once the Islamic State had realized its vision of a caliphate, it was unashamed—indeed, proud—about its application of sharia punishments, for blasphemy (execution), fornication (stoning; for some, a hundred lashes and banishment for a year), homosexuality (execution), theft (cutting off the hand), drinking wine (eighty lashes), apostasy (execution). Moreover, the Islamic State endorsed the institution of slavery, permitting its fighters to take captured women as sex slaves. The Islamic State's propagandists mocked Muslims who denied the legitimacy of such barbarous practices.

The Islamic State's political-social vision and barbaric practices, Wood shows, are firmly grounded in Islamic religious texts and tradition. The group's sincerely held beliefs form "a coherent view of the world rooted in a minority interpretation of Islamic scripture that has existed, in various forms, for almost as long as the religion itself."

The group belongs within the Salafi tradition of Sunni Islam. The term "Salafi" derives from an Arabic term meaning "pious forefathers," referring to the first three generations of Muslims. In Wood's summary, "Salafis take the Koran, the example of the Prophet, and the actions and beliefs of these men and women as their primary sources of religious authority, and they reject the opinions of many Muslims who came later." They reject other sects, notably the Shia, for their "innovative" practices, and regard themselves as the chosen sect of real Muslims.

The Islamic State regards itself as meticulously following the beliefs and example of Islam's founders. Just as they waged holy war, so does the Islamic State. The practices that horrify us—slavery, beheading—are well supported in holy texts and a long history. "These practices may be rejected by mainstream Muslim scholars today," Wood writes, "but for most of Islamic history, it barely occurred to Muslims to doubt that their religion permitted them." There is hardly a text on Islamic laws of war, in the pre-modern period, that "neglects to mention the rules concerning enslavement of women and children." Slavery was practiced by "Muslims for most of Islamic history, and it was practiced without apology by Muhammad and his Companions, who owned slaves and had sex with them." Moreover, to doubt that "apostasy has ever been a capital crime is a misreading of scripture and history."

Wood's book, which grew out of an influential article at *The Atlantic*, weaves together the history of the Islamic State, the religious basis for its views, and profiles of some of the group's followers and sympathizers. These portraits are fascinating, because Wood is disarmingly polite, yet relentless, in drawing out their beliefs. For example, we meet an Australian convert who became a YouTube preacher. Like many followers of ISIS, he sincerely believes in the goal of the caliphate and the group's effort to hasten a *literal* apocalypse.

From these profiles and Wood's analysis of the Islamic State, we also learn why counter-explanations for ISIS, which emphasize non-religious factors, fall apart. Aren't the soldiers of Islamic State simply psychopaths? What about the jihadist fighters who appear largely ignorant of Islam? Or the claim that the Islamic State was at its core a group of former officials of Iraq's ruling Baath Party? Wood convincingly refutes each of these counter-explanations. A "crushing weight of evidence" shows us that "religion matters deeply to the vast majority of those who have traveled to fight."

Part of what emerges from these profiles is how religion is a "way of thinking and living," providing a kind of "culture unto itself." Being an Islamist, we learn, is in significant part adopting a religious identity.

Wood also responds to the counterargument that Islamic State is a minority sect within Islam. It is. But every religion has minority sects that coreligionists find embarrassing or abhorrent. Think of the Westboro Baptist Church, whose followers believe that "God hates fags." Yet, Protestants have to recognize that the group's members study the Bible and believe Jesus died for their sins: they are fanatics, but they are *Christian* fanatics. And being a minority sect means just that. It's a separate issue whether a minority sect's interpretation is legitimate, which turns on questions of dogma.

The fact remains that "the Islamic State consults the same texts as other Muslims, and dips into the same Sunni historical tradition. The Islamic State's scholars do not cite Marx, the *philosophes*, the laws of Manu, or Paul the Apostle. They cite Koran, hadith, and carefully selected thinkers within the Islamic tradition. Their fanaticism is a Muslim fanaticism." The upshot is that even Muslim critics of ISIS are "compelled to acknowledge that the group is led and supported by Muslims, albeit Muslims with whom they vociferously disagree."

Given the evidence, Wood observes, it "takes astonishing levels of denial to claim, as uncountable Muslims and non-Muslims have, that the Islamic state has 'nothing to do with Islam,' merely because the group's heinous behavior clashes with mainstream or liberal Muslim interpretation." After studying jihadists and their sympathizers, Wood reflects that he "came to think of them as the visible surface of a cause that was stirring the emotions and convictions of tens of millions of others, and that would continue to inspire them for decades to come, even if it [Islamic State] lost its core territory in Syria and Iraq."

How that same cause has stirred the emotions and convictions of so many in France is a major focus of Gilles Kepel's *Terror in France*.

Fostering an Islamist Identity

Behind the 2015 eruption of jihadist violence in France, Kepel writes, there loomed "the implantation of Salafism—a model for breaking with the values of the [French] Republic and its secularism." This "is not an isolated phenomenon—and later jihadi developments in Belgium and Germany showed that it is not exclusively French." Kepel argues that this implantation has followed a distinct strategy which entails fostering a primarily religious collective identity among French Muslims.

This strategy, Kepel argues, contrasts with the approaches in earlier waves of the modern jihadist phenomenon. The first, roughly 1979 to 1997, centered on waging a holy war in Afghanistan, Algeria, and Bosnia. The next (1998–2005) was marked by al-Qaeda's rise to prominence: the attack of September 11, 2001, embodied a new strategy of targeting the "far enemy," the United States. From 2005 onward, Kepel argues, we can observe a third strategy emerging. A driving force behind it is Abu Musab al-Suri, an Islamist ideologue. The al-Suri strategy focuses on fomenting war on European soil. The idea is to recruit European Muslims, notably second generation immigrants, to carry out violent attacks. Gradually, such attacks lead to wars that destroy the West. Thus a path is cleared for a world dominated by sharia rule.

Key to this strategy is inducing French Muslims to embrace Islam as their primary identity. Reinforcing that goal is another, related one: to alienate them from secular society, so that they eventually take up arms against it. Facilitating these goals was the growing cultural influence of Islamic advocates, who vied to dominate France's Muslim communities. Muslims were encouraged to become self-assertive about their religious identity, for example, on the issue of wearing the Islamic veil, respecting the halal diet, and demonizing same-sex marriage. Such issues moved to the fore as growing numbers of Muslim citizens began to vote, run for public office, and lobby their representatives.

More and more in the *banlieues*—suburbs of Paris and other cities mainly populated by immigrants and their descendants—Islam was becoming "an irrepressible marker of identity." According to Kepel, it is "undeniable that Islamization is now more widespread in the *banlieues* of France" than it was thirty years ago. In some *banlieues*, for example, "it has become socially difficult or even impossible to break the daytime fast in public during Ramadan if one 'looks like' a Muslim."

The impact of this trend was manifest not only in the jihadist attacks in Paris in January 2015, at *Charlie Hebdo* and a kosher supermarket. It was also evident in the reactions to those attacks by segments of the country's Muslim community.

The ringleader of the attacks, Amedy Coulibaly, followed a path to jihad that fit the al-Suri strategy. Important in his path was the formation of an Islamist identity—and a growing hostility toward France's secular society. He was a small-time criminal, repeatedly imprisoned. Prisons in France, Kepel notes, are incubators for jihad, and, like many other released prisoners, Coulibaly emerged with a deeper commitment to the Islamist cause. Before launching the attacks in January 2015, Coulibaly recorded a detailed video statement justifying the attacks and anticipating his own martyrdom. Kepel's analysis of this video is illuminating. Coulibaly disavows his identity as a French citizen, and instead views himself—and encourages others to view themselves—first, and above all, as a Muslim. The basic narrative of Coulibaly's video presents him as fighting in "self-defense" against an infidel, "Islamophobic" society of which he, like all Muslims, is a victim. A goal of the video is to encourage other Muslims in Europe to emulate Coulibaly's violent attacks— and in fact, in the ensuing months and years, some did.

The Coulibaly-led attacks elicited a massive public reaction. Not only within France, but also globally, the empathetic hashtag #JeSuisCharlie (I am Charlie) trended for days. On the streets of Paris, millions came out with signs bearing that slogan and held aloft pencils, symbolizing freedom of speech. World leaders, arms interlocked, led a march through Paris.

Less noticed, however, was the reaction of some Muslims in France. For them, the reassertion of the nation's secular ideal and the principle of free speech meant endorsing blasphemy against their religion. In their view, the million-strong march after *Charlie Hebdo* was a further manifestation of "Islamophobia." Online, other hashtags began surfacing: #jenesuispasCharlie (I'm not Charlie), #cheh ("well done!" in North African Arabic), and #JeSuisCharlieCoulibaly. This last hashtag honored Amedy Coulibaly.

It's telling that as many as nine hundred people chose to leave France and journey to the Middle East to fight for the Islamic State. Remarkably, a senior official at the mosque where a number of them worshipped refused to condemn them. Later, an "imam of the Lunel mosque finally decided, in response to many requests, to criticize from the pulpit the departure for jihad in Syria. This earned him death threats from other activists."

Kepel's book is an in-depth case study, which delves into France's political and cultural scene. At times the analysis dwells on minute details while the book's overall logical structure fades from view. Nonetheless, Kepel offers some worthwhile comments on the rise of nationalist and racist groups. Particularly eye-opening, though all too brief, is his perspective on the French Left. He argues forcefully that elements of France's political Left have contributed to obscuring the true nature of jihadism and its impact in France.

Finally, some aspects of Kepel's argument are not fully developed or convincing. For example, Kepel seems to regard the complaints of "Islamophobia" as largely, or exclusively, contrived. On that assumption, his analysis bears out how such complaints serve an Islamist agenda. But he does not unpack this confusing idea of "Islamophobia." The concept mashes together, on the one hand, legitimate scrutiny, criticism, and debate of Islamic ideas and, on the other, actual cases of anti-Muslim prejudice. Some analysis of this issue would clarify and likely reinforce Kepel's case.

Shining a Bright Light on the Islamist Phenomenon

The chief value of these books by Wood and Kepel is that they help us better understand the Islamist phenomenon. A key lesson is that the Islamist movement is united by a deeply religious goal rooted in Islam, which its followers pursue by diverse means and strategies. For al-Qaeda, the caliphate would come later, and the apocalypse eventually. For Islamic State, it is caliphate *now*, the apocalypse *imminently*. Contrasting with both of these (and still other Islamist groups) is the al-Suri strategy of imploding the West by inciting jihad within Europe. The common end, however, is a society wherein the individual's life is defined in every detail by the mores and religious law of Islam, and religion essentially defines his identity.

PART 6

America's Incoherent Foreign Policy

American foreign policy is a confused hash of diverging, inconsistent goals, desperately lacking a principled approach. This is evident in the incoherence and intellectual bankruptcy of U.S. Mideast policy, particularly in our handling of the Israeli-Palestinian conflict and the U.S.-Saudi relationship.

The year 2018 marked a quarter century since the advent of a historic peace accord between Israel and the Palestinians, a deal endorsed by the United States. That accord, the much-celebrated culmination of the so-called Peace Process, in fact aggravated the conflict and undermined U.S. interests.

In that same year, America's relationship with Saudi Arabia made headlines. The new de facto ruler, Mohammed bin Salman, was widely hailed as a "reformer." But then came the grisly murder—inside the Saudi consulate in Turkey—of Jamal Khashoggi, a Saudi dissident who worked as a journalist for the *Washington Post*. The Khashoggi killing opened many people's eyes to the brutal nature of a regime that the U.S. has long embraced as a stalwart ally.

Let's Stop Normalizing the Palestinian Movement

Elan Journo November 10, 2017

Consider this nightmare: Imagine that the United States helps create a militant regime hostile to individual liberty. Suppose this U.S.-funded, authoritarian regime becomes notorious for inciting violent attacks. Now imagine that Washington enables jihadists to gain political power within the regime. Then, the authoritarians and jihadists join forces.

Chilling? Yes. Irrational? Yes. Far-fetched? Sadly, no. That, in a nutshell, is America's actual relationship with the Palestinian Authority, a state-in-the-making. Now, a new "unity" deal aims to reconcile the two major Palestinian factions: the quasi-secular authoritarians of Fatah; and the jihadists of Hamas. This deal opens the door for Hamas to share in the running of the Palestinian Authority.

To fathom how we ended up in this absurd situation, look at America's approach toward the Palestinian movement. A core problem is that our intellectual and political leaders push aside the need for a serious moral assessment of the Palestinian movement's nature and goals. They disregard, play down, even whitewash the movement's hostility to individual freedom. The situation today is the result of a bipartisan failure across many years.

In the 1990s, the U.S. helped establish the Palestinian Authority, a transitional quasi-state designed to become fully sovereign. It was supposed to be a step toward a lasting Israeli-Palestinian peace. Its first "president" was the arch terrorist Yasser Arafat, who led the Palestinian movement. With an indifference to genuine moral judgment, the Clinton administration brushed aside Arafat's heinous crimes and militant agenda, embraced him as a peacemaker, and whitewashed his vicious record.

Why? The Palestinian movement claimed it would recognize Israel and end the campaign to destroy that country, the region's only free society. Those promises were empty, yet Arafat became one of the most frequent foreign visitors to the White House and co-winner of a Nobel Peace Prize.

229

Instead, since its birth the Palestinian quasi-state has been yet another brutal, militant Middle East dictatorship, mocking the rule of law and methodically violating the individual rights of its own subjects. It has enabled and sponsored Palestinian attacks on Israel. In the first decade of its existence, more people were injured or died in Palestinian attacks than in the preceding quarter century. By a factor of two.

Despite these facts, the United States and European patrons played down the regime's authoritarianism and militancy, and continued backing it. Washington has lately given it about $400 million a year.

George W. Bush's administration compounded the problem. President Bush, like President Clinton, endorsed the goal of a fully sovereign Palestinian state. While the U.S. had for years given de facto backing to that goal, Bush was the first formally to go on the record in support of it. And despite his reputation as a morally principled leader, we have Bush to thank for handing Palestinian jihadists greater power.

Ultimately Bush was embarrassed into admitting the obvious fact that Arafat was a "committed terrorist," when the Palestinian Authority, in the midst of waging a terror war on Israel, was caught smuggling in a fifty-ton arsenal of weapons and explosives aboard a freighter.

Bush called on Palestinians to bring to power new "leaders not compromised by terror." Yet the White House insisted on allowing the jihadists of Hamas to field candidates in a 2006 legislative election. In doing so, the administration disregarded the abundant evidence that jihadists were ascendant across the region and within the Palestinian community. Washington shut its eyes to the moral significance of that fact.

The jihadists of Hamas made their name by out-martyring rival factions with suicide bombings, proof of the group's uncompromising commitment to destroying Israel. Hamas won the 2006 election by a landslide. Hamas leaders were now entitled to play a role in controlling the Palestinian Authority.

Lest American dollars reach the blacklisted jihadists, the Bush administration scrambled to "isolate" Hamas financially. Soon, however, Hamas and Fatah (which runs the Palestinian Authority) waged a gangland-style civil war, and they remained at odds for a decade, until the recent "unity" deal.

Like Bush, Obama continued to normalize the Palestinian Authority, despite its ongoing violation of individual rights and incitement of violence. The PA's current "president" Mahmoud Abbas is in the second decade of a four-year term in office. Yet, like Obama, President Trump has hosted Abbas at the White House, granting him the moral status of a reputable political leader.

Now if the "unity" agreement goes through, the two major Palestinian factions, Hamas and Fatah, may reconcile. Thus: A militant authoritarian regime that Washington helped create and bankroll could become honeycombed with jihadists, who've redoubled their commitment to wipe Israel off the map.

That prospect is one more marker of the moral bankruptcy in America's approach. By negating the need for objective moral judgment and acting on it, our policymakers have landed us in a dead-end situation that sells out our ideal of individual freedom and harms our regional ally, Israel.

We need to begin undoing that pattern. For a start: Stop normalizing the Palestinian movement. Stop brushing aside and playing down its crimes and vicious aims. Stop pretending that one faction, Fatah, is somehow well-intentioned—a fact refuted by its murderous, tyrannical history, not to mention its openness to allying with Hamas. Let's recognize that the Palestinian movement is deeply hostile to individual freedom, and treat it accordingly.

* * *

A version of this article originally appeared in *The Hill*.

What Would a Palestinian State Actually Look Like?

Elan Journo May 23, 2018

The Trump administration is poised to announce a "deal of the century" to resolve the Israeli-Palestinian conflict. Hints and leaks suggest that the proposal would stop short of endorsing the goal of a sovereign Palestinian state. That prospect has pushed some into mourning.

The Trump plan, writes William Burns, a distinguished American diplomat, will likely be "a eulogy for the two-state solution." The administration is about to "bury the only viable plan" for Israeli-Palestinian peace.

The goal of a Palestinian state is commonly seen as an obvious good—and the fact that it has yet to be realized, a mark of shame for Israel and the United States. But, whatever the actual terms and merits of Trump's proposal, we need to question the diplomatic article of faith that Palestinian statehood is necessary for peace.

If you care about justice and the rights of individuals—of Palestinians *and* Israelis—here is a crucial question seldom asked. What would such a Palestinian state actually look like?

No need to speculate; there have been four Palestinian quasi-states that provide ample data. In Jordan (1968–1970); in Lebanon (1970–1982); the Palestinian Authority in parts of the West Bank and Gaza (1993 onward); and most recently, the Hamas regime in Gaza (2007 onward).

To the extent the Palestinian movement has gained any semblance of self-rule and territorial control, it has built quasi-states that are militant and dictatorial—much to the detriment of the Palestinian people themselves and the goal of peace.

In Jordan in the late '60s, the Palestinian movement created a mini state with autonomous shadow-government institutions in all spheres—military, political, social. Palestinian factions ran their own police forces and law courts, arresting people and punishing them at will. This authoritarian regime was a base of operations for launching attacks on Israel. A plot to overthrow the Jordanian regime led Jordan to liquidate this militant Palestinian quasi-state.

In 1970s Lebanon, the Palestinian movement established its dominion within refugee camps. It imposed taxes, operated courts, conscripted men of fighting age, and reshaped the school curriculum—to ensure thought control. The Palestinian movement also seized several coastal towns in Lebanon and parts of the Lebanese administration, and "enforced its will with an iron hand." From southern Lebanon, Palestinian fighters launched rockets on Israeli towns. This Palestinian quasi-state fell apart after Israel retaliated by sending forces into Lebanon.

The Palestinian Authority (since 1994) was the fruit of an Israeli-Palestinian peace deal. An interim step toward full sovereignty, the PA enjoys formal recognition and far more autonomy than the previous quasi-states—and it has been correspondingly more oppressive and militant.

The Palestinian Authority quickly became yet another Middle East dictatorship, notorious for controlling the press and silencing opponents. The PA operated multiple, competing security forces. Its courts lacked any semblance of judicial independence. Arbitrary arrests were common, and leaders of the regime expropriated their own people's money and property.

Even with only limited self-rule, the Palestinian Authority provided space and abundant resources to foment and carry out attacks on Israel. In the early 2000s, the regime orchestrated a brutal terror war against Israel.

By 2007, the Palestinian Authority split in two: one quasi-state headed by the Palestinian Liberation Organization (PLO) in parts of the West Bank; and the second run by the jihadists of Hamas in Gaza, a militant regime shaped by Islamic religious law.

Hamas methodically indoctrinates its subjects on TV, in print, on radio, at the mosque, hammering the themes of holy war and martyrdom for the cause. True to their ideas, the jihadists of Gaza have launched thousands of rockets targeting Israeli cities. These led to several wars and many skirmishes—the most recent in early May.

A common denominator among these four Palestinian quasi-states?

Whenever the Palestinian movement has attained a modicum of self-rule over a stretch of territory, it has subjugated its own people and waged war against Israel.

No honest error or inexperience with governance can explain this pattern. It reflects the ideas animating the leading factions of the Palestinian movement. For many years, the movement's spearhead was the PLO. Its numerous factions espoused a mixture of Marxism-Leninism, watered-down socialism, and variations on Arab nationalism. Since the 1980s, Islamists have moved to the vanguard of the Palestinian movement. All these factions are self-consciously hostile to freedom and individual rights.

Some argue we must disregard the evidence of these quasi-states, because they fall short of full sovereignty. We should suspend judgment until a sovereign, independent Palestinian state is realized. That's absurd. Why expect that handing authoritarians and theocrats *more* political power will convert them into champions of individual freedom?

The idea of national self-determination cannot be a license to subjugate. No individual, no group of individuals, no self-identified national community has the moral right to create a tyrannical regime.

Is the Israeli-Palestinian conflict solvable? Actually, yes, as I argue in my book *What Justice Demands*, and a crucial starting point is to fundamentally rethink our past approach to the conflict. Anyone concerned with the fate of individual Palestinians and Israelis who desire freedom and justice must question the lethal premise of the "two-state solution." Handing the Palestinian movement even greater political power is a recipe not for peace, but for continued strife.

* * *

A version of this article originally appeared in the *Jerusalem Post*.

U.S. Exit from UN Human Rights Council Is a Good Start

Elan Journo June 23, 2018

At long last, the United States will leave the UN Human Rights Council—a morally corrupt UN organ that flagrantly betrays the ideal it supposedly upholds. The Human Rights Council is a microcosm of the UN's fundamental moral bankruptcy. Even as we should cheer the decision to step away from it, we must demand even more: a principled commitment to individual rights.

The UN's Human Rights Council is infamous for serving the agenda of authoritarian and dictatorial regimes—while obsessively rebuking one particular free society that actually upholds rights: Israel.

In my book *What Justice Demands: America and the Israeli-Palestinian Conflict*, I note how in the first ten years of its existence, the Human Rights Council passed more resolutions targeting Israel than it has against any other member state, and—by a wide margin—more than the rest of the world combined. More than North Korea, which starves is own people and enslaves them. More than Syria, a dictatorship that has used chemical weapons on its own people. More than Saudi Arabia, a medieval, Islamist monarchy. More than Iran, a theocracy that murders its own people in the streets. By focusing on Israel, the Human Rights Council not only damns a nation that actually respects human rights, it deflects attention from the actual crimes of such tyrannical regimes.

What lends the UN's Human Rights Council a shred of legitimacy is the participation of a few better, freer member nations—principally, the United States. So it's good that the Trump administration has withdrawn.

But the problems of the Human Rights Council reflect the UN's fundamental vice. A defining feature of the UN has been its policy of opening membership non-judgmentally to all nations, whether free or oppressive, peaceful or belligerent. This amoral neutrality is supposed to make evil regimes better. In fact, it enables and abets their violation of individual rights.

UN membership did not prevent the USSR from herding its citizens into forced-labor camps, murdering untold numbers of them, and invading other states. Nor China from crushing under its military boot peaceful ideological dissenters as well as pro-freedom demonstrators at Tiananmen Square. The list goes on.

And the UN has long provided a global stage for dictators and theocrats such as Iran's Hassan Rouhani, Russia's Vladimir Putin and Cuba's Fidel Castro to deliver speeches justifying and laundering their crimes. By elevating such vicious tyrants to the dignity of statesmen, the UN gives them moral cover.

When UN ambassador Nikki Haley announced the U.S. withdrawal from the Rights Council, she said it was "not a retreat from our human rights commitments" but an affirmation of them.

True, it was a good step in the right direction: To be a member of the Human Rights Council is to serve as an accessory to its lies, injustices and crimes. But so too is remaining in the UN. To uphold the ideal of freedom, withdrawal from the UN should be a further goal.

But there's even more the U.S. should do to resolve the contradictions in its foreign policy. It's a longstanding problem that U.S. policy often cozies up to tyrannical regimes, a problem that has escalated with President Trump's effusive comments on a number of authoritarians. Consider that just days before the U.S. withdrawal from the Human Rights Council, Trump praised North Korea's Kim Jong-Un as "very talented" and a leader who "loves his people."

The decision to withdraw from the UN Human Rights Council was correct. But truly to uphold the principle of rights, the U.S. itself needs to take seriously the moral difference between freedom and tyranny. A start would be to recognize the vicious character of the dictators and tyrants whom the UN enables.

* * *

A version of this article originally appeared in *The Hill*.

How 25 Years of Israeli–Palestinian Peacemaking Aggravated the Conflict

Elan Journo September 13, 2018

From the vantage of a quarter-century later, there's a tragic irony in the history-making vibe that marked the signing of the Oslo peace accord between Israel and the Palestinians.

When President Clinton proclaimed the event a "victory for peace," he voiced not empty rhetoric, but many people's fervent expectations. Let us go "from this place to celebrate the dawn of a new era," Clinton said, "not only for the Middle East but for the entire world."

Flanking Clinton on the White House lawn that day, September 13, 1993, were Israeli prime minister Yitzhak Rabin, a decorated war hero, and Yasser Arafat, leader of the Palestinian Liberation Organization and pioneer of international terrorism. Stepping back from the podium, Clinton reached to his left and to his right, and ushered Arafat and Rabin toward each other.

They shook hands.

Applause and cheers punctuated the moment. "The jaded were awed," observed one reporter, noting that "there were a lot of men in the audience crying."

What has been the legacy of this acclaimed venture in peacemaking? Not peace, but worse conflict.

In the years that followed, Palestinian suicide bombers struck buses, coffee shops, pizzerias, discotheques. More than 20,000 rockets from Hamas-controlled Gaza targeted Israeli population centers. Israel has had to retaliate against the Hamas regime in two major wars.

To begin to understand why this peace process aggravated the conflict, consider one crucial factor and its implications: *Fundamentally, the peace process was morally bankrupt.*

It reflected the idea that you can bargain with anyone; the moral character of the adversaries is beside the point. This negation of moral judgment meant disregarding the moral difference between Israel, a basically free society, and the Palestinian movement, a political-ideological force seeking to subjugate people. Under the land-for-peace formula of the peace process, Israel would cede land to the Palestinian movement, for the creation of a future state, and in exchange, the Palestinians would stop their violent attacks. To gain moral credibility as a partner for peace, the Palestinian leadership just had to utter a promise, a promise it constantly flouted.

Evading that reality and its moral significance, the peace process worked to enable the Palestinian movement through the creation of a new quasi-state, the Palestinian Authority. This regime, an interim step toward a fully sovereign state, was granted broad powers within its jurisdiction in areas of the West Bank and Gaza Strip—along with millions of dollars in international aid.

The Palestinian Authority was Arafat's dictatorship. The regime distinguished itself by the pervasive "intimidation of the media and human rights organizations, to the point that it became virtually impossible to transmit any message other than one personally approved by Arafat." It has brutally trampled the rights of its own people and fomented attacks on Israel.

A turning for the worse came in 2006. During George W. Bush's crusade for Mideast democracy, the U.S. demanded elections within the Palestinian Authority—and insisted on allowing the jihadists of Hamas to run candidates. Even more fervently committed to Israel's destruction than rival factions, the jihadists won handily. Soon the Palestinian Authority fractured. Hamas took over the Gaza Strip, making it a quasi-state under Islamic religious law. They began launching rocket attacks. These led to major wars in 2008–09 and 2014. The rockets have continued sporadically. One new tactic: incendiary kites and balloons that set fire to Israeli farmlands.

The Trump administration is planning to launch its own Israeli-Palestinian peace deal. Some of its decisions so far—recognizing Jerusalem as Israel's capital and withholding aid from Palestinians and from the UN's agency for Palestinian refugees—have departed from earlier U.S. policy. It seems the administration is resetting the negotiating terms in preparation for rebooting the failed land-for-peace approach. What's needed instead is a fundamental break with the amoral peace-process mindset.

We need to take seriously the lesson of the last 25 years. It is *because* the peace process negated the principle of moral judgment, that it enabled the Palestinian movement to subjugate, indoctrinate, and impoverish its people while continuing to attack Israel.

And, over time, it empowered the jihadists within the Palestinian movement.

The peace process *did* usher in a "new era in the Middle East," but one that only dictators and jihadists have reason to celebrate. Going forward, we need new, clear-eyed thinking about what justice demands and America's actual stake in the Israeli–Palestinian conflict.

* * *

A version of this article originally appeared at *The Hill*.

Trump's Dangerous, Amoral Loyalty to Saudi Arabia

Elan Journo December 14, 2018

The CIA has concluded that the Saudi crown prince ordered the grisly murder of journalist Jamal Khashoggi. After a closed-door CIA briefing, GOP senators emerged convinced of the Saudi regime's complicity, and the Senate has unanimously voted to hold Mohammed bin Salman responsible for the murder. But, despite the mounting evidence, Donald Trump has remained stalwart in his support of Saudi Arabia and Mohammad bin Salman (a "truly spectacular ally"). Why?

The president and his team insist that "standing with Saudi Arabia" best serves "America first!"—not only to reap a Saudi arms deal but also to counter Iranian influence. But far from being a hard-nosed, grounded-in-the-facts approach, this is a vacuous caricature of pursuing American interests.

To rationally define our interests, it's necessary to look at the Saudi regime and evaluate it by our own standards. But the Trump administration willfully clings to the U.S.-Saudi alliance *in defiance* of the facts and *at the expense* of our ideals.

Let's name the elephant in the room: the Saudi regime deserves to be counted an enemy.

The Khashoggi murder awoke many people to the heinous nature of Saudi Arabia. But it is not just a tyrannical monarchy subjugating its people under the barbaric strictures of Islamist religious rule. It has also been a major financial and intellectual backer of the jihadist cause globally.

Saudi money has paid for the worldwide spread of the regime's own (Wahhabi) strain of Islamic totalitarianism, through Islamist schools, books, mosques. Such proselytizing is a gateway to jihad. Saudis have funded charitable organizations that support jihadist ideologues and groups. Recall that all but four of the 9/11 hijackers were Saudis. And the regime has supported Taliban insurgents in Afghanistan.

Saudi Arabia bears massive responsibility for the global rise of jihadist ideology—a worldview that demands our subjugation and destruction.

That reality is precisely what any rational conception of American interests would have to take seriously. For the Trump administration, however, none of that matters.

Instead, the paramount concern is to preserve the Saudi alliance by trying to make the Khashoggi scandal go away.

Despite the CIA's conclusions, Trump uncritically repeated the denials of despotic monarchs: "King Salman and Crown Prince Mohammad bin Salman vigorously deny any knowledge of the planning or execution of the murder of Mr. Khashoggi." Then Trump echoed the regime's line that Khashoggi was an "enemy of the state" (as if that somehow makes summary execution OK). "Maybe he [the crown prince] did [know], and maybe he didn't!" Hammering on that theme of unresolvable doubt, Trump mused on Fox News, "Will anybody really know?" In other words, he manufactured a fog of doubt and uncertainty, unfocusing his eyes to the facts and urging the rest of us to do the same.

Why is the Trump administration so eager to protect the Saudi alliance? The answer—to secure an arms deal with the Saudis and to counter Iran—lays bare the complete vacuity of Trump's concept of U.S. interests.

Any rational view of our interests would recognize that Iran—*along with* Saudi Arabia—is a wellspring of the jihadist movement. Both Iran and Saudi Arabia are variations on the theme of religious authoritarianism. Both propagate the ideas of Islamic totalitarianism. Both are hostile to our ideals. Our policy toward both should reflect that.

But it does not. The Trump administration points to Iran's backing of jihadists and imperialism in the region (which we do need to confront)—but there's no reckoning with Saudi Arabia's longstanding nourishment of the jihadist cause. We hear Secretary of State Pompeo criticize the persecution of minorities in Iran and the legal requirement that women don a hijab in public in Iran—but he's conspicuously quiet on the *same* vile practices in Saudi Arabia.

To call this hypocrisy is to assume that the Trump administration upholds some standard or principle, but fails to live up to it. Yet the White House has shown a concern neither for facts nor principles.

That amoral mindset lies behind the Trump team's staggeringly myopic goal of strengthening the Saudi regime—by selling them arms and collaborating with them against Iran. No financial "gain" justifies arming a regime whose core ideas and aims are hostile to our own. And the claim that we need Saudi help to counter Iran is implausible. The Saudis have long worked to oppose Iran for their own, partly sectarian, reasons. Let them continue. We should seek to eliminate the menace not only from Iran, but also the Saudi regime.

Behind Trump's stalwart backing of the Saudi alliance is a dangerous idea, often mistaken for nuanced, clear-eyed policy-making. It's the amoral idea that we can define America's interests in the Middle East in defiance of facts and our ideals. But it is a delusion. Far from advancing America's actual interests, it means shutting our eyes to critical facts and laundering enemies.

* * *

A version of this article originally appeared in *The Daily Caller*.

The Sordid US–Saudi Alliance: Betraying Individualism

Elan Journo October 1, 2019

In the chaotic mess that is American Mideast policy, one scandal stands out for its longevity and brazenness. Longevity, because it has festered under both Republican and Democratic administrations. Brazenness, because instead of keeping the problem at a shameful arm's length, many of our political leaders evade its nature and eagerly look for opportunities to whitewash the problem.

I speak of America's amoral alliance with the Islamist monarchy of Saudi Arabia.

When in 2017 President Trump set off on his first foreign trip, he chose Saudi Arabia as stop number one. Like Presidents Obama and Bush before him, Donald Trump bowed before the Saudi king. Hardly a pioneer in cozying up to authoritarian Mideast leaders (the Bush clan were particularly friendly with the Saudi royal family), Trump hailed the U.S.-Saudi relationship, and he emphasized the newly signed deal to sell the Saudis upwards of $100 billion worth of American weapons.

For its part, the Saudi regime is eager to deflect attention from its tyrannical nature. Earlier this year, Saudi Arabia's crown prince, Mohammed bin Salman, visited the United States. The crown prince is next in line for the throne, but he's already essentially running many aspects of the kingdom. In countless interviews, he labored to convince anyone who would listen that he's pushing Saudi Arabia down the path of "reform."

During his U.S. tour, the crown prince received a warm welcome at the White House. President Trump told reporters that he and the 32-year-old crown prince have "become very good friends over a fairly short period of time." Thomas Friedman, a columnist for the *New York Times*, has praised him, with mild caution, for ushering in a new "Arab Spring, Saudi style."

The crown prince has enacted some changes—and promised various others—that deserve note. Among these: Women are now allowed to attend soccer games. The Saudi regime has permitted movie theaters to open their doors again. And, finally, *in the waning*

243

years of the second decade of the twenty-first century, Saudi women are allowed to drive cars.

It's important, albeit shocking, to recognize that these developments *are* indeed advances. And we should welcome these changes, because they lessen—if only ever so slightly—the Saudi regime's oppression of its people. But the fact *that* these are advances is profoundly revealing of the Saudi regime's nature.

To appreciate the perversity of America's approach to Saudi Arabia, take a closer look at the nature of that oppressive regime and some implications of our evasive approach. Our loyalty should lie with those who genuinely seek and fight for greater freedom in Saudi Arabia—the ones that the regime crushes underfoot. But by allying with Saudi Arabia's Islamist monarchy, we betray our own ideal of political freedom and sell out the regime's victims—thus conforming to a wider pattern in America's Mideast policy.

Embracing an Islamist Monarchy

Fundamental to America's approach is a failure to properly evaluate the Saudi regime and take seriously its horrendous character. Saudi Arabia is an absolute monarchy defined by Islamic totalitarianism. It is a political system set up to subjugate.

The Kingdom of Saudi Arabia differs markedly from Europe's few remaining monarchies. For example, there's still a monarch in the United Kingdom, where I grew up, but Queen Elizabeth II is a figurehead. The royal family are a kind of living, breathing tourist attraction. Politically, the British monarchy is a vestige of the country's cruel, barbaric, medieval past. It lingers on at the periphery of what is essentially a free, modern, scientifically advanced society. Not so with Saudi Arabia: although its leaders invest in the trappings of modernity and technology, seeking to present a forward-looking, welcoming face to the outside world, at the core its political system is cruel, barbaric, medieval.

The king of Saudi Arabia *actually runs the country.* Assorted princes serve in ministerial roles and as ambassadors. The present king, Salman, is steps from the grave, so he needed to pick a successor from among the teeming ranks of the royal family. After some actual court intrigues, he picked his son, Mohammad bin Salman, who has effectively taken over. By design, the king's subjects have no say in the direction of the country, no power to select their leader. Regardless of what they believe or judge best for their own country's future, there's no legal way for them to change their government.

The role of Islamic religious law, or sharia, is foundational to the Saudi monarchy. The royal family draws its legitimacy partly from its status as the custodian of two of Islam's holy sites, Mecca and Medina. Islam is not merely one religion that Saudis can choose to live by; to be a Saudi citizen, you have to be a Muslim. Islam is the official state religion, it is funded lavishly, and it is the source of the law.

The regime compels its subjects to obey religious dogma. During the month of Ramadan, for example, when Muslims fast during daylight hours, it's forbidden in Saudi Arabia to eat, drink, or smoke in public. To enforce obedience, the Saudi regime (like Iran) has deployed an actual "morality police" that seeks to prevent vice (e.g., by enforcing bans on alcohol, mingling between unmarried men and women, and worship of religions other than the officially approved strain of Islam) and to promote virtue (e.g., by enforcing the five daily prayer times).

Saudi Arabia's sharia legal system seems calculated to terrorize the population into submission. The law exacts severe, medievalist punishments. For "blasphemers," public flogging. For "adultery"— an endlessly elastic term—a woman can be sentenced to death by stoning. For theft, the criminal's arm will be amputated. For some kinds of robbery, the punishment is "cross amputation": cutting off the thief's right hand and left foot. The Saudi regime beheads criminals in public squares.

Selling Out the Saudi Regime's Victims

Saudi Arabia subjugates all of its people, but a special living hell is reserved for women. The Saudi regime's so-called guardianship laws infantilize women. Women may not leave home without a male chaperone, known as a guardian. The guardian is usually a male relative—a husband, father, brother, even a son. Consider what that looks like day to day: Do you want to go to the bookshop? Meet friends for lunch on your day off? What about getting a job? Or going to university? Getting married? Only if your guardian permits it. To hell with what you want. To hell with what you judge best for your life.

Listen to how a few Saudi women describe life under the "guardianship" laws.

> "My sister went to a bookstore without taking permission from her husband, and when she returned, he beat her up without restraint."
>
> "[My guardian] forbids visits to my female friends or going to shopping malls by myself. It is a complete and total isolation from all the joys in life."
>
> "[My guardian] won't allow me to work, even though I need the money. He also doesn't provide all my needs. I can't recall the last time he cared about what I needed or wanted. He is married to four women and completely preoccupied with them, and he doesn't allow me to travel with my mother. I suffer a lot, even in my social life. He controls it completely and doesn't allow me to have friends over or go to them. He forces me to live according to his beliefs and his religion. I can't show my true self. I live in a lie just so that I wouldn't end up getting killed."
>
> [A 30-year-old medical doctor says] "I've had to give up on a number of educational opportunities because he (my guardian) didn't think a doctor needed a cultural exchange program or a symposium he didn't understand. I've been trying to have him let me marry the man I love for the past two years…. I'm in charge of people's lives every day, but I can't have my own life the way I want."

The subordination of women reflects the Saudi regime's Islamist nature. Two examples underscore the regime's religious totalitarianism. One is the newly lifted ban on women driving; another, the regulations on women's dress and conduct in public.

Why prohibit women from driving? Consider some of the rationalizations. Some Saudi clerics have claimed "it was inappropriate in Saudi culture for women to drive, or that male drivers would not know how to handle having women in cars next to them." Others argued that "allowing women to drive would lead to promiscuity and the collapse of the Saudi family. One cleric claimed—with no evidence—that driving harmed women's ovaries." The leaders of Iran, the Taliban, and the Islamic State (or ISIS) share the same view of women: temptresses who by their mere presence incite men to debauchery, but who are acceptable as vessels for bearing children—so long as they're covered up in public and segregated from men.

This is precisely what the Saudi regime requires of women. In public places, men and women are segregated. In the name of piety and modesty, women are required by law to wear a religious veil. They are also generally expected to wear sack-like black gowns that obscure their figures.

Failure to comply can lead to punishment. When a video clip of a Saudi woman strolling down a street in a miniskirt and crop top made its way online, the police tracked her down and arrested her. The video—and the story of her arrest—went viral. The fact that she was arrested elicited shock and dismay around the world. Perhaps because of that embarrassing media coverage, the Saudi authorities decided to release her without charge.

That incident epitomizes the Saudi regime's distinctive union of religion and monarchy. It captures not only the Islamist zeal to dehumanize women, hide them behind veils, and make them dependent on their "guardians," but also the arbitrariness of a dictatorship, a regime under the rule of men, not laws.

It is *this* deliberate, methodical subjugation—especially of women—in Saudi Arabia that U.S. policymakers should decry, oppose, and hold against the Saudi regime. But, apart from some occasional rhetorical gestures, they look the other way. Instead of standing alongside and speaking out in the name of Saudi Arabia's many victims, American policy sells them out. And it betrays our ideal of freedom—a fact writ large in the story of one Saudi dissident.

Betraying Saudi Dissidents

Let me introduce you to Raif Badawi, 34, a married man with three children. He used to be a writer and blogger. In a society with pervasive censorship and thought control, his choice simply to express his ideas required immense courage. Lately, I read a short book of Badawi's collected articles and blog posts. Encountering a writer with the views he holds was not only bracing, but it was also a moving experience—mainly because I know what he's suffering today because of his writings.

If his articles had been published in, say, the *New York Times* or the *Wall Street Journal* or Vox.com or *National Review*, they would fit within the bounds of public discourse, standing out, perhaps, mainly for their frankness. But in Saudi Arabia, they were explosive.

For Badawi, "Freedom of speech is the air that any thinker breathes; it's the fuel that ignites the fire of an intellectual's thoughts"—true indeed, but a forbidden thought in Saudi Arabia. "Throughout the past centuries," he went on, "nations and societies advanced through the work of their intellectuals, who present their ideas and philosophies. The people, thereafter, can pick from that pool of viewpoints whichever intellectual style suits them; they can even develop it to reach the deep seas of knowledge, progress, civilization, and prosperity." True, but yet another forbidden thought.[51]

What's holding back Saudi Arabia, Badawi argued, is the saturation of life with religion. Incisively, he observed that

> [a]ny religion-based state has a mission to limit the minds of its people, to fight the developments of history and logic, and to dumb down its citizens. It's important to stand in the way of such a mentality, to deny it from continuing its mission to murder the souls of its people, killing them deep within while they are still alive and breathing.[52]

He saw this happening not only under the Islamists, notably Hamas in the Palestinian territories, but particularly in his home country. The "religious philosophy controlling our lives in Saudi Arabia is fighting a daily war to plant and impose the lines of Salafi religious ruling, which was forced upon us hundreds of years ago."[53]

To drive home his point, he wrote that if Hamas were ever to "liberate Palestine" by wiping Israel off the map, he would be "the first person to stand and fight Hamas." It's not because he reveres Israel (in fact, he doesn't); it's because he opposes "replacing Israel with a religious entity built on its ruins. Such a state [under the Islamists of Hamas] would only seek to spread a culture of ignorance and death within its people."[54]

What he championed were "secularism" and "liberalism." He explained: "Secularism respects everyone and does not offend anyone.... Secularism...is the practical solution to lift countries (including ours) out of the third world and into the first world," and, "For me, liberalism simply means, live and let live." Elaborating in another article, he noted that a "political system that takes liberalism as its guidance is an optimistic regime that believes in the ability of human unity to establish advancement through dialogue and to learn from its mistakes by repeated experimentation."[55]

The premise underlying such a political system is that human beings are "mature enough and capable of making [their] own decisions and deciding [their own] future without external guardianship."[56] It is a premise not merely absent but opposed in Saudi Arabia. Moreover, Badawi objected to the infantilization of women and called for them to be treated as equals of men, thus striking at one more Saudi taboo.

In his book, Badawi explains his motives: "I wanted to break the walls of ignorance, to shatter the sacredness of religious clerics. I wanted to advocate for change and respect for freedom of speech, to call for women's and minorities' rights, and the rights of the indigent in Saudi Arabia."[57]

Bear in mind that Badawi's arguments often invoke Koranic verses to justify his viewpoint. This indicates a degree of respect for Islam. The salient theme of his essays is the call to separate religion and state in Saudi Arabia. That's different from demanding that everyone repudiate Islam (though some might do so, if the regime somehow stopped indoctrinating its citizens and punishing impiety). I stress this point, because it's material to the accusation leveled against Badawi.

"1000 Lashes Because I Say What I Think"

For expressing his own views of what society should look like, for voicing criticisms of the Saudi regime, Raif Badawi was accused of "apostasy." This is the crime of consciously abandoning the religion of Islam. In Saudi Arabia, it carries the death penalty. Raif Badawi faced a death sentence. He narrowly avoided that fate. His reduced sentence?

Ten years imprisonment.

One million Saudi riyals (about $250,000).

And 1,000 lashes.

The punishment was calculated to shut down dissident voices, intimidating into silence anyone else who might dare speak out.

If he withstands the lashes, if he survives jail time among "killers, thieves, drug lords, and pedophiles," the crushing financial penalty threatens to pauperize him and his family. (The book of his writings, which I mentioned earlier, is titled *1000 Lashes: Because*

I Say What I Think, and it's a means of raising funds to support his family.)

Badawi has been confined to a filthy prison cell since 2012. The first installment of his 1,000 lashes was inflicted in January 2015. In front of a mosque in the city of Jedda, Badawi was given fifty lashes for the crime of "insulting Islam." That first flogging triggered an international outcry, and a medical doctor concluded that Badawi likely could not withstand further lashings. The remaining lashes have been postponed several times. Coincidentally, within a few days of Badawi's flogging, thousands of miles away in Paris, three self-identified jihadists massacred the editorial staff of the magazine *Charlie Hebdo*—for the same crime: "insulting Islam."

This parallel is a reminder that the Saudi regime shares essentially the same worldview—a totalitarian society shaped by Islamic law—that animates the Islamist movement across the globe, a movement the Saudis have encouraged and funded. It's crucial to understand that the prosecution, sentencing, and punishment of Badawi was no miscarriage of the Saudi legal system. On the contrary. This is what it looks like when the system *works*.

Because of the "many pressures placed upon them," Badawi writes, his wife and three children were forced to emigrate from Saudi Arabia.[58] They now live in Canada. His wife, Ensaf, actively campaigns for her husband's release in the media, in the halls of parliament buildings around the world, and through the Raif Badawi Foundation. Badawi's remaining hope is that he might be granted a pardon by royal decree.

A Wider Pattern of Ignoring What Justice Demands

Badawi is precisely the kind of freedom-seeking dissident who deserves our moral support. And yet when President Trump visited the Kingdom of Saudi Arabia in 2017, he uttered no criticism of the Saudi regime's subjugation of individuals. Not a word about the fate of any dissidents or political prisoners, many of whom face execution under a legal system that flouts the principle of rule of law. Not a word about the pervasive infantilization of women. Not a word about the abhorrent treatment of Raif Badawi. None.

The failure meaningfully to speak out for freedom and freedom-seekers is no oversight. Nor was Donald Trump the first president to evade the Saudi regime's fundamental hostility to human life and freedom. The president conformed to a wider pattern in American Mideast policy.

There's a through line in America's approach not only toward the Saudi regime, but to the entire Middle East. In various ways, our approach disregards the need for objective judgment. That's a crucial point that I illustrate in my new book, *What Justice Demands: America and the Israeli-Palestinian Conflict*. One of the chief problems of America's approach to that conflict is the failure properly to judge the adversaries by our own moral standards and define a policy that aligns with our evaluations. What's missing from our entire approach to the Israeli-Palestinian conflict—to Saudi Arabia, to the entire Middle East—is recognition of the fundamental moral distinction between freedom and tyranny. We should use the principle of freedom to guide our evaluation of regimes, movements, developments.

To do that would mean that we uphold freedom and individual rights consistently across time, in every situation—rather than haphazardly, or only when it suits us, or only in some cases. In reality, however, America's approach is haphazard, unprincipled, at times amoral.

For example, U.S. policy for years has blurred the stark moral inequality between Israel—an essentially free society—and the Palestinian movement and its anti-Israel allies. We turn a blind eye to the character of the Palestinian movement, with its commitment to authoritarianism and war-making against Israel, on the notion that whitewashing it can somehow hasten peace. By doing so, we sell out a free society, Israel, and the genuine freedom-seekers (however few remain) among the Palestinian community.

The same pattern can be traced in our approach to the Middle East. Our political leaders not only disregard the moral difference between freedom and tyranny, they sell it short. Instead of denouncing, ostracizing and shunning the region's monarchs, dictators, authoritarians and theocrats, we cozy up to them and grasp at any opportunity to see them as latent or actual "reformers"— whatever might rinse off the blood stains.

For example: Prior to the outbreak of civil war in Syria, American diplomats sought to befriend Bashir al-Assad, who was then supposedly committed to reforms, and we actually re-opened the American embassy in that country. Yes, *that* Assad, the one who was always a brutal dictator and who's now infamous for deploying chemical weapons against his own people.

Or consider the Obama administration's pursuit of a nuclear deal with Iran. Whatever you think of that now-defunct agreement, the diplomatic initiative to reach the deal was predicated on evading both Iran's nature as a leading jihadist regime and its vicious subjugation of its own people. Those facts, amply documented in State Department reports for years, were put aside, and Iran was treated as a legitimate, civilized regime.

The shameful U.S.–Saudi alliance is one more case in point. We turn a blind eye to the character of the Saudi regime, with its commitment to religious tyranny. Which explains some of the motivation behind the adulation heaped upon the Saudi crown prince.

It's true, as we've seen, that he has enacted several notable changes, including the reopening of movie theaters (subject to government censors) and the lifting of the ban on women driving. Some of these changes promise to have a positive impact on the lives of Saudi people. Despite his stated aim of remaking the country's future, however, notice what's taken as unchangeable—the centrality of Islamic law—and what's conspicuously absent—intellectual freedom, the freedom of speech, the rule of law.

Indeed, the crown prince himself, the celebrated "reformer," has exercised the same authoritarian powers that characterized other Saudi monarchs. Last November, apparently as part of the machinations to solidify his hold on power, he lured hundreds of businessmen, many of them members of the royal family, and imprisoned them at a Ritz Carlton hotel in the capital, Riyadh, in what the regime called an anti-corruption campaign.

> Most have since been released but they are hardly free. Instead, this large sector of Saudi Arabia's movers and shakers are living in fear and uncertainty.
>
> During months of captivity, many were subject to coercion and physical abuse, witnesses said. In the early days of the crackdown, at least 17 detainees were hospitalized for physical abuse and one later died in custody with a neck that appeared twisted, a badly swollen body and other signs of abuse, according to a person who saw the body.... Many were prevented from contacting their lawyers, but Prince Alwaleed spoke weekly with some of his managers, his associates said. He remained out of public sight until January, when the royal court allowed a journalist from Reuters to interview him in

the Ritz to counter a BBC report that he was being kept in a cell-like room.

To all appearances, the prince was seeking to neutralize rivals and strip them of their wealth. Perhaps the most alarming aspect of this incident was the government's insistence that the investigations of these captives was carried out "in full accordance to Saudi laws." To the extent that this is true, it's a stark reminder of the regime's profound authoritarianism.

In other crackdowns, the regime has arrested a number of dissidents and activists. One sweep took place just weeks before the lifting of the ban on women driving, and among those detained and held incommunicado were several activists who had long campaigned against the driving ban. Recently, Samar Badawi, the sister of Raif, and another rights activist were detained. And in the case of another activist, Israa al-Ghomgham, arrested for nonviolent protest, the regime has called for the death penalty.

The eagerness to embrace the crown prince as a reformer suggests a sordid motive: making him and his regime appear better than they are. Doing so cannot alter the facts, and it makes us accessories to the injustices committed against Raif Badawi—and other freedom-seekers like him.

To begin to understand why America's Mideast policy is such a deplorable mess, I argue in my book, look at the pervasive failure to engage in moral judgment of regimes and movements. If we are to properly define and attain our interests in the region, and if that part of the world is to reach a brighter future of freedom and progress, one step is indispensable. We need to recognize the fundamental moral divide between freedom and tyranny. We should uphold the ideal of freedom and lend our moral support to genuine freedom-seekers—and stand against the region's tyrants, dictators and theocrats.

Presidential Candidates—and Trump —Are Wrong About Iraq

Elan Journo November 1, 2019

On the 2020 campaign trail, opposition toward the Iraq war has become a litmus test of moral stature. Witness Elizabeth Warren (who "never believed what Cheney and Bush said about Iraq") signaling her virtue and shaming Joe Biden (and Trump), who supported it. And Trump denies he was ever for it. The common, underlying assumption is that not only the rise of ISIS, but so much of the Middle East's chaos is ultimately rooted in the 2003 U.S. invasion of Iraq.

The Iraq war was a debacle that sacrificed thousands of American lives and sowed chaos. But is it *fundamental* to understanding, and responding to, the threats emanating from the Middle East?

No.

Look, instead, at America's initial encounters with the ascendant Islamist movement. The first happened forty years ago this week.

Decades before ISIS made headlines, Iran's 1979 Islamic revolution created a totalitarian society defined by Allah's law. The cleric Ayatollah Khomeini vowed that the revolution cannot be limited only to Iran's borders; it must be spread by force—through jihad—everywhere. Amid that revolutionary tumult, on November 4, 1979, Khomeini loyalists stormed the U.S. Embassy in Tehran, seizing the compound and taking American diplomats and guards hostage. The hostages endured a living hell. They were, by turns, beaten, paraded on television, terrorized with mock executions. This was not merely a humiliation for Washington. It was an act of war.

How did Washington respond to this outrage? Did it recognize the ideological threat Iran embodied? Did the U.S. immediately threaten (if necessary) to deploy retaliatory military force to free its citizens?

The response from Washington was foreshadowed by orders given to the American guards on the day of the embassy takeover.

254

Facing the invading militants, the guards were instructed not to fire their weapons—lest they anger the mob. Such reluctance to stand up to aggression pervaded the response of Jimmy Carter's administration, which committed to a path of appeasement (late in the game, there was a military rescue mission, but it was an embarrassing failure). After 444 days of captivity, the 52 American hostages were finally released.

How? Only after Washington essentially paid a ransom. By condescending to negotiate with Iran at all, Washington conferred on it the undeserved status of a civilized, moral equal.

Speaking of the hostage crisis, Ayatollah Khomeini famously observed that America cannot do a damn thing. Iran was an inspiration for Islamists everywhere.

Washington's policy in the Iran hostage crisis fit a haphazard pattern of evasion, appeasement, and sporadic half-measures. It was a license and invitation to further Islamist aggression.

In 1983, Islamists struck American targets in Beirut, Lebanon, first at the U.S. Embassy (17 dead) and, later, a barracks housing Marines, serving as peace keepers (241 dead). Iran had a major role in these attacks, but conspicuously missing from Washington's response was an explicit recognition of Iran's culpability. Having fired off a few inconsequential shells at terrorist camps, President Ronald Reagan ordered a "re-deployment" of American forces— essentially a retreat that fulfilled the wishes of the Islamists.

Looking back on that retreat, Osama bin Laden took the lesson—and taught his followers—that America was a paper tiger.

Following 9/11, George W. Bush fundamentally evaded Iran's centrality to the Islamist movement. Bush went after Saddam Hussein's Iraq—a regime at most peripheral to the Islamist movement. The Iraq war was the centerpiece of the Bush administration's "democracy crusade," which empowered Islamists in Iraq, Lebanon, Egypt, the Palestinian Territories, and elsewhere.

And, without deliberate irony, Bush invited Iran (the leading state sponsor of terrorism, according to the State Department) to join a post-9/11 coalition against "terrorism." Bush temporarily tagged Tehran as part of an "axis of evil" before rapidly dropping that phrase, and spending the waning years of his administration coaxing the Iranians to the negotiating table.

It was Barack Obama who managed that diplomatic "feat," in the 2015 Iran nuclear deal, which served to entrench Iran's theocratic regime. Donald Trump walked out on the Iran nuclear deal, but he apparently imagines himself able to broker a better deal—as if the Islamist regime in Tehran can be counted on to abide by any diplomatic agreement.

The underlying problem is the persistent U.S. failure to understand and confront the ascendant Islamist movement, which Iran has spearheaded since 1979. That failure has fueled a spiral of Islamist aggression far beyond the Middle East. Absent that pattern, al-Qaeda would have never felt emboldened to strike; nor would the Islamic State. Nor would Iran have come to exert massive influence in Lebanon, Syria, Iraq, Yemen, and across the region, while seeking nuclear capability.

Which makes the posturing about the Iraq war on the 2020 campaign trail such a disgraceful spectacle. Everyone who supported the war, everyone who changed their minds, *and* everyone who originally opposed it: they're all wrong. Iraq was never the fundamental issue. The Iran-led ascent of the Islamist movement was. It still is.

Unless we grasp that, and change course, there's no hope that whoever sits in the Oval Office, whether Republican or Democrat, can define a sensible foreign policy in the Middle East.

* * *

A version of this article originally appeared in *The Daily Caller.*

Why Did the Saudis Expect to Get Away with Murder?

Elan Journo May 12, 2021

The victim was lured to his death on a seemingly innocuous pretext, relating to paperwork for a marriage license. The killing was straight out of a horror movie. The body was butchered into pieces, with a bone saw, so it could be disposed of without a trace. This was the fate of Jamal Khashoggi, a Saudi journalist and activist, employed by the *Washington Post*. The murder set off a global scandal. Who killed him? and why?

These are questions that a new documentary, *The Dissident*, helps us answer. It vividly tells the story of what happened to Khashoggi that day in October 2018 when he was put to death inside the Saudi consulate in Istanbul. The documentary prompts us to weigh a related issue that provoked so much of the outrage at the time of the scandal: why did the Saudi rulers believe they could literally get away with murder?

A Dictatorship's M.O.

The film presents compelling evidence that indicts the Saudi regime, all the way up to the crown prince. Often referred to as MBS, Mohammed bin Salman is a millennial, self-declared "reformer," and the country's de facto ruler. A number of Khashoggi's killers belonged to an elite force that reports directly to MBS, who has absolute control over the country's security and intelligence organizations. The agents, including an autopsy doctor and a forensics expert, came to Turkey aboard a private jet with diplomatic clearances, and eight of the 15 men held diplomatic passports.

Although there has been speculation that their mission was merely to abduct him back to Saudi Arabia, *The Dissident* suggests otherwise. In an audio recording of the killers as they awaited Khashoggi's arrival at the consulate, they discuss how his body would be dismembered and disposed of. We hear one of them ask if the "sacrificial animal" had arrived yet.

The documentary puts the Khashoggi scandal in the wider context of how the Saudi regime deals with dissidents and critics.

We meet one of Khashoggi's friends, Omar, a young Saudi activist self-exiled in Canada. To coerce Omar into shutting up, Saudi agents tried to lure him to a local consulate. They tried to intimidate him. Later, they rounded up and imprisoned 23 of his friends in Saudi Arabia. Then they exploited his family as leverage, detaining and severely torturing his brother. Elements of Saudi Arabia's m.o. were evident in the Khashoggi case.

Insider-Turned-Critic

Khashoggi was lured to the consulate in Istanbul, because he needed some paperwork so he could re-marry. We hear from his bereft fiancée about the life they had planned together. To most people Khashoggi is known only from headlines about his grisly death, and the filmmakers take pains to humanize the man, although at times this aim is over-emphasized. But what we learn about Khashoggi's views, particularly his criticisms of the regime, casts the murder in an even worse light, if that's possible.

Khashoggi used to be an insider at the Saudi court, and at first he supported the "reform" agenda launched by Mohammed bin Salman, which promised to uproot corruption and somewhat modernize the kingdom's society (MBS, for instance, finally granted women permission to drive a car in 2018[!]). But Khashoggi became increasingly critical of some features of MBS's rule.

There's no freedom of speech in Saudi Arabia, but to the extent there are voices questioning the royal family's rule, however gently, MBS had them crushed. The regime muzzled assorted "thought leaders" active on Twitter. Moreover, in a notorious purge-cum-shakedown operation, MBS rounded up hundreds of prominent Saudis, including rivals within the royal family, and held them captive at a Ritz-Carlton, until they coughed up millions of dollars. A number were hospitalized with signs of physical abuse.

Khashoggi's wish was to see some approximation of freedom of speech. We're not asking for democracy, he said in an Al Jazeera TV interview, only that people be allowed to speak.

One of his friends suggests that Khashoggi was naïve, never fully grasping the evil of the regime, which views its people like slaves or serfs. We can surmise some of what this friend had in mind; there's strong reason to believe that MBS wanted to be seen as involved in the murder, because that would intimidate other critics and dissidents.

An International Furor

When the truth about Khashoggi's murder came out, the Western reaction was outrage. The outrage focused particularly on the brazenness of the Saudi regime, and later, on the regime's lies about Khashoggi's disappearance (among the lies: he suffocated accidentally; he died in a fistfight). It was as if the Saudis fully expected to kill him without consequences, much less an international furor.

Why? *The Dissident* provides a lead to the answer when it briefly looks at the global reactions.

In this illuminating, but underdeveloped part of the film, assorted politicians decry the Saudi regime's conduct. An outlier was President Trump. Initially, Trump expressed doubts about the allegations of Saudi involvement, even echoing a Saudi talking point that the killing was a "rogue" operation. Trump evaded the CIA's report implicating the regime. The Saudis were spending billions of dollars on weapons, and Trump refused to jeopardize that by facing the truth.

Trump's approach was dismaying for another reason. In at least one respect, the Khashoggi case was different from the untold number of dissidents who languish in Saudi jails or perish in its torture chambers. Khashoggi worked for an American company, the *Washington Post*, and was a resident of the United States. This should have factored into the U.S. response, but it did not. When Congress passed legislation to block arms sales to Saudi Arabia, Trump vetoed it, and refused to make the CIA's report public.

Trump's loyalty to Saudi Arabia and MBS (a "truly spectacular ally") stood out, but with time it became a perverse norm. Although the Khashoggi murder led to some international fallout for Saudi Arabia, that soon faded. Initially, the scandal scared away investors from a major conference (likened to "Davos in the desert") that MBS was to host in Saudi Arabia. Several major corporations withdrew from the event. But one year later, they were back. Moreover, no global sanctions or punishments were meted out against Saudi Arabia. *The Dissident* ends by leaving us to ponder this dismal fact.

One implication to draw from the film is that the Saudi regime believed it could count on Western regimes to compromise whatever moral principles they mouthed.

It was not wrong.

For decades, the U.S. and other countries have refused to confront the nature of the Saudi regime. They evade how the regime tyrannizes its people under the barbarous rules of Islamic religious law and how it funnels uncountable dollars to fuel and proselytize for the Islamist cause. Saudi lucre has underwritten schools, books, charities, and mosques that spread the Wahhabi strain of Islamic totalitarianism around the world.

Despite its significant responsibility for enabling the jihadist movement, after 9/11 Washington perpetuated the fiction that the Saudi regime was a friend. Although it was known that all but four of the 9/11 hijackers were Saudis, President George W. Bush hosted the Saudi ruler at his ranch in Crawford, Texas. The amity continued under President Barack Obama, who met the Saudi king four times (more than did Bush and Clinton combined). In a highly symbolic decision, Donald Trump's first foreign trip as president began in Saudi Arabia. And a mere six months before the Khashoggi scandal, Trump had warmly welcomed MBS to the White House, gushing that he and the crown prince had "become very good friends over a fairly short period of time."

If past U.S. appeasement led the Saudi regime to expect impunity, since the release of *The Dissident* the incoming Biden administration has provided further warrant for that assumption.

The Sordid U.S.–Saudi Relationship

When running for president, Joe Biden vowed to put the ideal of rights at the forefront of his foreign policy. He criticized the Saudi regime harshly—at least, "harshly" by the precious, offend-nobody rules of diplomacy-speak. He called the regime a "pariah" with "very little social redeeming value," promising to make it "pay the price" for the Khashoggi murder. In February, the Biden administration released a summary of the CIA's findings that Trump had buried, implicating the crown prince in the murder.

What did the Biden administration do? Speak out boldly in defense of the ideal of individual rights? Exert real pressure on the regime to respect rights? Forbid MBS from entering the United States? Expel the Saudi ambassador to Washington?

No, none of that. Instead it decided "not to rupture the [U.S.-Saudi] relationship but to recalibrate it." The administration announced the "Khashoggi ban": a visa restriction "on individuals who, acting on behalf of a foreign government, are believed to have been directly engaged in serious, extraterritorial counter-dissident activities." Under this policy, 76 Saudi citizens will be banned.

Why such a pitiful response? What happened to making the regime "pay the price"? The relationship with Saudi Arabia, explained Secretary of State Anthony Blinken, "is bigger than any one individual."

The de facto leader of the Saudi dictatorship orchestrated the murder of a dissident, a writer with ties to the United States, and nevertheless, the United States gave MBS a free pass. Part of what's so shameful about this outcome is that it fits the longstanding pattern of Washington's evasion of the monstrous nature of the Saudi regime.

If the Saudi regime believed it could murder and get away with it, that's because it had long ago come to rely on the unprincipled foreign policy and cowardice of Western—and particularly American—leaders who turn a blind eye to its murderous, tyrannical rule.

PART 7

The Distinctiveness of an Objectivist Approach to Foreign Policy

Winning the Unwinnable War (2009), edited by Elan Journo, discusses in-depth what an Objectivist approach to foreign policy would look like and how it could enable the U.S. to end the Islamist menace. The final part of the book illustrates the distinctiveness of that approach.

In 2012 Rep. Paul Ryan, a self-described fan of *Atlas Shrugged*, joined the GOP ticket as Mitt Romney's vice presidential pick. "Paul Ryan, Ayn Rand, and U.S. Foreign Policy" considers whether his views on foreign policy actually bear the mark of Rand's influence.

When Donald Trump took office, he appointed several avowed fans of *Atlas Shrugged* to his initial cabinet. The essay "How Much Ayn Rand Is There in Trump's 'America First' Foreign Policy?" evaluates the claim that in Trump's approach one can detect "an unintended reincarnation of Ayn Rand."

The final essay, "What Should a Distinctively American Foreign Policy Do?" (completed before the Trump administration's arrival), indicates key elements of a principled approach to foreign policy and draws contrasts with American policy from Bush to Obama.

Paul Ryan, Ayn Rand, and U.S. Foreign Policy

Elan Journo October 2012

Vice-presidential candidate Paul Ryan has credited philosopher Ayn Rand with inspiring him to enter politics—and made her 1,000-plus-page magnum opus, *Atlas Shrugged*, required reading for his staff. "The reason I got involved in public service, by and large, if I had to credit one thinker, one person, it would be Ayn Rand," he said in 2005 at a gathering of Rand fans. "The fight we are in here, make no mistake about it, is a fight of individualism versus collectivism." It is a theme that pervades Rand's corpus.[59] While Ryan has distanced himself from Rand's philosophy of Objectivism, he continues to express admiration for *Atlas Shrugged*.

The addition of the Wisconsin congressman to the GOP ticket naturally unleashed a flash-mob of analysts parsing his speeches, articles and signature proposals for evidence of her influence. On domestic policy, the impact[60] of Rand's ideas[61] on Ryan's outlook[62] is marked, though uneven and sometimes overstated. Religion, in particular, has driven a wedge between Ryan, who would enact Catholic dogma into law,[63] and Rand, an atheist, who championed the separation of church and state. But what has received far less attention is Ryan's outlook on foreign policy—and whether it bears the mark of Rand's thought.

Ayn Rand's foreign policy, if we can construct one from her writings, would be grounded in her view of man's rights and the nature of government.[64] Like the Founding Fathers, Rand argues that the ideal government is the servant, not the master, of the individual. In her view, it is a vital institution strictly limited to one function: to safeguard individual rights. By "rights," Rand means freedom to take "all the actions required by the nature of a rational being for the support, the furtherance, the fulfillment and the enjoyment of his own life." Critically, the protection of an individual's rights "does not mean that others must provide him with the necessities of life."[65]

Domestically, this outlook entails a truly free market[66] with absolute legal protection of private property, and without

265

regulations, bailouts, corporate handouts or entitlement programs like Social Security, Medicaid and Medicare. (Ryan breaks with Rand by attempting to save, rather than end these programs.) In Rand's political philosophy, however, there is no gulf between economic rights and personal and intellectual ones: for instance, she wrote passionately of the crucial importance (contra Ryan) of the right to abortion,[67] and regarded freedom of speech[68] as sacrosanct.

Like her views on domestic policy, a Randian foreign policy would be guided exclusively by the goal of protecting the individual rights of Americans, and only Americans. Accordingly, the U.S. government shouldn't issue handouts to other countries (through foreign aid or international welfare schemes), nor treat its citizens as cannon fodder (through a military draft). Indeed, Rand was scathing in her analyses of the Vietnam War, arguing that it did not serve America's national interest. "[I]t is a pure instance of blind, senseless altruistic self-sacrificial slaughter," she wrote in *Capitalism: The Unknown Ideal.*[69]

Of course, there are times when government is obligated to go to war, according to Rand. The crucial standard here is whether the lives and property of Americans are imperiled. The only morally justifiable purpose for war, she wrote, is self-defense. This rules out so-called humanitarian missions, like the tragic 1992–93 mission in Somalia, and the notion that the United States is somehow obliged to serve as the world's policeman. The primary function of the military, in Rand's eyes, should be to deter and, when necessary, defeat foreign aggressors.

Rand regarded any form of pacifism[70] (including Ron Paul-esque passivity) as destructive to national defense. And undoubtedly she would have supported a strong military response to the 9/11 attacks (though, as I have argued in my book,[71] and sketch out below, she would have rejected George W. Bush's conception of the enemy and his entire prosecution of the war).

Rand viewed deterrence as an especially important—and effective—method of defending American freedom. In her view, the power of a morally confident, assertive United States was considerable, though largely unappreciated. For instance, she believed that if the West had truly stood up to the Soviet bloc by withdrawing its moral sanction, ending the flow of aid, and imposing an airtight boycott, the Soviet threat would have disintegrated many years before it actually did, without the need for war.

Perhaps most importantly, Rand argued in favor of genuine free trade—without trade barriers, protective tariffs or special privileges. In her words: "the opening of the world's trade routes to free international trade and competition among the private citizens of all countries dealing directly with one another." In the nineteenth century, she argued, free trade liberated the world by "undercutting and wrecking the remnants of feudalism and the statist tyranny of absolute monarchies." Not coincidentally, she observed, this era enjoyed the longest period of general peace in human history (roughly from 1815 to 1914).[72]

Taken together, Rand's approach entails a foreign policy based on the morality of "rational self-interest." To illustrate what that would look like, let us bring Rand's approach to bear on several of today's major foreign policy issues, starting with Iran.

Tehran is a leader of the Islamist movement, the cause animating al-Qaeda, the Taliban, the Muslim Brotherhood and kindred groups. Iran has inspired and funded jihadist terrorism and cast itself as an embodiment of the movement's political ideal. It's a regime that tramples on the rights of its own citizens. It ambitiously seeks to kill and subjugate beyond its borders, and, owing to its jihadist ideology, is vociferously anti-American. From Washington's capitulation in the hostage crisis of 1979–80, the regime concluded that it could get away with committing an act of war against America. Rand noted at the time that because we failed to march in with force within days after the hostage taking, the repercussions would be severe.

Since then U.S. policymakers, in effect, rewarded Iran's aggression with bribes and conciliation, and thereby encouraged a spiral of further Iranian-backed attacks.[73] Witness the Hezbollah hijacking of a TWA airliner; the kidnapping and torture of Americans in Lebanon; the 1983 bombings of the U.S. Embassy in Beirut and, later, the barracks of U.S. Marines, killing 241 Americans. The 9/11 Commission linked[74] Tehran to at least eight of the suicide hijackers. Later, Iranian forces trained and armed Iraqi and Afghan insurgents,[75] who murdered U.S. troops. Considering the U.S. failure to recognize the Iranian regime's character and goals, and assertively end its aggression, Tehran's defiance over its nuclear program should hardly surprise.

We are at war with Iran, but only that country knows it; in the name of self-defense, the U.S. government is morally obliged to eliminate this enemy. A military option is a non-starter, however, in the shadow of the Iraq and Afghanistan failures (more on those in a moment). But even when we have the opportunity to morally support the Iranian people in attempting to remove from power a regime hostile to the freedom of Americans and Iranians alike, as we did with the Green Movement, which arose after the 2009 elections, we refuse to do so. The reputedly crippling sanctions now in place are of course a forlorn hope, especially considering the large-enough-to-drive-a-truck-through exemptions[76] that have already been granted.

Part of what has magnified the tragedy of 9/11 is the failure of policymakers to properly identify and vigorously pursue the enemy that attacked us. It was not simply the hijackers' al-Qaeda cell, but the jihadist movement, spearheaded by Tehran and bankrolled by Saudi wealth, which had been waging attacks against us for years. In my book, *Winning the Unwinnable War*,[77] I discuss the nature and malignant goal of that movement, and explore what went wrong in the U.S. response, particularly the policy fiascos in Iraq and Afghanistan.

The goal uniting these two wars was Bush's messianic policy of "nation building" and bringing the vote to the oppressed and needy of the Middle East. Clearing out sewage pipes, fixing up hospitals, printing textbooks—these welfare and social services projects may be the province of the Peace Corps, but not the Army Corps, nor is it right to risk the lives of American soldiers for the sake of the world's needy. Just as Rand decried Vietnam as a selfless, purposeless war, so that same criticism applies, as strongly, in Iraq. Much of what went wrong in Iraq and Afghanistan stemmed from a policy of putting an altruistic welfare agenda first, above the self-interested goal of eliminating whatever threat we faced in those countries.

Tragically, despite its unparalleled military strength, the United States mired itself, needlessly, in no-win wars. Baghdad is now under Tehran's sway.[78] The continuing strife in Iraq, marked by only occasional suicide bombings,[79] is a testament to how the notion of success has been progressively defined down. In Afghanistan there are no longer good options. A minimum step toward the right policy—one with a modicum of justice to the now 2,000 American who perished there—is to properly redefine the mission from perpetual "nation building" to expunging the Taliban and allied Islamist forces in Afghanistan and the Pakistani borderlands.

One recent bright spot, seemingly, was the Arab Spring. But the upheavals across the Middle East, it turned out, shared only superficial similarities. One trend that did emerge, though, was the ascendance, notably in Egypt and Tunisia, of political parties sympathetic to or fully embracing Islamist goals. Here, then, is the consummation of Bush's "nation-building" democracy crusade. We now must contend with the emerging threat of an Egypt dominated by Islamists—a regime that our diplomats have been falling over themselves to encourage. At minimum we should refuse to endorse the regime (even though popularly elected) and even shun it.[80] To embrace it is to lend the regime an undeserved legitimacy; if any genuinely freedom-seeking Egyptians remain, would they feel anything but demoralized at the spectacle?[81]

U.S. policy has galvanized one group: Islamists. Further evidence of that came on September 11, 2012, in the form of the conspicuously timed attacks on our embassies in Cairo and Benghazi.

Storming the sovereign territory of the world's militarily strongest nation requires considerable temerity. Islamists in Egypt, however, thought nothing of attempting to invade the mission in Cairo and hoisting their flag. In Libya, in what looks like a meticulously calculated assault, the self-professed soldiers of Allah managed to murder the U.S. ambassador and three other Americans. The uproar and riots across the region, putatively in reaction to a YouTube video critical of Islam, brought to the surface (yet again) the assertiveness of those who seek obedience to religious dogma and revile the free mind and the individual's freedom of speech. What inspires not fear but contempt in the hearts of our Islamist enemies is the meekness of American foreign policy across decades.[82]

Meshing with that broad pattern, the Obama administration's response to the embassy crisis was deplorable. It's hard to imagine a more self-abasing reaction than to have the Cairo embassy apologize to the raging mob, while disparaging free speech. Nor can anyone take our government's commitment to freedom of speech seriously when it tries to lean on YouTube to take down the video, and rather than committing to protect the safety of the man behind the film, gives him a perp walk. Compared with that, the Romney-Ryan response was better: Yes, America has projected weakness; yes, Washington has undercut real allies, for example, by seeking to distance itself from Israel.

But that's far short of what was necessary. At minimum, our leaders should declare that American lives are untouchable and that our freedom of speech is inviolable, and demonstrate a willingness, in action, to retaliate with force. (When questioned about the embassy crisis in the vice-presidential debate, Ryan was handed an opportunity to speak forcefully in defense of freedom of speech and the sanctity of the rights of Americans. He dodged it.)

Consider, finally, our defense budget.[83] Clouding the debate over defense spending is the fact that our present foreign policy leads us to engage in a mess of contradictions: legitimate, self-defensive operations; illegitimate humanitarian, "nation building" efforts (along with all the support costs for long-term bases); and the occasional disbursal of bribes[84] to our enemies. First, strip out the global-welfare category. Next, consider whether we would need every single one of our permanent overseas bases—if our foreign policy demonstrated in word and deed our willingness, when necessary, to crush enemies. Arguably, we could make do with fewer—and realize considerable savings. To safeguard the freedom of Americans, a powerful, well-equipped and technologically advanced military—one that is peerless, efficient and formidable—is essential. Yet there's reason to think, under a principled, self-interested approach, we'd have the strong military we need, at a lesser cost.

What's distinctive to an approach informed by Rand's ideas is that it hinges on a rethinking of the moral values that should inform foreign policy. At its core is the idea that the individual[85] has a right to his life, that he's morally entitled to live it in line with his rational judgment,[86] and that his freedom to act on his judgment must be safeguarded from aggressors. And, crucially, he bears no duty selflessly to serve others—whether they are next door or overseas. This animating premise enjoins a firm, long-range policy of assertive national defense and strictly rules out altruistic[87] missions à la Bush.

Clearly, Paul Ryan does not share Rand's foreign policy. But is there nevertheless a discernible influence?

Reading Ryan's most substantive speech[88] on foreign policy, delivered at the Hamilton Society in 2011, you can certainly hear the reverberation of Ayn Rand's ideas. "[I]f you believe these rights are universal human rights, then that clearly forms the basis of your views on foreign policy," he said, partially echoing the Randian conviction that regimes are moral to the degree that they respect individual rights. For Ryan, as for Rand, championing rights leads "you to reject moral relativism. It causes you to recoil at the idea of persistent moral indifference toward any nation that stifles and denies liberty." Though as already noted, Ryan did not speak forcefully in defense of free speech in the aftermath of the Libyan attacks. But at least there is, in line with Rand, a thoughtful promotion of free trade. In his Hamilton Society speech, for instance, he argued in favor of an "expanding community of nations that shares our economic values as well as our political values" in order to "ensure a more prosperous world."

If these similarities between the two are meaningful, Ryan nevertheless seems to fundamentally part ways with Rand. In particular, he speaks of the need to "renew our commitment to the idea that America is the greatest force for human freedom the world has ever seen," and sees in the Arab Spring the "long-repressed populations give voice to the fundamental desire for liberty." (The ethnic-sectarian bloodbath that ensued in Iraq was proof, if any were needed, that political freedom and peace are not an innate yearning of mankind.[89]) Further, Ryan claims that it is "always in the interest of the United States to promote these principles in other nations." Like President George W. Bush, whose wars he supported, Ryan appears to subscribe to the quasi-religious view that freedom is written into the soul of mankind, and that it is somehow the moral duty of America, the freest and wealthiest of nations, to go forth and wage wars to unchain the world's oppressed. In all this, he could not be less aligned with Rand.

Rand certainly believed that the United States benefits from a freer world. Thus, she held, America should speak up for dissidents everywhere who seek greater freedom. But Rand would only ever consider deploying the military where the rights of Americans hang in the balance—when, in other words, it becomes an issue of self-defense. This critical distinction may well be lost on Ryan, if the media's parsing of his neoconservative leanings has been fair.

Perhaps, in these waning days of the campaign season, Ryan will consider rereading Rand's work, and sharing it with his running mate. Anyone seeking to inject more rational and more distinctively American ideas into our nation's chaotic foreign policy ought to seriously consider Ayn Rand's refreshingly clear-eyed perspective.

* * *

An earlier version of this article appeared in *Foreign Policy*.

How Much Ayn Rand Is There in Trump's "America First" Foreign Policy?

Elan Journo March 1, 2017

In Donald Trump's "America first" policy we can detect "an unintended reincarnation of Ayn Rand," suggests Arnold Steinberg in *The American Spectator*.

Rand's ideas may well have influenced Trump in some indirect way (the cultural impact of her philosophy is far-reaching). And I would welcome signs of such influence, having written two books that advocate aligning our nation's foreign policy with Rand's morality of rational egoism. But when we look past Trump's rhetoric, how committed is he to the principle of putting the self-interest of Americans first?

Trump differs profoundly from Rand's conception of American self-interest. Whereas Rand's distinctive approach upholds America's founding ideals of individualism and freedom, Trump exhibits an authoritarian and collectivist streak. We can see that by looking at Trump's approach with a wide-angle lens, one that includes aspects unaddressed in Mr. Steinberg's essay.

Let's start with the seeming echoes of Rand's approach in Trump's rhetoric. For Mr. Steinberg and many others (myself included), Trump's rhetoric about firmly confronting enemies resonates with a bracingly self-assertive tone. Regarding alliances, Trump has pointedly—and rightly—asked, what's in it for us? Trump might do some good, if he sticks to that path. Mr. Steinberg aptly notes, however, that Trump's foreign policy is "evolving," but reports that the president "remains a critic of using American boots on the ground to build nations or to spread democracy. And he is unlikely to give foreign aid to socialist idiots."

These points call to mind Ayn Rand's distinctive approach to foreign policy, which is predicated on her basic philosophic worldview. Rand was a thoroughgoing individualist, and her political views—from her support for laissez-faire capitalism to her view that our foreign policy should be guided by the principle of rational egoism—stem from that. Individualism regards every person as "an independent, sovereign entity who possesses an inalienable right to his own life, a right derived from his nature as a rational being." Man, in Rand's view, is capable of using reason to identify and pursue goals necessary for his own flourishing. Thus, for Rand, government's only proper function is to protect the individual rights of its citizens—domestically and in foreign policy.

Crucially, that rules out treating our citizens as cannon fodder (through a military draft and selfless missions, such as Vietnam and the nation-building in Iraq and Afghanistan), or disposing of their wealth by giving handouts to other countries (through foreign aid or international welfare schemes). For Rand, who vehemently opposed the Vietnam war as an instance of "senseless, altruistic, self-sacrificial slaughter," the only moral justification for war is self-defense: the elimination of threats against American lives and freedom—with decisive force.

But does the reality of Trump's actual foreign policy positions match his rhetoric? Consider two vital implications of a self-interested foreign policy: the paramount importance of moral judgment; and an uncompromising advocacy of free trade. From these positions, Trump diverges sharply.

Rational judgment is critical if we are to sort friend from foe (and everything in between), and act accordingly. What's true for an individual is doubly true for a nation's foreign policy. This entails a commitment to facts and judging other regimes by objective moral standards. We have much to gain from free nations, and a great deal to worry about from regimes that violate the rights of their own citizens, because these latter typically seek to do the same beyond their borders.

Consider Trump's startling assessment of the Russian tyrant Vladimir Putin. Trump fiercely admires Putin, whom he recently praised as a "bright and very talented man." This is the same Putin who imprisons reporters, murders political opponents, and wages wars of conquest. Isn't Putin a killer? asked Bill O'Reilly in a recent interview. Trump responded: "There are a lot of killers. We've got a lot of killers. What do you think? Our country's so innocent?" To admire this killer and then stick up for him is horrendous. To denigrate America as somehow morally on par with an authoritarian regime like Russia: that's the last thing we would expect from a president who really believes American interests are worth defending.

A self-interested foreign policy also entails a commitment to (genuine) free trade—without trade barriers, protective tariffs, or special privileges. It means, as Rand noted, the "opening of the world's trade routes to free international exchange and competition among the private citizens of all countries dealing directly with one another." That's a logical expression of individualism applied to politics and economics. Rand observed that free trade in the nineteenth century liberated the world by undercutting statist regimes and led to the longest period of general peace in human history.

Consider Trump's vociferous opposition to globalization and international trade. Trump's chief strategist, Steve Bannon, pushes "economic nationalism" and by all accounts, the president agrees with him. Reflecting that collectivist mindset, Trump vilifies foreigners for "stealing" jobs and luring away "our" factories. He promises to solve these "problems" through protectionism and strongman tactics. Trump has openly threatened to punish American companies that leave the country. This is one more example of Trump's marked authoritarianism. The president emulates his Russian hero.

Trump's collectivist and authoritarian streak underscores his divergence from a genuinely self-interested approach, which rests on the American values of individualism and freedom. Based on those values, what constitutes our national self-interest? It is nothing more than the aggregate interest of each individual American to the protection of his or her rights: the freedom to enjoy life, liberty, and property unmolested by foreign aggressors.

The idea of "American exceptionalism," in my view, captures the achievement of America's political system—a system predicated on the moral idea of protecting the individual's right to life, liberty and the pursuit of happiness. That's a virtue that Ayn Rand, who recognized the evil of authoritarianism and collectivism in all their forms, admired in America. In Trump's statements we can sometimes hear a welcome pro-America motif, but the president's signature positions don't live up to that ideal.

* * *

A version of this article originally appeared in *The American Spectator*.

What Should a Distinctively American Foreign Policy Do?

Elan Journo

This essay was first published in the 2018 book A New Textbook of Americanism: The Politics of Ayn Rand *(edited by Jonathan Hoenig). Drawing upon Rand's philosophy of Objectivism, this essay underscores the necessity of defining foreign policy by reference to rational moral principles. You can appreciate the need for such principles by observing what American foreign policy looks like in their absence, notably under the George W. Bush and Barack Obama administrations. It's a longstanding pattern. Although this essay was completed well before the election of Donald Trump, his administration continued that pattern.*

The raid began sometime around midnight, local time, on May 2, 2011. Swooping down aboard helicopters, SEAL Team Six breached Osama bin Laden's fortified compound. When the firefight ended, they had put to death the man culpable for the deadliest terrorist attack on American soil. Hearing news of the successful raid, crowds gathered spontaneously outside the White House and near Ground Zero and elsewhere in Manhattan, cheering, singing "The Star Spangled Banner," chanting "U.S.A! U.S.A!"[90] The emotional sum of that night was an elation so many of us felt at the power of our military, sledgehammer-bold yet scalpel-precise. Mingled together was the sense that this is the kind of thing we should do to defend our lives; that this was a down payment on justice, long delayed.

While our military is an awesome instrument, our foreign policy—responsible for directing when and how to deploy the instrument—is an embarrassment. The backstory of the bin Laden raid is one exhibit in the indictment. Recall that Pakistan was formally a "major non-NATO ally," supposedly committed to the fight against jihadists.[91] You might suppose we would seek Pakistan's help with the raid on bin Laden's compound. After all, the compound was located in the city of Abbottabad, a mere two-hour drive from the capital Islamabad and about a mile down the road from a Pakistani military base and academy. But we went in without a word to Islamabad—and for good reason. What our policymakers

275

well knew, but had been willfully blind to, was that for a decade, Pakistan had continued abetting Taliban and other Islamist fighters. Could it be trusted? No. Was the regime, which had received billions of dollars from us to combat Islamists, actually harboring bin Laden? So it would seem.[92] Why, then, proclaim it an ally?

The alliance with Pakistan, sealed with a handshake by George W. Bush, is hardly an outlier. Take the impossible-to-satirize situation with a major organ of American foreign policy that enjoys longstanding, bi-partisan support: foreign aid. Where does $28-odd-billion go every year?[93] To countries where many, many people view us as an "enemy." The Pew Global Attitudes Survey queried more than 325,000 people in 60 countries that receive U.S. aid. It asked whether they saw America as more of a "partner," or more of an "enemy" (or neither). The countries with the highest percentage of respondents who viewed us as an "enemy" were also among those receiving significant amounts of U.S.-backed aid: the Palestinian territories (76 percent of respondents saw us as an "enemy"), Pakistan (64 percent), Turkey (49 percent), Lebanon (46 percent), Venezuela (39 percent).[94]

So, yes, we are the world's mightiest nation, but we serve as a global ATM for people hostile to us and our interests. We spend years chasing down Osama bin Laden and fighting his minions in Afghanistan, while at the same time we support Pakistan's jihadist-enabling regime. Look broadly and deeply at American foreign policy, and you will find it crowded with many more instances of the same depressing theme. When considered as a whole, American foreign policy does not add up to a whole. It is a bewildering mishmash of diverging, inconsistent goals. It lacks a unifying, guiding principle.

What principle should direct American foreign policy and define our interests?

What Should the Goal of American Foreign Policy Be?

The place to start is not with the Sunday morning talk shows, nor the debates on Capitol Hill, nor scholarly arguments. We should look instead to the distinctive American approach to government, and consider the more basic question: What, in that original system, is the government's proper job, domestically? The answer provides the principle for guiding its conduct of foreign affairs.

The political vision of America's Founders, little understood today, was groundbreaking. They upended the traditional relationship between man and the state. For eons, man was subservient to some ruler, expected dutifully to kneel before some authority—the king, the church, the mob—commanding the power to dispose of his wealth, property, life. Rejecting that, the Founders held that government exists not to lord over men, but to serve as the protector of their freedom. Government derives its "just powers from the consent of the governed," and its only reason for being is to protect the inalienable rights of citizens to live and pursue their own happiness.

In the twentieth century, Ayn Rand championed the full realization of the Founding Fathers' vision of a free society. What precisely does the government's protection of rights entail? Rand observed:

> Man's rights can be violated only by the use of physical force. It is only by means of physical force that one man can deprive another of his life, or enslave him, or rob him, or prevent him from pursuing his own goals, or compel him to act against his own rational judgment. The precondition of a civilized society is the barring of physical force from social relationships—thus establishing the principle that if men wish to deal with one another, they may do so only by means of reason: by discussion, persuasion and voluntary, uncoerced agreement.[95]

The government, through the police and objective law, acts as our agent of self-defense. That is its essential role in securing our freedom to pursue our goals, to trade, to prosper. Just as the police and courts are essential to protect our rights domestically, so we need an effective military force to protect our freedom from foreign threats.

For the same reason that the police must apprehend criminals domestically, the military must deter—and when necessary eliminate—foreign threats to our ability to live our lives and trade freely. Just as there are times when the police are morally justified in using retaliatory (even lethal) force to capture a dangerous criminal or end a threat, so there are times when the government must use retaliatory military force to thwart foreign aggressors.

And the only morally justifiable purpose for war? Self-defense. To echo the Founders, we delegate our right of self-defense to the government so that it can protect our freedom—both within our borders and outside them.

The overarching goal that should guide our foreign policy is the principle of individual rights. What is in our interest as a nation in the arena of foreign affairs is nothing more than the aggregate interest of each American to the protection of his individual rights. The distinctive American approach to the purpose of government entails a foreign policy that is exclusively concerned with protecting our own rights. It means a policy of pursuing America's self-interest.

That approach would radically transform how America interacts with the rest of the world.

What Does a Self-Interested Foreign Policy Look Like?

The U.S. military operations in Iraq and in Afghanistan, at least on the surface, seemed to be about ending the real threats to our security. If only that were so. In my book *Winning the Unwinnable War*, I exposed in detail how Bush's policy sacrificed the proper goal of eliminating whatever threats we faced.[96] In reality, the Bush "war on terror," distinguished by its hollow with-us-or-against-us rhetoric, left untouched the leading state sponsors of jihadist terrorism (notably, Iran, Pakistan, and Saudi Arabia). Where we deployed military forces, the primary mission of our troops was nation-building—re-opening schools, clearing sewers, guarding ballot boxes. On the battlefield, our troops clashed with Islamist fighters (seeking political domination under Allah's laws), even as U.S. officials leading the "reconstruction" endorsed new constitutions installing sharia (Islamic religious law) as the supreme legal framework of Iraq and Afghanistan. Our policy's actual aim was: enabling the poor and oppressed of the Middle East to voice their (predictably hostile) opinions at the ballot box and install jihadist-friendly leaders—which they did.

A full catalogue of the myriad inconsistencies in U.S. foreign policy would fill several tomes. Consider: even as our policy in Afghanistan was to fight the Taliban regime, al-Qaeda fighters, and their allied holy warriors, the Bush administration made diplomatic overtures to the local branch of Syria's Muslim Brotherhood, the progenitor of the Islamist movement from which al-Qaeda and many other jihadist groups derived. How does that add up? Or take another example, on a far larger scale. Compare our policy response to the Arab Spring uprising in Libya with our response to the post-election protests in Iran a couple of years earlier. What you find is that, yet again, instead of advancing our interests, we shrank from that goal.

Recall the massive street demonstrations in Iran in 2009. The clerics in Iran have led crowds in chants of "death to America" for 30-plus years, but here we saw spontaneous protests against the regime itself, with crowds reportedly shouting "death to the dictator" and "death to Khamenei."[97] The cleric Ayatollah Khamenei is the supreme leader in a regime predicated on the supremacy of religious rule; the protesters were, in effect, challenging the very legitimacy of the Iranian theocracy. Defying a government that seeks totalitarian control, the protesters risked death at the hands of regime-backed militia sent to crush them.

We had ample reason to encourage the implosion of the Islamist regime in Tehran. Tehran is a leader of the Islamist movement, the cause animating al Qaeda, the Taliban, the Muslim Brotherhood, and kindred groups. Iran has inspired and funded jihadist terrorism, embodying the movement's political ideal. It is a regime that tramples on the rights of its own citizens, and it ambitiously seeks to kill and subjugate beyond its borders. Our State Department has designated it as an active State Sponsor of Terrorism since 1984.[98] Through proxies like Hezbollah, Iran has committed numerous acts of aggression against the United States and other Western interests. Iran's Revolutionary Guard Corps helped create and train Hezbollah, which hijacked a TWA airliner and which kidnapped, tortured and killed Americans. Iran was behind the 1983 bombings of the U.S. Embassy in Lebanon and later bombed the barracks of U.S. Marines, killing 241 people. Iran also orchestrated the 1996 car bombing of Khobar Towers in Saudi Arabia, killing 19 U.S. servicemen.[99]

For decades, Iran has been at war with us, but we pretend otherwise. In the name of self-defense, the U.S. government is morally obliged to eliminate this enemy. A military option is widely viewed as off the table, however, because of the Iraq and Afghanistan failures. But when Iranians themselves marched in protest, seeking to remove from power their theocratic regime, we faced a prime opportunity to provide (at least) moral support to those brave protesters. If successful, their efforts could have brought to power a non-hostile regime, and drastically reduced the threat to American lives. That, after all, is the principle that defines our interest: to live in freedom and unmolested by foreign threats.

What did we do? Muttered a few limp words, belatedly, about being "appalled and outraged." Then we flouted even that perfunctory rhetoric. By reaffirming that "the United States respects the sovereignty" of Iran, we endorsed the regime.[100] Next, we hastened to invite Tehran, stained with fresh blood, to engage with us diplomatically. We forfeited an opportunity to safeguard our security and went out of our way to accommodate a belligerent regime that seeks nuclear capability.

With much at stake in Iran, we shied away from pursuing our own interests. But when we had little on the line, in Libya, we leapt into action, precisely because no one could validly accuse us of pursuing our self-interest. Under General Muammar Gaddafi, Libya was an abhorrent dictatorship. It was, however, at most a trivial threat to our security. During the so-called Arab Spring, protesters rebelled against Gaddafi.

Who were these protesters? What political goals did they seek? We didn't ask. Stating no clear purpose for our involvement in enforcing the NATO no-fly zone, we dutifully scrambled jet fighters and put American lives in harm's way.

Washington's response to Libya and Iran refutes the notion that our foreign policy is animated by self-interest. We have seen that in fact the disgrace that passes for U.S. foreign policy lacks a guiding principle. What can be discerned is a pattern of clashing, disparate goals that we feel we can pursue, because they aim at "humanitarian" ends and the needs of others, above whatever benefits we imagine might come our way. (None do.)

It is deemed "selfish" to advance our own interests, whereas serving others, well, that is a universally accepted rationale. Yet, that kind of foreign policy can only sow chaos: Much of what went wrong in Iraq and Afghanistan stemmed from putting a welfare agenda above the goal of eliminating whatever threat existed in those countries (and elsewhere).

Without a principle to direct it, our foreign policy is haphazard, warped, and ineffectual. It is hardly surprising that the hunt for Osama bin Laden took nearly ten years. That he spent nearly six tranquil years living in Pakistan serves as an exclamation point.

Why Moral Judgment in Foreign Policy Is Indispensable

Examine the questionable U.S.-Pakistan alliance and you can appreciate—by its omission—the vital importance of a key feature of a self-interested foreign policy: the imperative of judging other regimes objectively. Distinguishing friend from foe (and every gradation in between) is crucial if we are to protect the lives and freedom of Americans. But the failure to exercise actual moral judgment was at the core of our approach to Pakistan.

Prior to 9/11, Pakistan, having supported the Islamists for years, was one of only three countries formally to recognize the Taliban's totalitarian theocracy in neighboring Afghanistan. But post-9/11, the Bush administration claimed we needed Pakistan as an ally, and that the alternatives to dealing with the military dictatorship were far worse. Did we need Pakistan? Perhaps, but it is doubtful. Could we have formed an alliance with it? Only on one condition: if we treated this supposedly lesser of two evils as, in fact, evil, which means acknowledging the immorality of Pakistan's past backing of the Taliban, and demanding that it combat the Islamists as proof of repudiating them. We would have at most an arm's-length relationship, continually monitoring for evidence of Pakistan's commitment—or betrayal. We would have to state publicly that both the regime and the pro-jihadists among its people are immoral, that our alliance is delimited to one goal, and that we would welcome and support new, pro-American, genuinely pro-freedom leaders in Pakistan.

In a nutshell, the alliance could have served a self-interested mission of defeating Islamists in Afghanistan, if we followed the facts and judged that we need to cooperate with "a pickpocket for the purpose of apprehending a mass murderer."[101]

What we actually did was instantly canonize Pakistan and swallow its rhetoric about being "with us." By 2007 the evidence of its deceit was so egregious, *Newsweek* reported that Islamist fighters, once "restricted to untamed mountain villages along the [Pakistani-Afghan] border," now "operate relatively freely in cities like Karachi." The Taliban "now pretty much come and go as they please inside Pakistan." They easily slipped in and out of neighboring Afghanistan to arm and train their fighters.[102] But our foreign policy evaded Pakistan's true character, and thus we continually evaded mounting evidence that it was conning us, doing just enough to give the appearance of being an ally.

We acquired our new "ally" for the low, low price of $15 billion, and it betrayed us, again and again.[103] Even some Pakistanis inside the regime are aghast at our policy:

> The United States was neither speaking out against Pakistan nor changing its policy toward a government that was exporting terrorism, the [Pakistani] legislator lamented. "How many people have to die before they get it? They are standing by a military that protects, aids and abets people who are going against the U.S. and Western mission in Afghanistan, in Syria, everywhere."[104]

The Pakistan debacle illustrates a wider point about what our foreign policy must do. We should pass judgment and act on it, because otherwise we cannot successfully protect the lives and freedom of Americans. That holds true, not only in the Middle East, a flashpoint from which the above examples are drawn, but also across the board. The norm today is to shy away from the responsibility of judgment. The results speak for themselves.

It is in those rare moments of sobriety, when our policymakers face facts and empower our military to act in our own interests, that we achieve such wins as the raid in Abbottabad. That kind of success is what Americans expect—and deserve—as the norm. Quite obviously our soldiers can deliver. But will our policymakers let them?

A Vision for Peace and Prosperity

A foreign policy worthy of America is one that embraces our nation's distinctive founding principle, the ideal of individual rights. To understand how that principle should guide our foreign affairs is to recognize how little a role it plays in current policymaking—and how urgently it is needed. Guided by that principle, we would embrace our self-interested pursuit of happiness and arm ourselves with the means to safeguard our freedom, so that we may live in peace, start a business, engage in free trade, build a career, raise a family, and thrive.

LEARN MORE

About ARI
The Ayn Rand Institute fosters a growing awareness, understanding and acceptance of Ayn Rand's philosophy, Objectivism, in order to create a culture whose guiding principles are reason, rational self-interest, individualism and laissez-faire capitalism—a culture in which individuals are free to pursue their own happiness.
aynrand.org

Courses, Lectures, Articles and Books
Explore audio, video and written works by Ayn Rand—including some of her most important essays—and works by other Objectivist authors at ARI Campus or by downloading the Ayn Rand University mobile app.
courses.aynrand.org

The Objectivist Academic Center
The Objectivist Academic Center (OAC®), ARI's premier intellectual training program, features live classes with Objectivist experts conducted via videoconference, and personalized feedback on students' writing, speaking and understanding of Rand's philosophy.
aynrand.org/oac

New Ideal, Journal of the Ayn Rand Institute
New Ideal explores pressing cultural issues from the perspective of Ayn Rand's philosophy, Objectivism, which upholds the ideals of reason, individualism and capitalism.
newideal.aynrand.org

What You Can Do

Read

"Man's Rights" by Ayn Rand
"If one wishes to advocate a free society," writes Ayn Rand, "one must realize that its indispensable foundation is the principle of individual rights." This essay defines and explains the principle of individual rights.

"Nature of Government" by Ayn Rand
This is a presentation of the Objectivist view of the nature and proper role of government in a free society. The proper purpose of a government, Rand shows, is to protect individual rights from the initiation of physical force.

"The Lessons of Vietnam" in *The Voice of Reason: Essays in Objectivist Thought* by Ayn Rand
"The Vietnam war is one of the most disastrous foreign-policy failures in U.S. history," wrote Ayn Rand. In this essay, she analyzes the intellectual bankruptcy behind the Vietnam war and draws wider, enduring lessons from it.

"The Roots of War" by Ayn Rand
By the nature of its basic principles and interests, laissez-faire capitalism "is the only system that is fundamentally opposed to war," Ayn Rand observes. "If men want to oppose war," she argues, "it is statism that they must oppose."

The Foreign Policy of Self-Interest: A Moral Ideal for America by Peter Schwartz
This book advocates an approach to foreign policy based on Ayn Rand's morality of rational self-interest, under which our nation's self-interests are measured by only one standard: the individual liberty of its citizens.

*Winning the Unwinnable War: America's Self-Crippled
Response to Islamic Terrorism*, edited by Elan Journo

This book shows how our own policy ideas led to 9/11 and then crippled our response in the Middle East. Only by radically rethinking our foreign policy can we achieve victory over the enemy that attacked us on 9/11; we need a foreign policy based on Ayn Rand's morality of rational self-interest.

Defending Free Speech, edited by Steve Simpson

This hard-hitting collection reveals how the attacks on free speech are the product of destructive ideas—ideas that are eroding Western culture at its foundation. The book exposes those ideas and the individuals who hold them, and, importantly, it identifies the only ideas on which Western civilization can be sustained: reason, egoism and individual rights.

*What Justice Demands: America and the Israeli-
Palestinian Conflict* by Elan Journo

In this book, Elan Journo explains the essential nature of the Israeli-Palestinian conflict, and what has fueled it for so long. What justice demands, he shows, is that we evaluate *both* adversaries—and America's approach to the conflict—according to a universal moral ideal: individual liberty. From that secular moral framework, the book analyzes the conflict, examines major Palestinian grievances and Israel's character as a nation, and explains what's at stake for everyone who values human life, freedom and progress. *What Justice Demands* shows us why America should be strongly supportive of freedom and freedom-seekers—but, in this conflict and across the Middle East, it hasn't been, much to our detriment.

Watch

America vs. Americans by Leonard Peikoff (April 21, 2003)
In this talk, Leonard Peikoff analyzes and rejects—as appease-ment-ridden and ineffectual—the entire George W. Bush adminis-tration response to the terrorist attacks on the United States, from 9/11 through early 2003. America should have reacted to 9/11 as it did to Pearl Harbor, by waging a real war—a merciless war—not on Afghanistan or Iraq, but on Iran: the ideological fountainhead of Islamic totalitarianism.

The Failure of the Homeland Defense: The Lessons from History by John David Lewis. (Recorded March 23, 2005)
With the creation of the Department of Homeland Security, America has accepted a permanent, institutionalized state of siege on its own soil. In this lecture, John David Lewis examines exam-ples from history and argues that such a policy is suicidal. Rather than bracing against further attacks at home, America should destroy her enemies.

Free Speech and the Danish Cartoons: A Panel Discussion with Yaron Brook (April 11, 2006)
The Danish cartoons depicting Muhammad have sparked a world-wide controversy. Death threats and violent protests have sent the cartoonists into hiding and have had the intended effect of sti-fling freedom of expression. This unflinching discussion—which includes an unveiling of the cartoons—addresses key questions, including: Why is it so important to hold events like this? What is freedom of speech? Does it include the right to offend? What is the significance of the worldwide Islamic reaction to the cartoons? How should Western governments have responded to this incident? How should the Western media have responded?

Freedom of Speech or Tyranny of Silence? (January 21, 2015)
Following the massacre of journalists at *Charlie Hebdo* in Paris and a growing climate of self-censorship, this panel opens up a con-versation on the future of the freedom of speech. In the discus-sion, Onkar Ghate talks about the meaning of the right to free speech, the "exceptions" to free speech, the relation between faith

and force, and the need for the separation of church and state. The panel includes Flemming Rose, Harvey Silverglate, Jeff Jacoby and Gregory Salmieri.

The Jihadist Movement by Elan Journo (July 2015)
What motivates the jihadist movement? Pushing back against the dominant perspectives on the issue, Elan Journo shows that the Islamist movement is fundamentally animated by a religious goal of subjugation and conquest.

The Israeli–Palestinian Conflict by Elan Journo (July 2015)
What is at the core of the Israeli–Palestinian conflict? Why has the conflict come to seem intractable? What, if any, is America's stake in it? By exploring key elements of the Israeli–Palestinian conflict, this talk by Elan Journo makes a forbidding, convoluted subject lucid.

Charlie Hebdo, the West and the Need to Ridicule Religion by Onkar Ghate (July 2015)
Attacks like the one against the newspaper *Charlie Hebdo* in Paris are becoming all too common. The Islamic totalitarian threat goes all the way back to 1989 with Ayatollah Khomeini's fatwa against Salman Rushdie. In this talk, Onkar Ghate explains why and how to defend freedom of speech in the face of religious attacks.

Flemming Rose on Islamist Threats to Free Speech, interview by Elan Journo (December 9, 2020)
What's the climate in Europe for freedom of speech, specifically on the topic of Islam, five years after the massacre at *Charlie Hebdo*? What became of the visceral outpouring of support for freedom of speech, embodied in mass protests and the hashtag #JeSuisCharlie ("I am Charlie")? What can we make of the response of European governments? Elan Journo interviews the author Flemming Rose, who was an editor at the Danish newspaper *Jyllands-Posten* when it published cartoons on the subject of Islam that led to an international crisis.

The *Charlie Hebdo* Assassinations: Six Years Later [Podcast]
by Onkar Ghate and Elan Journo (January 6, 2021)
In this episode of the *New Ideal* podcast, on the sixth anniversary
of the murderous attacks on the *Charlie Hebdo* newspaper in Paris,
Elan Journo and Onkar Ghate discuss the attacks as a symptom of
the erosion of free speech in the West. Among the topics covered:
The history of Islamist attacks on free speech; the ineffective public reaction to the *Hebdo* attacks; why free speech—and intellectual
freedom more generally—is so important to defend; the West's failure to take a principled stand in defense of free speech; why it's
important to criticize religion; and how unopposed threats to free
speech engender self-censorship.

Listen

Faith and Force: The Destroyers of the
Modern World by Ayn Rand (1960)

The twentieth century was bloody, with two world wars and dictatorships arising around the globe. What is the deepest cause of this warfare and destruction? In this talk, Ayn Rand identifies the cause in our intellectuals' rejection of reason in favor of faith and the morality of altruism. Only by rejecting faith and altruism and embracing reason and a new morality of rational egoism will freedom and peaceful co-existence be possible.

The Wreckage of the Consensus by Ayn Rand (1967)

In this 1967 lecture, delivered at Boston's Ford Hall Forum, Ayn Rand questions the morality of fighting a war in Vietnam that "does not serve any national interest." Rand also explains how the military draft violates the rights of those conscripted.

Global Balkanization by Ayn Rand (1977)

Drawing her title from the Balkan Peninsula, where ethnic groups have splintered and warred against each other for centuries, Ayn Rand argues in this Ford Hall Forum lecture that the global trend toward political organization based on race, language and religion bodes ill for the future of Western civilization.

Freedom of Speech, "Islamophobia," and the Cartoons Crisis [Podcast]
by Elan Journo (December 18, 2014)

In this podcast, Elan Journo interviews Flemming Rose about his new book, *The Tyranny of Silence*, which explores the Danish cartoons crisis, the reaction to it and the future of free speech. The interview covers questions such as: What incidents prompted the commissioning of the cartoons? What lies behind the push to outlaw "defamation of religion"? Why is the invalid term "Islamophobia" so destructive?

The Yaron Brook Show: Freedom of Speech
and the Muhammad Drawings

In this special episode, guest host Onkar Ghate analyzes the appeasing, victim-blaming attitude among many intellectuals toward the Islamist attack on a cartoon contest in Garland, Texas.

Speak Up

Three Things You Can Do Right Now ...

1. Contribute to ARI

The book you are holding—like all the content and projects of the Ayn Rand Institute—was made possible thanks to the many individuals, foundations and corporations whose financial contributions fund our work. Your contribution will multiply ARI's impact and help fuel our mission to make people aware of the philosophy of Objectivism and its crucial value to human life.

To donate online and to learn about convenient ways to sustain ARI's work, please visit **aynrand.org/donate.**

2. Recommend This Book
- Write a review of this book on Amazon.com.
- In conversations, let people know what you found illuminating in this book and encourage them to read it.
- Give away copies of this book (and *Winning the Unwinnable War*) to five of your friends.

3. Tell Three (or 3,000) People
- Engage people in conversation about American foreign policy, correct their misconceptions by pointing to the actual facts of Washington's self-crippled approach, and encourage them to question the basic assumptions shaping U.S. policy.
- Write op-eds, letters to the editor and blog posts to express your view and to indicate the proper ideals that should guide our foreign policy.
- Many of the articles and blog posts in this book are available on ARI's website; share them with your friends on social media.

About the Contributors

Onkar Ghate

Onkar Ghate is the chief philosophy officer and a senior fellow at the Ayn Rand Institute. He is the Institute's resident expert on Objectivism and serves as its senior trainer and editor. For two decades, he has taught philosophy at the Institute's Objectivist Academic Center.

Ghate is a contributing author to many books on Rand's fiction and philosophy, including *Essays on Ayn Rand's "The Fountainhead"*; *Essays on Ayn Rand's "Atlas Shrugged"*; *Why Businessmen Need Philosophy: The Capitalist's Guide to the Ideas Behind Ayn Rand's "Atlas Shrugged"*; *Concepts and Their Role in Knowledge: Reflections on Objectivist Epistemology*; and *A Companion to Ayn Rand* (Blackwell Companions to Philosophy).

His writings have appeared in venues across the ideological spectrum, from *Huffington Post* to CNN.com to FoxNews.com and Businessweek.com. He's been interviewed on national and international radio, including NPR and BBC Radio, and has appeared as a television guest on CNBC, KCET, Fox News Channel and the *CBS Evening News*.

A Canadian citizen, Ghate studied economics and philosophy as an undergraduate student at the University of Toronto and worked in the financial industry prior to joining ARI in 2000. He received his doctorate in philosophy in 1998 from the University of Calgary.

Elan Journo

Elan Journo is a vice president and senior fellow at the Ayn Rand Institute. He writes and speaks for ARI; he is a senior editor of *New Ideal*, the Institute's journal; and he teaches at the Objectivist Academic Center. In 2012 he launched ARI's Junior Fellows Program and led it until 2018.

Journo specializes in the application of Rand's ethics of rational egoism to public policy issues. His research and writing focus on the intersection of moral ideas and American foreign policy. His 2009 book, *Winning the Unwinnable War: America's Self-Crippled*

Response to Islamic Totalitarianism, analyzes post-9/11 U.S. foreign policy from the perspective of Rand's philosophy. He is a contributor to *Defending Free Speech* and *A New Textbook of Americanism: The Politics of Ayn Rand*. His most recent book is *What Justice Demands: America and the Israeli-Palestinian Conflict*.

His articles have appeared in a wide range of publications, from *Foreign Policy* and *Middle East Quarterly* to *The Hill* and *The Los Angeles Times*. He has been interviewed on PBS, NPR and hundreds of radio programs nationally and internationally.

He holds a BA in philosophy from King's College, London, and an MA in diplomacy from SOAS, University of London. Find him on Twitter: @elanjourno.

Leonard Peikoff

Leonard Peikoff has spent more than sixty years studying, teaching and applying the philosophy of Ayn Rand. Having been Rand's foremost student, he is today the world's preeminent expert on Objectivism.

A great admirer of *The Fountainhead*, he first met Rand in 1951, when he was, in his own words, "an ignorant, intelligent seventeen-year-old." He read *Atlas Shrugged* in manuscript and was invited "to ask the author all the questions I wished about her ideas." For thirty years, Rand was his mentor, editor and friend. "We talked philosophy late into the night on countless occasions," he recalls. "It was, for me, an invaluable education." On her death in 1982, Rand named Peikoff heir to her estate.

Born in Winnipeg, Canada, in 1933 (but now a U.S. citizen), Peikoff studied philosophy at New York University and taught at several colleges and universities between 1957 and 1973. For decades he lectured on Objectivism to worldwide audiences through live appearances and audio recordings of his courses. His 1976 course on Objectivism's entire theoretical structure earned Rand's endorsement (she also participated in some of the Q&A periods) and became the basis for his book *Objectivism: The Philosophy of Ayn Rand* (1991), the first systematic presentation of her philosophy.

Peikoff is also the author of *The Ominous Parallels: The End of Freedom in America* (1983), *The DIM Hypothesis: Why the Lights of the West Are Going Out* (2012), and *The Cause of Hitler's Germany* (2014, excerpted from *The Ominous Parallels*).

Asked once to name his life's greatest achievement, Peikoff said: "I mastered Objectivism and presented it to the world."

Yaron Brook

Yaron Brook is chairman of the board of the Ayn Rand Institute and its former executive director.

He hosts *The Yaron Brook Show* and is a frequent guest on national radio and television programs. He is a co-founder and contributor to Ingenuism.com

Brook is a highly sought after public speaker around the world, discussing and debating the ideas of Ayn Rand and the morality of capitalism.

Brook's most recent book (with Don Watkins) is *In Pursuit of Wealth: The Moral Case for Finance,* which argues that few industries are more vital to our prosperity—and more maligned—than the financial industry. Brook and Watkins also authored the national bestseller *Free Market Revolution: How Ayn Rand's Ideas Can End Big Government* and *Equal Is Unfair: America's Misguided Fight Against Income Inequality.*

Brook was a columnist at Forbes.com, and his articles have appeared in *The Wall Street Journal, USA Today, Investor's Business Daily* and many other publications.

Born and raised in Israel, Brook earned a BSc in civil engineering from Technion-Israel Institute of Technology, and an MBA and PhD in finance from the University of Texas at Austin. He became an American citizen in 2003. For seven years he was an award-winning finance professor at Santa Clara University, and in 1998 he cofounded BH Equity Research.

Brook is chairman of the board of the Ayn Rand Institute and serves on the board of the Clemson Institute for the Study of Capitalism. He is a member of the Association of Private Enterprise Education and the Mont Pelerin Society.

Keith Lockitch

Keith Lockitch is the vice president of education and a senior fellow at the Ayn Rand Institute. He oversees the Institute's educational programs, including free books to teachers, essay contests on Rand's novels, the Objectivist Academic Center, conference content and other programs.

Lockitch is a senior instructor in ARI's Objectivist Academic Center, where he has been teaching courses on written and oral communication skills since 2003. He also teaches classes on Rand's novels and ideas in a variety of settings, from high school and college classrooms to ARI's internship program to ARI Campus.

As an Institute fellow, Lockitch writes, speaks and edits for ARI, serving in particular as a senior editor for its journal, *New Ideal*. He specializes in the application of Rand's philosophy to scientific topics, in particular to environmental issues such as energy and climate. His writings have appeared in such publications as *The Daily Caller, Washington Times, Orange County Register, Pittsburgh Tribune-Review, Canberra Times, San Francisco Chronicle* and the science policy journal *Energy and Environment*. He is a contributor to *Why Businessmen Need Philosophy: The Capitalist's Guide to the Ideas Behind Ayn Rand's "Atlas Shrugged."*

Lockitch received his PhD in physics from the University of Wisconsin, Milwaukee, and prior to joining ARI he conducted post-doctoral research in relativistic astrophysics.

Acknowledgments

We wish to thank Rikki Nedelkow, Simon Federman, Donna Montrezza, Chris Locke, Keith Lockitch, Richard Ralston, Thomas Bowden, Amanda Maxham, Melissa Pranger, Steven Dougherty and Lew Hendrickson. Carl Svanberg, Grant Parker and Christopher Machold assisted in the preparation of the manuscript. Steve Simpson offered valuable editorial feedback on the project.

* * *

This book was made possible thanks to the many individuals, foundations and corporations whose financial contributions fund the work of the Ayn Rand Institute.

Endnotes

1. https://youtu.be/7tSpWLq8vVM

2. The group is known by various names, including ISIL (Islamic State in Iraq and the Levant), ISIS (Islamic State in Iraq and Syria), and Daesh. For simplicity, I'll refer to it as the Islamic State or ISIS, since these have gained some currency.

3. There are also several "provinces" of the Islamic State (for example in Libya, the Sinai peninsula, and Yemen) run by groups that have sworn allegiance to it.

4. Qutb used the term "jahiliyya" to denote this state of affairs, which he regarded as comparable to the barbaric ignorance that obtained in pre-Mohammedan times.

5. Sayyid Qutb, *Milestones* (New Delhi, India: Abdul Naeem for Islamic Book Service, 2007), 63.

6. Qutb, *Milestones*, 72.

7. Note, for example, that the official slogan of Hamas (officially: the Islamic Resistance Movement) is "Allah is its target, the Prophet is its model, the Koran its constitution: Jihad is its path and death for the sake of Allah is the loftiest of its wishes." See, The Covenant of the Islamic Resistance Movement, 1988, http://avalon.law.yale.edu/20th_century/hamas.asp.

8. On some of the ways these thinkers diverge, see for example, Vanessa Martin, *Creating an Islamic State: Khomeini and the Making of a New Iran* (New York, London: I.B. Tauris, 2003), 120–21, 138–39.

9. A discussion of these two senses can be found in, for example, David Cook, *Understanding Jihad* (Berkeley: University of California Press, 2005), ch. 2.

10. On Iran's galvanizing role in the movement, see Gilles Kepel, *Jihad: The Trail of Political Islam* (Cambridge, MA: Harvard University Press, 2000); on the regime's long history of backing jihadist groups, see, for example, Ilan Berman, *Iran's Deadly Ambition: The Islamic Republic's Quest for Global Power* (New York: Encounter Books, 2015), and United States Department of State, *Country Reports on Terrorism*, 2016 and earlier, https://www.state.gov/j/ct/rls/crt/.

11. "Why We Hate You & Why We Fight You," *Dabiq*, no. 15, July 2016, 31 (an English-language magazine published by the Islamic State), accessible at http://clarionproject.org/wp-content/uploads/islamic-state-magazine-dabiq-fifteen-breaking-the-cross.pdf. All words in brackets are in the original. "Jizyah" is a special tax on non-Muslims permitted to live under Islamic rule. The quoted verse about Abraham ("There has already been for you an excellent example in Abraham...") appears to be from the Koran (60:4); the

296

passage about fighting unbelievers ("we have been commanded to fight the disbelievers...") seems to be a paraphrase of Koran (9:29); and the quoted verse ("And fight them until there is no fitnah...") echoes Koran (8:39).

12. John L. Esposito, *Islam: The Straight Path*, 3rd ed. (New York: Oxford University Press, 1998), 88.

13. Esposito, *Islam*, 88.

14. Esposito, *Islam*, 90.

15. The foregoing survey draws on Esposito, *Islam*, 88–93.

16. Sayyid Qutb, *Milestones* (New Delhi, India: Abdul Naeem for Islamic Book Service), 47.

17. Esposito writes that "Quranic principles and values were concretized and interpreted by the second and complementary source of [sharia] law, the Sunna of the Prophet, the normative model behavior of Muhammad." These "Prophetic deeds" were "transmitted and preserved in tradition reports (*hadith*, pl. *ahadith*)." (Esposito, *Islam*, 79–80) These are two major sources of religious law—the Koran and the example of Muhammad; Esposito notes a number of subsidiary sources, too.

18. Esposito, *Islam*, 87–88.

19. Qutb, *Milestones*, 78.

20. Quoted in Karsh, *Islamic Imperialism: A History* (New Haven: Yale University Press, 2006), 208.

21. Qutb, *Milestones*, 59–60.

22. Words in brackets appear in the original translation, by Abdullah Yusuf Ali, accessible at https://archive.org/details/Quran_English_Text. "People of the Book" is taken to mean Jews and Christians; "jizya" is a special tax levied on non-believers who are permitted to live under Islamic law. Notice that this Koranic verse is paraphrased in the statement from the Islamic State, which I quoted at length above.

23. Cook, *Understanding Jihad*, 6.

24. Quoted in Karsh, *Islamic Imperialism*, 217.

25. See, Maajid Nawaz and Tom Bromley, *Radical: My Journey Out of Islamist Extremism* (Lanham, MD: Globe Pequot Press, Lyon Press, 2013).

26. One version of this argument can be found in Obama's speech at a 2015 summit titled "Countering Violent Extremism." He argues that Islamists are at "war with Islam," that they are "desperate for legitimacy," and that they exploit religious themes to draw people in. The task of combating them, he insists, largely entails resolving economic and political grievances that they rely on. See Barack Obama: "Remarks at the White House Summit on Countering Violent Extremism," Feb. 18, 2015. Online by Gerhard Peters and

John T. Woolley, *The American Presidency Project*, http://www.presidency.ucsb.edu/ws/?pid=109652.

27. One example is "Jihadi John." Born in Kuwait and raised in the UK, he went to university and worked as a computer programmer before joining ISIS. See Cahal Milmo, Kim Sengupta, Jamie Merrill, "'Jihadi John': Mohammed Emwazi—from British Computer Programmer to Isis Executioner," *Independent*, Nov. 13, 2015, http://www.independent.co.uk/news/uk/home-news/jihadi-john-was-a-computer-programmer-known-to-mi5-for-at-least-four-years-10073607.html. Another example is Osama bin Laden. Although raised in the Middle East, he was born to a wealthy family, he was educated, and thus he had many opportunities in life.

28. See Osama bin Laden's "The Betrayal of Palestine" (Dec. 29, 1994) and "Declaration of *Jihad*" (Aug. 23, 1996) in *Messages to the World: The Statements of Osama bin Laden*, ed. Bruce Lawrence, trans. James Howarth (New York: Verso, 2005).

29. See Thomas Hegghammer and Joas Wagemakers, "The Palestine Effect: The Role of Palestinians in the Transnational Jihad Movement," *Die Welt des Islams* 53, no. 3–4 (2013).

30. Note that Osama bin Laden describes Bosnia as one of several places where Muslims are being assaulted; see "Declaration of *Jihad*" (Aug. 23, 1996) in *Messages to the World*.

31. Nawaz, *Radical*, 56–61.

32. For an in-depth analysis of the Israeli-Palestinian conflict and how it intersects with the Islamist movement, see my book *What Justice Demands: America and the Israeli-Palestinian Conflict*.

33. See, for example, Osama bin Laden's statement: "The legal duty regarding Palestine and our brothers there—these poor men, women and children who have nowhere to go—is to wage *jihad* for the sake of God, and to motivate the *umma* [global Muslim community] to *jihad* so that Palestine may be completely liberated and returned to Islamic sovereignty," *Messages to the World*, 9.

34. *Dabiq*, 32–33.

35. Peter Neumann, *Radicalized: New Jihadists and the Threat to the West* (London: I.B. Tauris, 2016), 90–92, 93, 93–97.

36. Pakistan is another significant regime enabling the Islamist movement, notably the Taliban in Afghanistan.

37. On Qatar's backing of jihadists, particularly Hamas, see Jonathan Schanzer, "Assessing the U.S.–Qatar Relationship," Testimony Before the House Foreign Affairs Committee, Subcommittee on Middle East and North Africa, July 26, 2017, http://docs.house.gov/meetings/FA/FA13/20170726/106329/HHRG-115-FA13-Wstate-SchanzerJ-20170726.pdf.

38. In my book *Winning the Unwinnable War,* I explore Bush's rationale for targeting Iraq, and the administration's evasive policy toward the regime in Pakistan, which was instrumental in the Taliban's rise to power in Afghanistan (and later, following the U.S. invasion, in the Taliban's resurgence).

39. See, for example, Obama, "Combatting Violent Extremism."

40. For example, in his 2018 State of the Union speech, Trump stated that two recent attacks "were made possible by the visa lottery and chain migration" (both forms of legal immigration); in 2016, after the massacre at the Pulse nightclub in Orlando, Florida, Trump stressed that the killer was born of Afghan parents, who immigrated to the United States. It's worth noting that the killer was born in New York (like Trump himself).

41. For example, see George W. Bush's characterization of his own view, and these statements by Vice President Dick Cheney. Michael Chertoff, secretary of Homeland Security, used a slightly different term, stating that we're in an "existential struggle."

42. *The News Hour with Jim Lehrer,* PBS, October 16, 2009.

43. See, for example, Michael Flynn (former national security advisor to President Trump) and Michael Ledeen, *The Field of Flight: How We Can Win the Global War Against Radical Islam and Its Allies* (New York: St. Martin's, 2016), 8, 114. See also the view of Steve Bannon, Trump's former chief strategist and advisor, in "This Is How Steve Bannon Sees The Entire World," BuzzFeedNews, November 16, 2016. Mike Pompeo, the secretary of state, reportedly told a church gathering in 2015 that "we are engaged in a struggle against radical Islam, the kind of struggle this country has not faced since its great wars."

44. John Mueller and Mark G. Stewart, "The Terrorism Delusion," *International Security* 37 (Summer 2012): 100.

45. Mueller and Stewart, "The Terrorism Delusion," 100.

46. John Mueller, *Overblown: How Politicians and the Terrorism Industry Inflate National Security Threats, and Why We Believe Them* (New York: Free Press, 2006), 7.

47. Mueller, *Overblown,* 7.

48. Mueller, *Overblown,* 8 (emphasis added).

49. Mueller and Stewart, "The Terrorist Delusion," 103.

50. "CTU Presents: What ISIS Wants - Univ. of Rochester," Ayaan Hirsi Ali Foundation, April 22, 2019, https://youtu.be/VXhneojKEMY.

51. Raif Badawi, *1000 Lashes: Because I Say What I Think,* trans. Ahmed Danny Ramadan, ed. Constantin Schreiber, Lawrence Krauss, contrib. (Vancouver: Graystone Books, 2015), 1.

52. Badawi, *1000 Lashes,* 16.

53. Badawi, *1000 Lashes,* 17.

54. Badawi, *1000 Lashes*, 15–16.

55. Badawi, *1000 Lashes*, 42.

56. Badawi, *1000 Lashes*, 42.

57. Badawi, *1000 Lashes*, xxv.

58. Badawi, *1000 Lashes*, xxviii.

59. The quote from Ryan appears in Ryan Lizza, "How Paul Ryan Captured the G.O.P.," *New Yorker*, 6 August 2012, http://www.newyorker.com/reporting/2012/08/06/120806fa_fact_lizza#ixzz24lX7Q8jX (accessed 25 September 2012).

60. Don Watkins, "Ryan, Rand, and Rights," *Daily Caller*, 17 August 2012, http://dailycaller.com/2012/08/17/ryan-rand-and-rights/ (accessed 25 September 2012).

61. Onkar Ghate, "Ayn Rand's Appeal," Fox News, 21 August 2012, http://www.foxnews.com/opinion/2012/08/21/ayn-rand-appeal/ (accessed 25 September 2012).

62. Don Watkins, "Why Paul Ryan Is No Ayn Rand on Social Security," *Christian Science Monitor*, 21 August 2012, http://www.csmonitor.com/Commentary/Opinion/2012/0821/Why-Paul-Ryan-is-no-Ayn-Rand-on-Social-Security (accessed 25 September 2012).

63. Michelle Goldberg, "Paul Ryan's Extreme Abortion Views," *Daily Beast*, 11 August 2012, http://www.thedailybeast.com/articles/2012/08/11/paul-ryan-s-extreme-abortion-views.html (accessed 25 September 2012).http://www.thedailybeast.com/articles/2012/08/11/paul-ryan-s-extreme-abortion-views.html

64. Ayn Rand, "The Nature of Government," *The Virtue of Selfishness* (New York: Signet, 1964), http://www.aynrand.org/site/PageServer?pagename=arc_ayn_rand_the_nature_of_government.

65. Ayn Rand, "Man's Rights," *Capitalism: The Unknown Ideal* (New York: Signet, 1986), http://www.aynrand.org/site/PageServer?pagename=arc_ayn_rand_man_rights.

66. "Capitalism," *The Ayn Rand Lexicon*, http://aynrandlexicon.com/lexicon/capitalism.html.

67. "Abortion," *The Ayn Rand Lexicon*, http://aynrandlexicon.com/lexicon/abortion.html.

68. "Free Speech," *The Ayn Rand Lexicon* http://aynrandlexicon.com/lexicon/free_speech.html.

69. Ayn Rand, *Capitalism: The Unknown Ideal* (New York, NY: Signet, 1967), p. 224.

70. "Pacifism," *The Ayn Rand Lexicon*, http://aynrandlexicon.com/lexicon/pacifism.html.

71. Elan Journo, *Winning the Unwinnable War: America's Self-Crippled Response to Islamic Totalitarianism* (Lanham, MD: Lexington Books, 2009), http://www.amazon.com/dp/B003UERGVY.

72. "Foreign Policy," *The Ayn Rand Lexicon*, http://aynrandlexicon.com/lexicon/foreign_policy.html#order_2.

73. Thomas Joscelyn, *Iran's Proxy War Against America*, The Claremont Institute, 2007, https://www.claremont.org/repository/docLib/20071127_ProxyWarAgainstAmerica.pdf.

74. Daniel Pipes, "Iran's Link to Al-Qaeda: The 9/11 Commission's Evidence," *Middle East Forum*, Fall 2004, http://www.meforum.org/670/irans-link-to-al-qaeda-the-9-11-commissions (accessed 25 September 2012).

75. Michael R. Gordon and Andrew W. Lehren, "Leaked Reports Detail Iran's Aid for Iraqi Militias," *New York Times*, 22 October 2010 http://www.nytimes.com/2010/10/23/world/middleeast/23iran.html (accessed 28 September 2012); Sanjeev Miglani, "General McChrystal Says Afghan Insurgents Trained in Iran," Reuters, 30 May 2010, http://www.reuters.com/article/2010/05/30/us-afghanistan-iran-idUSTRE64T0U920100530 (accessed 28 September 2012).

76. David Feith, "Obama's Iran Loopholes," *Wall Street Journal*, 2 July 2012, http://online.wsj.com/article/SB10001424052702304211804577502912009234948.html (accessed 25 September 2012).

77. See: http://winningtheunwinnablewar.com/.

78. Josh Rogin, "US Struggles with Iran for Influence in Iraq," *Foreign Policy*, 23 March 2012, http://thecable.foreignpolicy.com/posts/2012/03/23/us_struggles_with_iran_for_influence_in_iraq (accessed 25 September 2012).

79. Yasir Ghazi, "Wave of Attacks Kill Dozens in Iraq," *New York Times*, 16 August 2012, http://www.nytimes.com/2012/08/17/world/middleeast/at-least-39-killed-in-wave-of-attacks-in-iraq.html?_r=1 (accessed 25 September 2012).

80. Christopher Bartolotta and Jordan McGillis, "A Conversation with Yaron Brook and Elan Journo," *Whitehead Journal of Diplomacy*, Winter/Spring 2012, http://blogs.shu.edu/diplomacy/2012/04/a-conversation-with-yaron-brook-and-elan-journo/ (accessed 25 September 2012).

81. Nick Meo, "US Secretary of State Hillary Clinton Meets Egypt's Muslim Brotherhood President Mohammed Morsi in Historic First," *Telegraph*, 14 July 2012, http://www.telegraph.co.uk/news/worldnews/africaandindianocean/egypt/9400749/US-Secretary-of-State-Hillary-Clinton-meets-Egypts-Muslim-Brotherhood-president-Mohammed-Morsi-in-historic-first.html (accessed 25 September 2012).

82. Elan Journo, "Our Self-Crippled Foreign Policy Encouraged Deadly Embassy Attack," FoxNews.com, 28 September 2012, http://www.foxnews.com/opinion/2012/09/28/our-self-crippled-policy-encouraged-deadly-embassy-attacks/ (accessed 28 September 2012).

83. http://www.economist.com/blogs/democracyinamerica/2011/12/defence-spending

84. Amit R. Paley, "Iraqis Joining Insurgency Less for Cause than Cash," *Washington Post*, 20 November 2007, http://www.washingtonpost.com/wp-dyn/content/article/2007/11/19/AR2007111902022.html (accessed 25 September 2012).

85. "Individualism," *The Ayn Rand Lexicon*, http://aynrandlexicon.com/lexicon/individualism.html.

86. "Independence," *The Ayn Rand Lexicon*, http://aynrandlexicon.com/lexicon/independence.html.

87. "Altruism," *The Ayn Rand Lexicon*, http://aynrandlexicon.com/lexicon/altruism.html.

88. House of Representatives Committee on the Budget, http://budget.house.gov/news/documentsingle.aspx?DocumentID=244386.

89. Richard A. Oppel Jr., "Number of Unidentified Bodies Found in Baghdad Rose Sharply in May," *New York Times*, 2 June 2007, http://www.nytimes.com/2007/06/02/world/middleeast/02iraq.html (accessed 25 September 2012).

90. Peter Baker, Helene Cooper, and Mark Mazzetti, "bin Laden Dead, Obama Says," *New York Times*, May 1, 2011, http://www.nytimes.com/2011/05/02/world/asia/osama-bin-laden-is-killed.html.

91. Islamic totalitarianism seeks to impose a global regime under sharia (religious law), enveloping the totality of human life and society. The terms "Islamist" and "jihadist" are used interchangeably in this chapter to denote a member of the movement.

92. Carlotta Gall, "What Pakistan Knew About bin Laden," *New York Times*, March 19, 2014, http://www.nytimes.com/2014/03/23/magazine/what-pakistan-knew-about-bin-laden.html.

93. U.S. government data for FY2013, http://foreignassistance.gov/web/DataView.aspx#DataSetAnchor.

94. Pew Global Indicators Database, updated with polling data from 2013 spring survey, http://www.pewglobal.org/database/indicator/55/survey/15/response/Enemy/. The Palestinians are among the highest per-capita recipients of aid. An exception is Israel, a major beneficiary of aid and an ally. But it's an odd man out for an additional reason: it is also home to a vibrant economy teeming with high-tech startups, and is itself a donor of aid to other nations.

95. "The Nature of Government," in *The Virtue of Selfishness*, 108.

96. *Winning the Unwinnable War: America's Self-Crippled Response to Islamic Totalitarianism* (Lexington Books: Lanham, MD, 2009).

97. Cf. this video which apparently aired on CNN, https://www.youtube.com/watch?v=iNDTpYlR48g. See also, Karim Sadjadpour, *Reading Khameini: The World View of Iran's Most Powerful Leader* (Carnegie Endowment for International Peace: Washington, 2009), v.

98. *Country Reports on Terrorism 2013*, U.S. Department of State, http://www.state.gov/j/ct/rls/crt/2013/224826.htm.

99. An accounting of Iran's role in these attacks can be found in Thomas Joscelyn, *Iran's Proxy War Against America* (Claremont, CA: Claremont Institute, 2007).

100. What was widely viewed as the administration's firmest response came, eventually, more than a week after the upheaval began. To regard Obama's full statement as even remotely "firm" is to hold a pitiably low standard for what counts as strength. "Text – President's Press Briefing," *New York Times*, June 23, 2009, http://www.nytimes.com/2009/06/23/us/politics/23text-obama.html.

101. Peter Schwartz, *The Foreign Policy of Self-Interest: A Moral Ideal for America* (Irvine, CA: Ayn Rand Institute Press, 2004), 33–34. Saudi Arabia is the illustration offered in Schwartz's argument.

102. Ron Moreau, "Where the Jihad Lives Now," *Newsweek*, October 20, 2007.

103. The figure cited is for "security-related" aid only; if "economic-related" aid is counted as well, the figure climbs to approximate $24 billion. "Direct Overt U.S. Aid Appropriations and Military Reimbursements to Pakistan, FY2002-FY2017" prepared by the Congressional Research Service, https://fas.org/sgp/crs/row/pakaid.pdf.

104. Gall, "What Pakistan Knew About bin Laden."

Made in the USA
Middletown, DE
21 January 2022

59108233R00186